KT-495-553

A GIRL'S BEST FRIEND
IS HER MONEY

A GIRL'S BEST FRIEND
IS HER MONEY

Jane Mack and
Jasmine Birtles

BOXTREE

First published 2002 by Boxtree,
an imprint of Pan Macmillan Ltd
Pan Macmillan, 20 New Wharf Road, London N1 9RR
Basingstoke and Oxford
Associated companies throughout the world
www.panmacmillan.com

ISBN 0 7522 6171 1

© The Motley Fool UK Ltd 2002

The right of Jane Mack and Jasmine Birtles to be identified as the
authors of this work has been asserted by them in accordance
with the Copyright, Designs and Patents Act 1988.

All rights reserved. No part of this publication may be
reproduced, stored in or introduced into a retrieval system, or
transmitted, in any form, or by any means (electronic, mechanical,
photocopying, recording or otherwise), without the prior written
permission of the publisher. Any person who does any unauthorized
act in relation to this publication may be liable to criminal
prosecution and civil claims for damages.

1 3 5 7 9 8 6 4 2

A CIP catalogue record for this book is available from
the British Library.

Designed and typeset by seagulls
Printed by Mackays of Chatham plc

Contents

Acknowledgements

This book couldn't have been written without the various perspectives on women and finance that have come our way over the last few years. Men and women alike have contributed to our thought processes when we've been trying to evaluate the general Zeitgeist. The help has been enormous and we'd particularly like to single out Frances Lindsay, Colin Taylor and Sarah Wilson who have put their valuable knowledge and experience at our disposal for certain chapters as well as, of course, our editor, Natalie Jerome and publisher Gordon Wise. The press offices of the Inland Revenue and the Department for Work and Pensions have also been remarkably helpful.

There are also friends, family and work colleagues such as Duncan Mack, Tom Johnsen, David Berger, James Carlisle, Pam Garner, Bruce Jackson, Helen Roy, Zoë Sanderson and Stuart Watson who either took the time to read what we'd written to ensure we were going in the right direction or urged us on with the kindness and support we needed when we were struggling.

Talking of 'struggling', there are people on our Motley Fool discussion boards who have given us more motivation than they have probably ever realised – even though we have mostly been onlookers. We may not know their real names but when Clariman, ffwl, Grafter, Gerrymander10, IMBalance, Jimsusan, KingMcKong, maggiethomas, raimesh, Ronniepurple and Struggling, to name but a few, post messages on our boards, you know that if someone wanted the answer to a question, they will have done their level best to help. (Thank you so much for your unfailing willingness to provide a kind word or a bit of advice to others in times of need)

We'd also like to thank our mothers for giving birth to us (sob), our fathers for trying to teach us basic maths (sob, blow nose), all our teachers at school, university, our cats (break down into uncontrollable sobbing). Apologies if we've forgotten anyone. There are many others we could mention but there's still the whole book to read and we reckon you might be getting fed up with our mini-Oscar nomination list.

Introduction

Act 1, Scene 1

The scene opens in the lounge of a top London hotel. Jasmine and Jane, gorgeous, gifted and immaculately dressed (hey, they can dream!), are indulging in a cream tea and chatting elegantly. The audience gets the feeling that this is something they do on a regular basis (it's a dream, right?). Suddenly they notice they're being watched and look up.

Jasmine: Hello, you're there! You've opened the book...

Jane: ... you've dipped your toe in the water...

Jasmine: ... and you're now wondering whether you should buy it, whether you could stand an entire book full of facts and figures about pensions, mortgages and ISAs and stuff.

Jane: Well, naturally, we think you can. Particularly as it isn't *just* facts and figures. There's a lot of serious advice packed into these pages, but it is readable and really quite fun. Honest!

Jasmine: You see we know what it's like to feel that you ought to do something about your finances but be put off by the arse-achingly tedious financial jargon you have to wade through. Also, we don't like maths one bit – well, Jane doesn't, anyway.

Jane: Nor do you – you don't even like timetables.

Jasmine: True – stupid 24-hour clock.

Jane: But the thing is, a few years ago we both realised, quite independently of each other, before we even knew of each other's existence, that we really, *really* had to get our finances in order if we were to have any sort of life.

Jasmine: I mean the debt!

Jane: Tell me about it. Living off an overdraft ain't much fun. And those letters from creditors can be a little, shall we say, unfriendly?

Jasmine: And me – it was only a few years ago that I was over £8,000 in debt, with very little idea of what was going on with my pension and no concept of the vital importance of investing in the stock market to provide a decent income for my retirement. I do now though... Oh yes! There's no stopping me now!

Jane: But we know that we're the lucky ones. The vast majority of people in this country spend far too much and save way too little. And the majority of women are facing an impoverished retirement unless they do something *now*. Women tend to earn less than men, they take time off to have children, they generally come off worse financially after divorce and they live longer than men so they need more money to keep them going.

Jasmine: Yes, women have special financial needs and many don't know where to go for help. That's why we wrote this book.

Jane: Obviously, much of what we've written in this book applies to men as well as women, but there are differences. Women tend to have different responsibilities than men: for a start, the vast majority of single parents are women and the care of children tends to fall to women whether they are in a relationship or not.

Jasmine: The rates we can expect to get when we draw our pensions are lower than those for men and we tend to be more interested than men are in owning our own home.

Jane: Of course, although there's much that unites us, all women are different. For instance, I'm married, Jasmine's not...

Jasmine: ... yet...

Jane: ... yet, neither of us has children, although *you* might or you might be planning to have them.

Jasmine: We've tried to cover the major areas of women's lives in this book, but it's unlikely that they'll all apply to you right now.

Mind you, some of the chapters will apply to everyone.

Jane: We suggest that you definitely read Chapter One and then the chapters on compound interest, ISAs, debt (even if you're not in debt, there are useful tips there) and pensions. Apart from that, it's up to you to decide what's relevant to you.

Jasmine: We can't give you all the answers because we don't have them. (Do you think we'd be spending weeks and months writing some book on personal finance if we did? Ha! No way, we'd be sunning ourselves on a beach in the Bahamas, that's what we'd be doing.) But we do have a load of help and information here that will answer many of the financial issues in your life and set you on the road to solving the others yourself.

Jane: Because you can do it.

Jasmine: You have to do it.

Jane: No one else is going to do it for you.

Jasmine: And that's the other point of this book.

Jane: Empowerment. The fact is that the best person – the most qualified and most dedicated person – to deal with your finances and make all the most important financial decisions in your life is you.

Jasmine: Little you.

Jane: Little, quite brilliant, you. Let's face it, who else in the world cares more about your future and your financial health than you? Not even your nearest and dearest give it as much thought as you, so why hand over these massively important decisions to someone else who just does it for a living or happens to share your toothpaste occasionally?

Jasmine: Oh, they're the worst! Definitely don't do that.

Jane: We're confident that by the time you finish this book...

Jasmine: ... devouring every dot and comma...

Jane: ... not only will you have worked out how to get out of debt, start saving and get your mortgage and pension in order, but you will know how to invest easily and safely in the stock market and you may start investing in individual shares.

Jasmine: After all, once they get the idea, it's been proven that statistically women are better at investing than men.

Jane: ... *statistically* mind you. You will also find out, if you haven't already, what a useful tool the Motley Fool is. You will rush to the website and register immediately, stunned at the wealth and breadth of information hidden in its archives and discussion boards.

Jasmine: More tea?

Jane: Thanks, but go easy on the scones. I need to make room for the champagne.

Jasmine: Cheers, my dear!

Jane: Cheers!

End of scene 1.

The Importance of Being Earnest

It wasn't until I met my boyfriend, Grant, that I realised it is actually illegal for large-breasted women to handle money.

Gayle Tuesday, Page Three Stunner (a.k.a. Brenda Gillhooley)

Do you suffer from Knight in Shining Armour Syndrome? It's a little-known ailment that afflicts a huge number of women. Strangely, it's not talked about endlessly on TV or in women's magazines, unlike pretty much any other syndrome, real or imagined. It particularly affects women in their twenties and thirties, but can last even into their forties and beyond if they have been fed on an unhealthy diet of soaps and slushy novels.

Sufferers are easy to spot if you know what to look for. They are the glassy-eyed ones with the latest fashions and the scariest credit card bills. They usually say things like, 'Oh, I don't understand money. It's so boring.' Or, waving their store cards about, they happily tell you that, 'You've got to spend it while you've got it. We could all be dead next week anyway.' (Sufferers are usually not too hot on probability theory, either.) They tend to resist suggestions that they should save for the future or, if they do decide to be sensible and invest for their retirement, they go to their bank manager ('who is so sweet') and put money into the first poor-performing fund he suggests.

They live for the short term. They spend money on things that could snare an unwary Prince Charming into sweeping them into his arms and sorting out all their tiresome money-type problems. But what the photo-

love stories and Hollywood films don't tell you is that, even if Prince Charming does turn up, he's just as likely to mess up money matters and force you into poverty as he is to care for your needs. Princes are notoriously bad with money and just can't be trusted with anything more important than the royal lawnmower. And don't forget, love can quickly go out the back door when money problems come in the front door.

Sometimes princes get confused and mistake you for an heiress who will keep them in the manner to which they would like to become accustomed. Frogs like these can turn out to be a financial liability and may have to be chucked back into the pond. But, even if his armour does stay shiny and his charger doesn't turn out to be an old nag, you still can't be sure of living happily ever after. Life could throw in divorce, sickness or even widowhood, so every woman, married or single, needs to have an eye on her own financial security throughout her life.

It is essential that not one woman should assume a lovely man will come along and pay for everything for the rest of her life. Face it, girl, that ain't gonna happen. You may get a lovely man, you may get a rich man. But lovely *and* rich? That's pretty damn rare in our experience. Even if you do hit the jackpot, or if you already have, there's nothing like being sure in your own mind that your future is secure. You never know when you might suddenly be without him. After all, arguments about money are the biggest single cause of rows in the home. This is because women and men usually have different attitudes towards it and are often on very different levels of income. The more independent you are financially, the more secure you are with or without a man and, therefore, the less pressure you will put on your relationship, so the more harmonious it will be.

The sad fact is, traditionally, women have not held control of their own purse strings and, even now, on average, they are very poorly provided for when it comes to their futures. Look at the facts.

- Women generally earn less than 80% of men's salaries.
- Women usually give up their careers, for a few years at least, to care for their children, which drastically cuts down their earnings.

- The divorce rate is currently running at about 40% and generally it is women who fare worse financially from these break-ups.
- Women usually outlive men but have much less money invested for their future.
- It is anticipated that within twenty years more than half of the adult population will be living alone.

With less of a human support network around them than ever before, women particularly need to get real about how they are going to keep themselves going financially later on. We have a way to go. At the moment, fewer than 40% of women in the UK have *any* sort of pension provision and those who do don't have enough for their needs. Do women realise this yet? Who do you think is going to finance your retirement? Well, sorry to tell you this, girl, but it's you!

But you know this of course, otherwise why would you have bought this book? You are fully aware that you need to take charge of your finances and your future. Reading this book and putting our advice into practice will set you on the road to queenly fortunes and vast empires in your golden years. Or at least guarantee you a better diet than baked beans and Battenberg cake when you're a granny. Well done, you, keep going!

But what about those around you? Even if you have shaken off the Knight in Shining Armour Syndrome yourself, many of those close to you may still be infected on your behalf. Your dad may keep hoping for a nice man to come along and provide for you. Even your mum may not take your desire for complete financial independence seriously. What about your partner? Does he see it as his role to save for both your futures? And do you know how he is doing it?

Certainly many of the financial institutions, mortgage advisers, Independent Financial Advisers (IFAs) etc. are likely to assume that, even though you may be single at present, your financial future will necessarily involve a male partner at some point who will take care of your pension and savings needs. Maybe you already have such a partner.

They may even suggest that you don't want to worry your pretty little head about stock market investments when there are nice, allegedly safe, mediocre-performing with-profits bonds and managed funds to snap up. Of course the fact that those nice, safe, mediocre-performing products offer some of the best commission rates to Independent Financial Advisers has nothing to do with it. You're a woman, so you want some easy, safe investments to tide you over until a man comes into your life and gets you some real money.

Don't you believe it!

The message – if you haven't got it by now – is that every woman, whatever her age or income, needs to take control of her own financial future. And when we say take control, we mean *control*. It's up to each one of us, at whatever age, to acquire the knowledge – which is not hard to do – on which to base our own financial decisions, in our own way and at our own pace. You are not to trust it to anyone else because no one else, not even your own family members, has your financial future in his or her heart as much as you do.

My parents brought me up with the savings habit, and I'm eternally grateful to them. I received my pocket money every week and that was it. My dad was generous to a fault – still is – but he always had a low-paid manual job so money was tight. If I wanted anything, I simply had to save up for it. There was no other way. If you get the saving habit early in life, it never really leaves you. You can depend that it is one of the best and most rewarding habits you will ever pursue. You can, of course, take it up at any time of life – it's just that, like a lot of other things, the longer you leave it the harder it becomes.

From the Motley Fool discussion boards

You can do a lot with your finances if you can learn to live within your means, save and invest. If you are in your twenties, this can be particularly lucrative. For far too many people, early adulthood involves spending excessively and acquiring debt rather than assets. Yet these years are a priceless opportunity to acquire savings and make investments before the children come along.

But what do I want money for?

Good question. What indeed. This is the point where you sit back, have a sip of tea, a nibble on a chocolate éclair (go on, you know you want to) and let your thoughts drift into happy dreamland. Dream away. How do you see yourself in five years? In ten years? In thirty or forty years? Would you like to ditch your tiresome job and set up your own empire? Perhaps you'd like to learn to fly, have enough money to take four good holidays a year, travel round the Australian outback for six months or be able to send your yet-to-be-born children to university. What about retirement? That may be way off in the future or just a few years away. What, in an ideal world, would you like to be doing in your retirement? Does a pair of Dr Scholl sandals and holidays in Margate appeal, or would you prefer a cupboard full of Manolos and cruises round the Mediterranean on luxury liners? You do have a choice – more so the younger you are. Even if you are able to put aside only a little money each month, if it is invested in the right places it can make that cosy cottage in Provence a reality.

It's a question of actually thinking about the future. Facing it and taking a bit of time now, and then once or twice a year hereafter, to work out how much money you will need to support your dream. But – and we can't emphasise this enough, dear reader – you first *have* to consider your future and take it in your own hands in order to do this.

Oh yes, the future. Oops!

Oops, indeed. All you have to do is become a Fool. No, not a *fool*, Fool! A *Fool*!

In case you're wondering whether becoming a Fool is a good thing, rest assured that the Motley Fool name comes directly from that much-revered and rather classy writer, William Shakespeare. He wrote of jolly Fools who were paid to entertain the king and queen with a humour that instructed as it amused. In fact, Fools tended to be the only members of the royal entourage who could tell the truth without having their heads lopped off.

This is the mission of the Motley Fool: to educate, amuse and enrich. To tell it like it really is when your bank manager, your financial adviser and that nice man who deals with your pension are desperately climbing over each other to be first in the queue when you're wondering where to put all your hard-earned moolah. Conventional wisdom would indicate that these people know what they're doing and you can trust them. Beware, fledgling Fool. You can't. Indeed you mustn't. For they are the Wise, whose favourite quotation is 'A fool and his money are soon parted'. Alas, this is true. The Wise have years of experience of this phenomenon. That's why we call them the Wise.

Fortunately, you are not a fool. Well, not any more! You're about to dispense with Wisdom and become a Fool. And Foolishness means you control your own financial destiny.

The Foolish way to invest for the future is by selecting products that generate the best returns and by setting aside specific amounts of money each week/month/year to put into them.

Now you're not to be offended by this bit. In a moment we'll be telling you just how brilliant women are at investing to make money, but before that we've got to be strictly honest here. When it comes to pensions and setting money aside for a comfortable future, a lot of women (though not all) have been very neglectful. According to *Women and Personal Finance*, a survey published in April 2001 by the Financial Services Authority (an organisation that oversees the finance industry), generally men are at least twice as likely to have pensions as women. It's particularly bad if you're married or cohabiting. Less than one in three married or cohabiting women have a pension, often because they have left it to their partners to sort out. Recent legislation that entitles women to part of their spouse's pension on divorce will help to protect some of them in these times of uncertain relationships. But how much better would it be for them to have at least their own pension pot to comfort them in their old age?

It's not that we at the Motley Fool are desperately pro-pension-owner-ship. We're not, particularly in the case of women. Admittedly the arrival of Stakeholder Pensions in April 2001 increased their value by restricting the charges fund managers can levy, but the big downside to pensions is that once you come to draw one, you are allowed to take out *only* 25% of it to invest as you see fit. The rest of it *must* be used to buy an annuity, an insurance-related product that provides an income for life. Currently annuity rates are generally unimpressive across the board, but they are even lower for women as we are supposed to live longer. So, however good the fund is, you are always going to be held back by the annuity rate.

What we *are* keen on – very keen actually – is that *all* women have some sort of investment vehicle for their future. This may or may not include a pension. (We're not counting the state pension because, frankly, by the time we get to draw that it probably won't even buy our individual tin of Spam each week.) The fact is that ownership of a pension of some sort – ideally a company pension to which your employer contributes too – gives you some sort of income in your golden years, and that, whatever your age, is something you should be confident of having. For those of us who don't quite have the discipline to resist dipping into our 'rainy-day money', a pension can be a life-saver as, unlike most other investments, once you've put money in, you can't take it out until the day you retire.

If you don't contribute to a pension and you'd like to, or you feel you should contribute more to your pension pot, take a look at Chapter Seven. This chapter guides you through the joys of Stakeholder Pensions, a scheme brought in by the Government with women particularly in mind as you can still contribute even when you are not working (when you take time off to have a family, for example).

One of the major benefits of pensions is that the money you put into them gets tax relief (although you do have to pay tax on the pension when you actually draw it), so this adds to your initial investment as well as cutting down your tax bill. Another very helpful tax vehicle is an Individual Savings Account, or ISA. An ISA is basically a kind of wrapper for your investments. It's not an investment itself: it's simply a 'bag' for you to put them in which protects them from tax. You can invest up to £7,000 each year in equity (share) products, such as tracker funds or individual shares, or you can invest that money in a mix of cash, equity products and insurance products, all the time protecting the income you gain on these investments from tax. Any woman keen on maximising her investments for the future should ensure that she uses as much of her £7,000 a year ISA allowance as possible. So long as you have the discipline not to take this money out later and spend it, ISAs are a really useful way of investing for your future. We give more in-depth information and guidance on ISAs in Chapter Six.

Pensions and ISAs are just two of the many vehicles in which you can invest your money. If you think of yourself as an investor, rather than just someone who pays into a pension plan or has a savings account, this changes the way you look at money. You may realise that you are wasting your money by keeping it in the building society or it may even lead you to decide that a pension is not the right investment vehicle for you. It broadens your outlook and, importantly, puts a level of responsibility on you to look after your savings and investments. You won't just set up regular payments into a pension fund and think that that will look after your future. You will take a look at the whole picture – your current earnings, your outgoings, your dependants and responsibilities – and how you may need to change your life and your earnings to be able to make the money you need for your future. It's not that great a shift, so don't let it put you off! From this moment forward, you are an investor (and you don't need a stripy shirt and red braces to do it).

Anyone who puts money aside for anything can be an investor. Looking after your investments means ensuring a maximum return with minimum costs, in terms of charges and tax, all within the limits set by your own attitude towards risk. The Fool is able to take an overview of all her investments (building society accounts, pensions, ISAs, shares, property) and think in terms of her Total Return. As long as an investment is pulling its weight in the Total Return category then it's fine. If it isn't, then it should be traded in for a better-performing vehicle.

So, lesson one in investing is that every woman, of whatever age, should be investing her money to some degree in order to provide for her future. Every woman should also make sure that all her various investments – and it's a good idea to have a few different ones – are working really hard on her behalf, giving her as good a return as possible within her own comfortable level of risk. And when we say good return, we mean *good*, because, as you will see in Chapter Two, in the long term, even one percentage point can make a massive difference to the level of wealth you end up with. Never underestimate the power of compound returns.

Female Fools beat the Wise

Now, if at this point you can feel your buttocks clenching and your shoulders tightening in an 'I can't do this, I don't know anything about money so how can I *not* have an impoverished retirement?' kind of a way, relax those muscles now and b-r-e-a-t-h-e. That's it. Take a deep breath. It's okay. We felt the same way too when we first started to look into organising our finances in a profitable way (and both of us have been in debt at various points in our lives so we know what it's like). But we can tell you it is really not that hard. If we can do it, so can you. In fact, we now know that the moment women are given the same financial knowledge as their male counterparts, not only do we do as well as they do, we actually do better. The only problem is that most of us don't realise that we can do this and, just as upsettingly, nor do those we pay to advise us. So we have to be even more wary of financial advisers than men.

For example, the Wise financial advisers – whether they are men or women – generally believe that women are more averse to risk than men. They tend to offer us apparently safer, less profitable investment options that are not much help to us in the long term. Relative risk aversion amongst women is a commonly reported statistic in the financial press. US studies have suggested that financial advisers are more likely to offer low-risk products to women and that some brokers give female customers inferior treatment compared with men. But when women are presented with the complete facts, they often make the same decisions as men and show no more bias for 'safe' products, proving that the possession of a womb does not stop one from making big money.

In fact, a recent academic paper examining the differing success rates of investments between men and women revealed that risk aversion was a good thing, and that if you want to do well, you shouldn't be a man! Economists at the University of California studied the investing habits of more than 35,000 stockbroker clients: they found that women get better returns on their investments than men because their risk aversion makes them inclined to think more about what they're buying and to trade less frequently. It's not that women have little confidence in their decisions: they just have less of a need to compete and make the aggressive moves that men do – particularly young men.

According to the University's research, men trade 45% more often but underperform women by 1.4% a year. Single men – clearly bereft of the stabilising factor of a good woman – trade 67% more frequently than single women but produce returns of 2.3% less per year. All this simply proves that being more risk-averse does not mean going for the safe option all the time. In the case of women it means investing and holding for good reasons, rather than buying and selling in the hope of making a fast buck.

See, you can do it, and do it well! And doesn't that show just why Fools, and particularly female Fools, should treat the Wise with extreme caution. Even Independent Financial Advisers to whom you pay an upfront or hourly fee may be working from the automatic assumption that all women prefer low-risk investments, and that they need some hand-holding. Nonsense!

Press reports of the stock market have always focused on its short-term volatility and precarious nature. Recently for example, they have cited the spectacular falls of all shares as proof. This fuels the widespread assumption that shares are risky and should not be touched by sensible investors. Rightly, IFAs are now strictly regulated and face heavy penalties if they suggest investments that don't tally with your risk preference. But as a Fool, you are not interested in investing for short-term gain (also known as gambling). You are interested in the long term, and in the long term the stock market is likely to do what it has always done, which is to grow steadily.

Stop before you go

So, feeling more confident now? Your back has relaxed, your buttocks are unclenched and you now know that you have the potential to make some seriously clever investments. Why not throw this book down right now, race out and stick your money in something, anything, that promises to make you money later? Well, hang on a moment. There are a few things to sort out first.

Number one is debt. There's absolutely no point trying to save or invest any money until you have paid off all your current debts. Get out of debt. With the exception of mortgage debt, all debt is bad for your wealth. There's simply no point in paying seriously large amounts of money in interest rates when that money could be going into your own pocket. Life has a habit of tripping you up just when you think you've got things under control. It's only then that you realise things remained under control only while everything stayed the same. Think about where you would stand if you suddenly lost your income tomorrow. Could you cope?

In Chapter Three we give hints and tips on how to get out of debt, so here we'll content ourselves with pointing out the obvious: most lenders (personal loans, credit cards, store cards, overdrafts etc.) charge interest rates that cost you far more than you might be earning on your savings. By a simple process of subtraction, you can see that if you are in debt and have savings at the same time you are quite simply losing money.

Strangely, millions of people in this country, both male and female, have yet to grasp this basic concept. The vast majority of lenders charge interest in double figures – in the case of some store cards around 30% – whereas the most interest you might be earning on savings these days is, at the time of writing, about 5% at best. On average, millions of people are making a loss every year just because they are not using their savings to pay off their debts.

Set up an emergency fund, and not just so that it's there for a rainy day. If you can build up savings of between three and six months' expenses, then you're practically ready for anything that life may chuck at you. Imagine not panicking when your car engine blows up or your child's teacher demands money for a school trip to France. Imagine the security of knowing that you have no debt and that you can afford to manage on your savings for a few months should you decide you can't stand your Toxic Boss for a single minute longer. Imagine being able to walk out on a controlling, emotionally retarded excuse of a boyfriend/husband because you know you have the wherewithal to manage on your own.

Next, where's your knowledge? In order to sort out your financial life, save and invest sensibly, you need to know what you are doing. That's pretty much the point of this book, so we suggest (well we would, wouldn't we?) that you have a good read of it – or at least the chapters you feel relate to your circumstances – and get a firm mental grip on the facts before you go spending any money anywhere.

Knowledge, as we all know, is power, and this is very much the case in the realm of personal finance. Many, many unscrupulous Wise types out there make substantial amounts of money out of consumers' lack of knowledge. They *depend* on your ignorance to earn a living. Even the honest ones could sell you unsuitable products because the explanations they give are full of financial jargon and other nonsense so you don't really know what you are agreeing to. Unless you do a bit of homework yourself and make sure you know what you want, and what you will *not* accept, you could find yourself spending good money on very poor products simply because you do not understand what the product is.

Every day, in banks, IFA offices and even in people's homes, bad financial products are being sold to people who really do not know what they are buying. We know, we were those people. Jasmine is still smarting from being sold a life cover policy (albeit dressed up as a savings vehicle) when she had just graduated, had no partner or dependants and had no immediate prospect of either. Who exactly was supposed to benefit if she died?

With no understanding of what these products are, you may find yourself having serious conversations with a financial adviser-type in which you make a major decision about your future without realising the full implications of what you are doing. It may go a little like this:

You: I'd like to invest £100 every month into something that will make me rich later in life. What do you suggest?

IFA: Ah. Well, given your age, income and circumstances, I would suggest the 'Buy A Fund Manager A Porsche Boxter For Christmas' Bond, with an APR of 5.6% and air-conditioning as standard. You see, if you look at this unintelligible graph I'm holding up, the monster-raving aardvark quotient is set to rise by at least an ottoman each quartile – Julian calendar obviously – so that, pending a foreman's enquiry and assuming there's an 'r' in the month, you should end up with an income of at least £10,000 a year!

You: £10,000? That sounds nice... Um... Sorry, I didn't quite catch all of that. How does it happen again?

IFA: Of course, I'll put it in simpler terms. Your money will be divided up into stocks, bonds, ponds, fish, traffic, door stops and circus-performing seals, while overnight it'll be swept into a maximum-yield crop formation so that you can receive a regular income of two groats and a bag of sand every time the moon is in the ascendant. Basically, all you need to know is that you'll be very comfortable in your old age. Trust me, I've done the research.

You: I see. Well, if you think that would be the best thing then I'm sure you know best. I'll sign up for it now and put my hard-earned cash into it every month. Thank you so much!

Go on, be different!

Finally, as the last bit of our preamble before launching into the rest of this book, we would like to have a word about being different. Yes, the very thing you've been trying to avoid ever since Roger Watson got the whole school to point and laugh at you in the playground because of your enormous pink-rimmed NHS specs. To be truly in control of your finances you need to make decisions because you believe in them, not because you are following the crowd. The latter route is the way losses are made.

You'd be amazed how many of our thoughts and actions are not our own. Most of us spend much of our lives in a semi-hypnotic state. Advertising, overheard conversations, TV programmes, newspapers and magazines influence our thoughts sometimes consciously, but more often unconsciously. We yawn when others yawn, assume what they assume and, for no reason other than the fact that everyone else is thinking it, we suddenly decide that those pointy-toed shoes we laughed at on our grandmothers are actually the chicest footwear we have ever seen. Unless we check our thinking regularly and question even our own vaguely formed wants and desires, we can find ourselves following the herd in most aspects of our lives. And herds tend to think somewhat irrationally, and they're not particularly good at running their own finances.

On the other hand, Fools – real ones with a capital 'F' – are contrary by nature or by education. They believe in living by *their* rules, rather than by those of the Wise organisations and institutions that would like to take control of them and, more immediately, of their money. They enjoy the freedom and wealth of investing their own time and money as they see fit, according to their own research, interests and intelligence. They don't hand over the keys to their future wealth and happiness to some faceless fund-management company. They don't buy when the City journalists tell them to and sell when the tipsters cry panic. They don't rack up mounds of debt buying the latest gadgets and fashions just because everyone else has them. Nor do they depend entirely on the man in their life to look after them. But they do keep their heads while all around are filling theirs with nonsense. They weather the storms of crashing markets and stay sane during inflated ones. They make decisions quietly in markets full of bears or bulls, gradually investing according to their own decisions and refusing to be budged by scaremongers or get-rich-quick salesmen.

I believe that if you want a job doing especially well, it's better to educate yourself because, ultimately, only you have your and your family's best interests at heart. Middlemen, third parties, advisers, etc. all have their own interests at heart first and foremost, and in the case of financial advisers will always get paid whatever the quality of their work and regardless of the consequences that arise from it. In terms of learning about the basics of finance it is not too hard to understand them. By spending a weekend reading the Motley Fool message boards it is easy to gain an understanding of a down-to-earth approach to finance. This has been a massive eye-opener to me and it has completely changed my original outlook on finance. What has been even more pleasing is that it hasn't really taken that much effort or skill or even money to do this. I now have the confidence to look after myself financially and create a plan to live below my means so that I will be able to reap the rewards over my lifetime.

From the Motley Fool discussion boards

Fools think hard about their future and formulate a plan of action. Start thinking along the lines of 'high net worth = true wealth' as opposed to 'high income and consumption level = illusion of wealth'. In other words, don't think that a good salary and being able to go out and buy lots of things means you've got money. If you've spent it all, then you haven't! Think more along the lines of what you would have left in your hands if you sold absolutely everything you own right now and paid off everything you owe. If there's not much left over, then give yourself a pat on the back that you're reading this book!

There's nothing wrong with finding out about how to save for the future. You want a comfortable retirement, right? You'd like to own your own home? Be able to buy a decent car? Take nice holidays? Of course you would!

Well, by the end of this book, you will know how to start working on it. You'll know all about pensions and ISAs, how to get out of debt, how to start saving, how to buy a home, how to invest in your own future as well as that of your kids, even how to start again if you have to. We would all like a magic broom to sweep up our problems, but unfortunately you can't buy them anywhere. You are the broom! You are the one person you can truly depend on. Nothing is unachievable if you put your mind to it; you'll find that once you've started, problems have a rather miraculous tendency to solve themselves automatically.

When you have enough money to feel financially secure, your whole psychology changes. It brings confidence and self-esteem, and that can make all the difference in the world.

Wannabe a Fool and run your own life? Of course you do. Welcome to the club. And if you'd like to discuss this book or any of the issues in it, do go to the 'Women's Finance and Investing' discussion board on the Motley Fool site.

$(1+i)^n$ – A Formula for Success

There are three types of people in life: those that can count and those that can't.

Anon

Hands up who likes maths! No? We don't, either. In fact, we would go so far as to say that the neat little heading for this chapter might make an interesting stencil design for a frieze around the bathroom, but we wouldn't plan on using it for anything else.

If you're good at maths you'll probably recognise $(1+i)^n$ as the basic formula for calculating compound interest, but we're not going to go into detail about it because this book is not supposed to induce waves of panic. So we're going to skip over the explanation of $(1+i)^n$ here and tell you that, if you're really interested, you'll find one in the *Motley Fool's UK Investment Guide* for your perusal. Those who can do maths tell us that it's an excellent explanation of how it works, even if it does go over our own heads.

Nevertheless, the Miracle of Compound Interest is a subject that isn't just important: it's so vital that the Motley Fool UK would like it to become the number one lesson to be taught in schools. In fact, forget finger-painting and baking fairy cakes: we'd like to see toddlers being taught this in nursery school: 'Alicia, please! Stop trying to spoon jelly in your ear and give me the annualised rate for an 80% total return over 5 years, mischievous child!'

In truth, you need only to understand the principle of compound interest and the returns it can make for you in order to appreciate how important it is for your financial future. After all, you don't need to know how an engine works in order to drive a car.

Bear in mind that, as you read what follows, compound interest works in reverse if you are paying interest on debts. If you owe money, then it will be the lender who is rubbing his hands with glee at all the returns he's getting from *you*.

The Miracle of Compound Interest

Simply put, investing involves turning money into more money. This might seem laughingly obvious, but, although most people will be able to give you a broadly similar definition to the one we've just given you, it's remarkable how difficult the concept can be to take on board.

Go to the top of a mountain in Gstaad in the middle of winter, make a snowball in your hands and roll it down the hill. As the surface area of the snowball gets bigger, it'll gather more and more snow each time you roll it. You'll probably find when you arrive at the bottom that you've got yourself a snowball the size of a hot-air balloon. (It's a really high mountain, okay?)

So, the principle of compounding works like a snowball. Your initial capital has collected enough interest on the way down to provide you with a sizeable sum of money. Of course, you don't actually need to go to Gstaad to discover this, fun though it might be. The fact is if you save and invest your money as you walk down the mountain towards your retirement, it'll grow into a bigger pot of money. The more you save and the longer you save, the more you'll end up with. You start off just getting interest, but then you earn interest on that interest, and then you earn interest on the interest on that interest, and so on. Over a long timescale, it really adds up.

Real wealth – the stuff of dreams – is not created overnight. It is in fact created almost magically through the most mundane and commonplace of principles: Time plus the Miracle of Compound Interest.

Here's how it works: Let's say your granny decides to give you £1,000 on your birthday. You decide that, instead of blowing it on a new wardrobe, you're going to invest it in a simple index-tracking ISA. These are explained briefly later and in more detail in Chapters Five and Six, but for the moment all you need to know is that an index tracker is a very easy way of investing in the stock market and you already know from Chapter One that an ISA, protects your money from tax.

For the purposes of our example, let's say your £1,000 appreciates at a rate of 10% a year (before taking account of inflation). That's not an unreasonable estimate given that 10% is the average annual return from the stock market ever since 1869. So, over five years, the numbers should look like this:

Year 1	£1,100
Year 2	£1,210
Year 3	£1,331
Year 4	£1,464
Year 5	£1,611

Without doing anything at all, you've just made yourself a profit of £611! If you'd spent your £1,000 at, say, Gap, where would your 'investment' be now? Packed in a box earmarked for Oxfam?

Now let's introduce you to Kylie, a young woman who, on her twentieth birthday, decides to invest £100 a month into an index-tracking ISA. At the age of 30 she marries Wayne, stops work to have children and cancels her direct debit into the ISA.

Wayne, meanwhile, who has frittered away both his money and his twenties on pastimes too terrible to mention here, decides on his thirtieth birthday to start contributing the same £100 a month into the same scheme. Wayne continues working and contributing to the ISA until he is 60. Assuming an annualised growth rate of 10%, the numbers pan out like this:

	Kylie	Wayne
Age 20	£0	£0
Age 30	£20,146	£0
Age 40	£52,254	£20,146
Age 50	£135,532	£72,399
Age 60	£351,536	£207,929

Ouch! Extraordinary, isn't it? Kylie only contributed to her ISA for 10 years and yet she's ended up with more than twice as much as her husband. Not only that, overall Kylie contributed a total of £12,000 while Wayne paid in £36,000 – three times as much for only two thirds of the return!

From this we derive our first Law of Compound Interest: *Start early!*

Let's look at yet another example. Assume a number of women at the age of 20. All appreciate the importance of regular long-term investment but disagree about the best method. For the sake of argument, we'll assume they have each chosen investments that return different annual growth rates and they each contribute £100 a month until the age of 60. Let's look at the numbers:

	Fennella 4%	Felicity 7%	Ffyona 10%
Age 20	£0	£0	£0
Age 30	£14,718	£17,202	£20,146
Age 40	£36,503	£51,041	£72,399
Age 50	£68,751	£117,606	£207,929
Age 60	£116,486	£248,552	£559,461

	Frances 12%	Freda 15%
Age 20	£0	£0
Age 30	£22,404	£26,302
Age 40	£91,986	£132,707
Age 50	£308,097	£563,177
Age 60	£979,307	£2,304,667

Take a look at the bottom line for each woman. It speaks for itself, doesn't it? Over long periods of time, a difference of only one or two percentage points can have a huge impact.

So the second Law of Compound Interest is: *Small differences in the rate of return matter. A lot!*

It's obvious that the type of investment has a big influence on the return on investment, but there's another thing that needs to be taken into consideration. Any ideas? No? Give up? Oh, all right, then: charges! (Give yourself a pat on the back and treat yourself to a chocolate Hob Nob if you got it right.)

Imagine Frances with her 12% interest rate is actually investing in a fund with annual charges of 2%. She hasn't thought about it much, but every single year when her investment fund takes its cut, her cash pile reduces. By the age of 60, she'll have only the same as Ffyona – little more than half as much as she would have accumulated without the charges.

The same goes for initial charges. Initial charges are a type of entry fee to the fund and are payable as a percentage on everything you put in. Some funds charge as much as 5% for the privilege of buying into them – this is far too much! Imagine Freda with her 15% interest rate is paying initial charges of 5%, thereby reducing her £100 monthly contribution to £95. That extra £5 could have added about £100,000 to her fund over the 40-year period, if she'd been able to invest it.

Charges of any kind are extremely painful. Annual maintenance charges of much above 1% and initial charges – which can be as high as 5% for some unit trusts – are, quite simply, excruciating.

So the third Law of Compound Interest is: *Watch the charges!*

Can you see how, through the Miracle of Compound Interest, your savings nest egg can grow? Now you may be wondering whether the stock market really does produce these sorts of returns. After all, interest rates are extremely low at the moment and you'd be hard pushed to find even a simple building society savings account paying more than around 5%.

The fact is, though, the average stock market return since 1869 has been 9.5% while building societies have returned only about 4.7%. Even during times of crisis when the stock market has crashed and people have run around like headless chickens and jumped off tall buildings in a state of panic, the *average* annual return has still evened out at 9.5% a year. 'But what about inflation?' we hear you ask – well, those of you who are financially astute or have an economics background ask (clever you! What are you doing reading this book?). Good point. Currently inflation is quite low (about 2% at the time of writing) but it's worth taking into account when calculating your long-term potential returns so you can think in terms of today's money. While the nominal rate of return is 9.5% a year on average, the 'real' rate of return, ie: taking inflation into account, is 6.4%. Now, while that may not sound very much, when you know that the real rate of return for cash is a mere 1.8%, you'll realise that the stock market is the best place for your money.

What is an index tracker?

For the vast majority of the public, a cheap index-tracking fund is the ideal long-term investing vehicle. They're cheap, simple, efficient and, best of all, you don't have to do any complicated research. There's more information about them in Chapter Five, but essentially an index tracker follows the fortunes of the whole stock market. It 'tracks' them in the same way a stalker might – except it's legal and you don't get a heavy breather phoning you up in the middle of the night! Actually, it's more like 'keeping up with the Joneses'. A tracker simply copies the movements of a particular index by buying and selling shares in the companies included in that index.

For example, if you've heard of the FTSE 100 (or Footsie), you'll know that it is simply a list of the UK's 100 largest publicly traded companies. We also have another type of FTSE, called the FTSE All Share, which is a longer list of about 800 of the UK's largest publicly traded companies. It's usually pretty safe to invest in these vast companies that make up a particular index – especially when you're spreading your dosh between so many. The chances of their suddenly all going down the pan are rather slim. (One or two companies might, of course, but most of them actually just keep growing.)

An index tracker simply buys a bit of all these companies (thus spreading the risk) and benefits from their steady combined growth. All you do is buy some units in an index tracker – via a lump sum or by investing on a monthly basis – so you can benefit too.

History proves that investing in the stock market over the long term can reap huge rewards – and using an index tracker is the easiest way of doing it. Although we often say that past performance is no guide to the future (and generally this is absolutely true), there are some facts you simply can't ignore. And, of course, tracking the stock market over the long term is even better when you take into account the enormous importance of compound interest.

You can buy your index tracker, or several of them, in an ISA. Remember an ISA is a tax-protective wrapper around your investments that stops the Chancellor of the Exchequer from getting his hands on any profits you make over the years. It will depend on your personal circumstances as to whether you really need an ISA – there are other tax breaks such as the Capital Gains Tax allowance against which you offset your annual profit – but an index-tracking ISA is probably worth considering if you're planning to save for the long term, and if you don't want to have to think about boring tax stuff. It's often cheaper to buy your tracker within an ISA, too.

Build a firm base for your future

When Jane got married in 1989, her husband-to-be decided to make the wedding cake himself. It was to be a three-tier affair and he spent hours slaving over a hot Magi-Mix to create this masterpiece. Unfortunately, once the three cakes of varying sizes had cooled down, he realised that the centre of the largest cake – the base – wasn't quite cooked through in the centre. Instead of making a new base, he simply cut out the middle and packed it with bits of the smallest cake and announced it was to be a two-tier masterpiece instead of three.

You can guess what happened, can't you? Upon arriving at the reception, the newly-weds were greeted by an anxious hotel manager who informed the happy couple that what was to be the centrepiece of the wedding photographs had collapsed shortly after being assembled. Oops!

Apart from it being one of the more amusing memories of Jane's wedding day, there is a point to this story. To put your initial savings into context, think of your finances and how you want to invest for the future as a three-tier wedding cake.

The top tier represents your day-to-day expenses and the second tier your short-term goals, such as saving up for a car or a deposit for a house. The bottom layer is your long-term savings. The goal is to compound that long-term money into a solid foundation. Ideally, your long-term investments should eventually be the biggest piece of your cake, broad enough to support a long and active retirement. Being the bottom of the cake, it is the least accessible and should be left until the proper time has come; otherwise, your cake will crumble.

3

Get Out of Debt

I'm living so far beyond my income that we may almost be said to be living apart.

e. e. cummings

It may sound a little presumptuous to suggest this, but if you've spent your way into debt then, ahem, you may well have a self-esteem problem. Yes, really!

Psychologists at Sussex University have carried out quite a bit of research into the phenomenon of retail therapy and have concluded that, generally speaking, we shop in order to plug the gap between our actual and ideal selves. The more materialistic a person is, the more likely they are to be big spenders since it may make them feel more like the person they want to be. And as clothes, jewellery and ornaments are closely linked to self-image and appearance, it explains why these are such popular consumer goods, particularly amongst women. 'I shop, therefore I am.'

Now, obviously, not everyone in debt has self-esteem issues. If you've unexpectedly lost your job through being made redundant then that's far more likely to be the reason for your being in debt. But it does mean that next time you enviously watch a woman walking down the street in her Gucci shoes and swinging her Prada handbag, at least you can consider it a possibility in a *schadenfreude* sort of way. It might make you feel better!

Regardless of our self-esteem issues, we've turned from a nation with a horror of debt into one that loves it. Consumer debt has reached record levels and, frankly, it's a bit scary. The 'Buy Now, Pay Later' syndrome has taken hold of the nation so much that even the current Government is perturbed! Figures from the Bank of England show that the level of borrowing (excluding mortgages) in December 1997 amounted to £87.5 billion. Three years later it had risen to £127.4 billion – an increase of 45%! Citizens' Advice Bureaux have been overwhelmed dealing with nearly one million enquiries about debt in 2000/01.

What's more alarming is that we're not just spending this money on durables such as cars, kitchens and double-glazing – we're apparently spending it on holidays, meals out and other forms of entertainment. Where's the sense in *borrowing* money to pay for a meal in Pizza Express?

The Motley Fool's debt discussion boards are peppered with people searching for help after realising that years of out-of-control spending have resulted in their being £20,000 or £30,000 in debt – and that's not even counting the mortgage! Don't let that be you in ten years' time. And if you're already there, then it's time to pull your head out of the sand and face it. You'll be richer in the long run, honest. There's a saying that quite a sizeable proportion of the population is only two pay cheques away from the streets. This is, of course, highly unlikely to occur in the literal sense, but you take the point. If you lost your job and couldn't find another for two or three months, would you be able to manage? That's the question to ask yourself.

So if you use the willy-nilly, scattergun approach with your credit card or you're getting bills that you're too scared to open because you went and bought that new dress/sofa/car when your bank balance was already screaming at you not to, for God's sake, *slow down*. Perhaps it's time to call a halt to your spending and evaluate your position.

I am thirty-four and, with the exception of one couple, every single person (or couple) I know who is either the same age or younger than me, either carries debt over on their credit card or runs into overdraft every month – usually both. I know a couple who earn nearly £60,000 a year between them, live in a £120,000 house and have no kids yet still have several credit cards with ten's of thousands of pounds worth of debt on them! I know a girl in her early twenties who was distraught because she could not pay her debts. She went to a debt management company, restructured her payments and then went on a two-week holiday abroad. Responsibility? None!

From the Motley Fool discussion boards

Think about what you spend your money on and try not to be taken in by the hype. The advertising and marketing industries are just as bad as the financial services lot when it comes to persuading you to part with your hard-earned dosh. Remember that what you earn is not quite the same as what you take home in your pay cheque. The Government helps itself to a sizeable chunk before it even goes in the bank, so, when you actually figure out how many hours you have to work for your *disposable* pounds, it can put what you spend it on in a very different light. That pair of shoes may *look* as if they cost £80 but if it works out that they actually cost £120 in terms of the hours you have to work to pay for them, are they still good value for money?

As we said in the previous chapter, the Miracle of Compound Interest works *against* you when you are in debt. The lenders are making money out of you in interest charges and the longer you take to pay off your debts, the more they make out of you. It's a lucrative business for them but it's wasted money for you. We believe that learning how to manage your finances is easy – and it's even easier once you've realised the extent to which some of those lending you money are really ripping you off. It makes you want to fight back!

The fact is, if you spend more than you earn, you're going to get into trouble eventually, so if you're in debt then batten down the hatches and get shot of it.

This doesn't mean depriving yourself of the good things in life; you are not lowering your standard of living by exercising control. You are raising your expectations of living *well*. Just do it within your means. Not all debt is to be avoided, of course. Mortgage debt is fine – assuming you haven't overstretched yourself – as it's an essential living expense and the rates of interest are comparatively low. Cheap student debt is arguably okay too, provided it really *is* cheap, and that's usually the Government-type of student debt, which is pegged at the rate of inflation. But that's about it. All other debt is *bad*. So get rid of it!

The first step is to try to change your thinking: if you can be indignant about the amount of money you're wasting in interest charges, then you might be more inclined to take control. At the very least, if you know you're being a bit stupid about your spending, then admit it to yourself and make a decision not to be stupid any more. We know a woman who over a period of six months wasted £36 in bank charges simply because she couldn't be bothered to walk from one side of Paddington Station to the other where there was a free cashpoint. (No, it wasn't Jane. Well, okay, it was.)

Where to start

So, if you've rolled up your sleeves and you've decided that you want to tackle your debt problems, then your first step is to get to grips with your financial affairs. Don't groan! You only need to get your latest bank and credit card statements together in one pile – it's not *that* hard to do! Put simply, you need to work out:

● How much do you earn after tax each month?
● What are your essential outgoings each month?
● What's left?

Do a proper audit of your income and outgoings, a ruthlessly honest one. This is called a 'Statement of Affairs' (see our sample on page 70). If the 'What's left?' is negative, you're being unrealistic. You are living above your means. You need to rein in your spending for a while and think about where your money's going. Let's tackle the three basic criteria in a different way so we can work towards a solution.

How much do you earn?
We all have an income of some sort, whether it's your/your partner's salary, maintenance payments, Income Support or the Job Seeker's

Allowance. But, if you have children, don't forget things like Child Benefit or, if you have a lodger, don't forget to include income from rent. This forms your Total Net Monthly Income. Tot it all up and see what you've got.

What must you spend?

Next comes your *essential* spending needed to keep body and soul together. We're not talking about your debts as that is a separate issue. What we mean is mortgage/rent payments, gas, electricity and water rates, council tax, TV licence, telephone, house and car insurance, pension, basic groceries etc. (If you're behind with any of these, don't include the arrears.) Note down all the things that amount to *Needs* rather than *Wants*, in other words your Essential Monthly Outgoings. Add it all up and see what it comes to.

What have you got left?

Using the two figures from above, deduct your Essential Monthly Outgoings from your Total Net Monthly Income and you will be left with the sum of money - your Net Disposable Income - that you can spare to tackle your debts. Have you got enough coming in each month to cover those essential bills, with a bit to spare? If you haven't then a visit to your local Citizens' Advice Bureau is probably in order! They should be able to help.

Debts

This is where you have to take a deep breath and make a list of your actual debts. These include bank overdrafts, credit cards, store cards, car loans any other loans, as well as any arrears from your list of Essential Monthly Outgoings. It's best in cases where an interest rate is charged - and there usually is - to state the annual rate of interest. That way you can see at a glance which debts are costing you the most.

Did you realise you owed that much? And you've probably just remembered that you were in such a good mood last Saturday that you bought yourself a new party frock, had a girlie night out on the town and finished up with a good gossip down at the local curry house. All money you probably shouldn't have spent.

What next?

I started tackling my debts again about six or seven months ago. The fact that I've been going for that long makes it easily my most successful attempt ever. Last month, my credit-card balance hit zero, for the first time since I acquired the damn thing. My only debt left is a graduate loan. And, even though I don't need to pay that off – it's at 8.9% APR, not a punitive interest rate – I'm going to. And the reason for that is, I'm pretty sure, the same reason that this attempt will hopefully end my relationship with debt entirely. The reason is: I want to. The difference between needing *to reduce your debt and* wanting *to reduce your debt is, I think, a really significant one. Lots of people need to reduce their debt simply so that they can live without fear of repossessions and County Court Judgements or even put food on the table. But mostly, I think, they don't want to pay their debts off.*

The change in my attitude that took me from needing *to* wanting *was part of a change in my life generally. I felt that perhaps I was lacking direction somewhat – professionally, financially, in a number of ways – and I decided to consciously think about and write down what I was trying to achieve. When I'd thought about what I was trying to do in life, and I had written it down, it became obvious to me that being in debt was completely incompatible with many of the things that I was trying to accomplish. For example, I would like to start my own business, and I would like to be financially independent from my work – I'd like to be able to walk away from it if I choose. Clearly, if I was committed to making repayments on credit cards and loans, I was not in a position to achieve these and other aims. Because these aims were important to me, paying off my debt became a priority. I no longer just needed to do it, I had a genuine desire to.*

From the Motley Fool discussion boards

Remember the difference between *Needs* and *Wants*? Think about where you can cut back and set a budget for your required spending. A *Need* is the mortgage payment, a *Want* is buying a sandwich and a cappuccino for lunch during the week. If you're doing the latter, for example, then you're probably spending about £25 a week. That's £1,200 if you work 48 weeks a year!

Getting out of debt means looking at the current state of your finances so that you know, literally down to the very last penny, where your money is going. Start looking at what comes out of your purse every day. People often say they haven't a clue where all their money goes. It's pretty easy to find out. Write down what you've spent whenever you hand over any money! You might be able to see perfectly well from your bank statement that you took £50 out of the cashpoint the other day and the remaining balance seems to be correct, but the question really is: do you know what you spent that £50 on? So, carry a small notebook around for about a month, keep all your receipts and, if you're handy with a spreadsheet, log it all into the computer. It's only when you can clearly see where all the loose change in your pocket disappeared to that you understand exactly what you might be doing wrong.

You will probably find that it's not really the big things that are hitting you where it hurts, but the small things. Spur-of-the-moment sessions in the pub after work and the frequent trips to Tesco on the way home, not to mention popping into the newsagent's round the corner for a can of cola every afternoon. It all mounts up, sometimes shockingly so. You may spot that you could cut back a lot simply by making your own sandwiches for lunch, doing your weekly grocery shop with a well-thought-out shopping list in your hand. If you're paying gym fees every month, ask yourself whether a brisk walk around the block might be a cheaper way of taking exercise.

Be aware, though, that you are highly unlikely to be suddenly and magically transported to the Land of Plenty. But this simple exercise of making a note of your expenditure for one month might just provide the push you've been looking for to get on the road to an even brighter future. It may take a few weeks or months to change the habits of a lifetime – perhaps even longer if spending money has been your number one favourite pastime since the day you acquired your first credit card! But it's not hard, and you don't necessarily have to do without. You'll just find yourself questioning your expenditure a bit more. Keeping an eye on your petty cash helps you to realise how much money you've been pouring down the drain for all those years.

So set a budget for your Needs and a separate budget for your Wants, then stick to it as if your life depended on it. Be strict but fair with yourself. The purpose behind setting these budgets is to free up extra cash to pay off your debts, not to punish yourself for finding you are in debt.

Once you've done that you'll be in a position to use the leftovers to tackle your debts. So let's do it!

The art of snowballing

Have you ever heard of 'snowballing'? Lots of people haven't and yet it's one of the easiest and simplest methods to use when trying to get shot of debts. It's also extremely effective and it works in exactly the same way as our compound-interest snowball. Just as snowballs get bigger and bigger as they roll down the hill, so do debts get crushed and annihilated at a faster rate the more you practise it.

The idea of snowballing is to single out one debt as your target and throw all the money you can at it whilst making minimum payments on all your other debts. Once you've paid off your first target debt, you then use all that freed-up money to tackle the next one on your list. Take a look at this example for three credit-card debts:

	Debt	Amount Owed	APR	Minimum Payment
CREDIT CARD DEBT	CC1	£1,000	22%	£50
	CC2	£5,000	12%	£150
	CC3	£10,000	6%	£300

You owe a total of £16,000 and your minimum payments each month are £500. It's quite a scary number and, obviously, it's going to take a long time to pay these credit cards off if you only make the stated minimum payments. Three years and one month, actually – and that's only if you keep paying the same amount each month. You'll be looking at many more years if you reduce your minimum payments whenever the credit-card companies tell you that you can. But let's say you've managed to pare down your expenditure so that you have a spare £200 available each month on top of the £500 minimum payments for all of the debts. Where do you start?

Well, logically, it makes sense to focus on the most expensive debt first – the £1,000 with an APR of 22%. It also has the added bonus of being the smallest debt, so you'll get a result pretty quickly, which should prove motivating. So, let's pay the minimum of £50 plus the spare £200 towards this debt – a total of £250 – whilst continuing to make only minimum payments on the others. Note that, as you gradually pay off this first debt, you'll be told that your minimum payment has been cut – but don't reduce the amount you are repaying! *Keep paying it off at the same rate.* You'll have cleared CC1 after five months.

Obviously, you'll then have a spare £250 a month to throw at the next debt. If you add that £250 to the £150 you're paying towards CC2, you'll have a total of £400 to chuck at this second debt. Because you've also been making minimum payments whilst paying off CC1, you'll have cleared CC2 seventeen months from now.

Eventually, you'll have £400 available to add to the £300 you're paying for CC3 – a total of £700 a month. Wow! You'll be shot of that debt in no time at all! Debt-free two years and one month after you started – and you'll have saved yourself a bundle in interest at the same time. Remember that, if you'd made only the same minimum payments listed in the table, it would have taken you three years and one month to clear your debts. But using this method, you'll be 'clean' a whole year sooner, you'll have saved a great deal in interest and you'll find yourself £700 a month richer! That's £700 of 'real' money – for you, not the credit-card companies.

Obviously, to snowball effectively you have to have more money available than what's necessary merely to meet the minimum payments. You need to look at your expenditure and see where you can make cutbacks so that you've got some extra money to start the snowball rolling. Find out how to get a better deal on your mortgage, your utilities and your credit cards and loans; free up some money for your snowball fund. You'll realise, for example, that our first credit-card debt – the £1,000 at the astronomical interest rate of 22% – could be transferred to another credit card with a much lower rate, which will make your snow-balling efforts even more effective.

If you have access to the Internet you can download a spreadsheet at http://www.geocities.com/schizeckinosy/Snowball.html, devised by one of our American Fools for people who are in debt. If you enter into the spreadsheets each of your debts, their relevant interest rates and the amount of money you have available to pay off these debts it will then tell you how quickly you can pay them off depending on whether you do this, that or the other.

There are other ways to make or save money (see our tips on page 67). Jasmine, for example, paid off an £8,000 debt inside a year by selling things, not going on holiday at all, doing babysitting and working for six and even seven days a week for a while.

Use your savings

Obviously, you need cash for essential expenses like mortgage payments, Council Tax, utilities etc., but if you have debts, *you do not need a savings account*. Think about it. A 19% interest rate on £1,000 of debt versus a 5% interest rate on the same amount in savings – you're not *saving* money, you're *losing* it. You would be daft to have savings and be borrowing money at the same time. Also, remember that any interest you earn on your savings will be taxed, whilst interest you pay on your borrowings comes out of your after-tax income. There's simply no point in paying vast amounts of interest on money that you owe if you're reaping much smaller returns on the money that you're saving.

Some people like to have a little bit of money in savings – an emergency fund – so they can meet any unexpected expenses that might crop up, and that's fair enough. Remember, however, if you've paid off your debts with your savings then, in an emergency, you could always resort to your credit card again, if you really have to. If you have the opportunity to get shot of your debts by using your savings, that's almost always the route you should take.

Use credit cards to your advantage

Switch as much of your debt as you can to a low-interest credit card – there are plenty of them around. If you don't want the hassle of switching frequently, the cards that offer low rates for the lifetime of the debt are better than the deals that last for only six months. *If you're going to do bad things, make sure you do the least bad things possible.* Shopping around pays off.

Watch out for those lenders who offer you something like 2% for balance transfers and 10% for *new* borrowings (in other words, that frock you spotted yesterday). Your monthly payments will go towards your original debt until you've paid it off, but any new borrowings will sit there for months on end getting bigger and bigger because of the higher interest rate. Crafty, aren't they? Your best bet is to move your debts to the most appropriate credit card for balance transfers and then use a different low-interest credit card for any new *emergency* spending.

Your next task is to cut up all your credit cards apart from the emergency one. Now put this one remaining credit card into a plastic container, fill it with water and hide it at the back of the freezer so it's there only if you really need it. At least it'll be out of temptation's way until you really do have an emergency, and you may find that by the time you defrost it, you'll have gone off the idea of buying whatever it was you so desperately wanted in the first place. (Don't cheat! If you're thinking of the microwave, it's a bad idea. It does terrible things to the magnetic strip!)

Watch your overdraft

Many people find themselves dipping into the red at the end of the month and being charged interest on their overdrafts. Overdraft debt is not sensible, but as we have said before, people sometimes behave in a – small 'f' – foolish way. The most important thing is never, ever let your bank balance slip into the red without already having arranged an overdraft with your bank. Unauthorised overdraft rates are even more extortionate than credit-card rates, and you are likely to find many other charges are piled on top, too. These unauthorised overdraft rates do not take into account any additional charges like arrangement fees, securities charges and monthly fees. Overdraft rates don't tell the whole story. Most banks and building societies add monthly fees while you're in the red.

Borrowing money using an expensive overdraft facility is just not sensible. But again, *if you're going to do bad things, make sure you do the least bad things possible.* If you know that you are likely to carry an overdraft on your current account, make sure you swap your account to a bank that offers you the best rates possible.

Consolidate your debts

As a last resort, if you really can't face filling in the forms for better-rate credit cards or using the snowball method to clear your debts, then get a low-interest personal loan so that you can pay off all your debts at once and be left with one simple monthly payment. We regard this as a last resort because it is extremely common for people to consolidate their debts with a personal loan, and then go on a spending spree using their newly cleared cards! They don't just end up back at square one with their credit cards: they've now got a personal loan to pay back as well. Another reason it is a last resort is that lenders sometimes require personal loans to be secured against your home. If you fall behind with your payments because you've racked up more debt again, then you could be in danger of losing the roof over your head.

So, be warned! Having just one big debt rather than half a dozen smaller ones doesn't mean you're sorted. You're not! A lot of adverts these days try to tempt you with personal loans by using the phrase 'clear your debts'. By consolidating your debts you are not clearing them at all: you are simply shifting them from one set of lenders to another. You've made life a little less complicated by bundling them all together, but that's all! Be careful not to run up further debts while you're paying off the loan.

Know how the system works

I recently applied for a new credit card and to my surprise was refused. I say surprise because my current credit card companies are always increasing my credit limit. I applied for the new card over the Internet and used an address that I have just moved into rather than the address of my current cards. Could this be the problem?

From the Motley Fool discussion boards

The question above is typical of those we often see on our discussion boards on the Motley Fool. Why is one organisation prepared to lend you money but another isn't?

In general, the answer lies in the credit scoring system adopted by each provider. Whenever you apply for a credit card, personal loan or mortgage, the prospective lender will run a credit check on you through one of the two main credit reference agencies: Experian and Equifax.

Between them these two agencies hold details on some 44 million people in the UK. Your file includes information about your other credit cards, your mortgage, your bank accounts as well as facts and figures on any unpaid bills, failure to pay hire-purchase debts and County Court Judgements, or CCJs. An adverse credit record will obviously count against you. Importantly, your credit reference also records whether you have applied recently for new loans or credit cards. As you'll see later, this is significant.

It is entirely up to the credit provider as to the amount of risk they are prepared to take, so varying degrees of importance are attached to the information gathered from the credit reference agency and from your application form. It works on a points system: the more points you get, the more likely it is that the provider will lend you money. However, while one provider may give you 40 points for being married (some lenders think that makes you a stable and reliable person!), another may not give you any points at all. It depends on the provider's target market: after all, a provider targeting students wouldn't expect many of them to be married.

A lender's individual credit scoring system is commercially sensitive information so it's sometimes difficult to find out exactly why you might have been turned down for a credit card or loan. However, here's a sample credit score with some examples that may give you an idea of how it works:

	Years in present employment	Points
	0–5	0
	6–10	+15
	11–12	+30
	13 or over	+50
	Marital status	**Points**
	Divorced	0
	Widowed	+10
	Married	+40
	Single	+12
	Age	**Points**
	21–25	0
	26–30	+5
	31–39	+40
	40–59	+55
	60 or over	+42

SAMPLE CREDIT SCORE

SAMPLE CREDIT SCORE continued

Number of children	Points
None	+30
1	+15
2	+5
3 or over	0

Age of most recent bad debt	Points
No debts	+5
Less than 3 months	-35
3–12 months	-30
1–2 years	-27
2–3 years	-15

Telephone	Points
Yes	+20
No	-30
Not answered	0

It's interesting, isn't it, how you get penalised for being divorced or for not having a phone? And why is a 24-year-old considered less responsible than a 34-year-old? Other criteria include how long you've lived at a particular address (the longer the better) and whether or not you're on the electoral roll. Your postcode is also relevant because it indicates whether you live in an affluent area or not. And your profession counts, too.

One very important factor is the number of applications for credit you've made. This is registered on your file and it counts against you if you've been applying for credit willy-nilly over a short period of time. It's far better to find out why a lender has turned you down in the first place instead of applying somewhere else, just in case it's something you can rectify. The reason it's as well to bear this in mind is that, if you decide to take up the gauntlet and work on getting yourself out of debt according to the advice in this chapter, you may well be looking for low-rate credit cards and personal loans as a means of doing it. If the first couple of lenders turn you down, then the third might wonder what's going on and turn you down as well. So, be very choosy about your first application. Phone your prospective lender and find out if you're *likely* to be accepted without their running a check on you and, only if the answer's positive, *then* apply formally.

Your credit file can also contain mistakes and, as you're allowed to correct any factual errors, it makes sense to obtain a copy of your file to check it. You're also allowed to add a brief statement to your file to explain a problem that might usually count against you, for example, why you briefly fell behind with your mortgage payments six months previously. There may be a good reason that would help the lender to make a more informed decision.

To that end, it's a good idea to get hold of your credit files before you start applying for any form of borrowing, just so you can see what your prospective lender will see. (See page 73 for the addresses of the two main credit reference agencies, Experian and Equifax.) They don't hold exactly the same information, so it's worth getting copies of both credit files for comparison.

Some tricks of the trade

It's true we should have more control over our spending as individuals, but it doesn't help that the moneymen confuse us with doublespeak. It's how they stay ahead of the game and why we fall further and further behind. The fact is credit is simply another word for debt. Think of phrases like 'to his/her credit' or 'creditable': it sounds like a good and reliable thing, almost the complete opposite of debt. Try substituting the word 'debt' for 'credit' wherever you see it: 'Debt card', 'easy debt terms', 'interest-free debt for six months', 'Poor debt rating? Don't worry – we can offer you debt today!' Do they still sound like attractive offers? Does 'good credit rating' really mean very much more than you are considered to be a reliable payer of interest?

The average credit card balance in the UK is £2,500 per person. Unless it is paid off in full each month then it is probably costing an Annual

Percentage Rate (APR) of at least about 15% – and that amounts to £375 per year. To some people £375 may not seem a lot of money, but think of it this way: if you lost your purse with £375 in it, would you be upset? Of course you would. Apart from anything else it's the price of a week's holiday in one of Europe's cheaper and sunnier climes, but instead you're freely giving it away to Spend-U-Like Finance or Buy-Now Plastic!

So think about what you're paying in interest. Make sure that whenever you borrow anything, you know how much you will be paying overall. A £10,000 car loan at 15% APR from a high-street bank over four years will cost, approximately, £3,350 in interest payments alone. How long does it take you to earn £3,350? And what else could you do with that £3,350 over those four years?

Be aware that credit-card companies love it when you make only the minimum payment each month. Minimum payments are usually worked out at between 2% and 5% of the total outstanding balance or £10, whichever is the greater. But if you choose to pay just the minimum amount of, say, 2% on a £500 credit card bill that charges an 15% APR, it will take you over six and a half years or 79 payments to clear your debt. Furthermore, you will have paid almost £290 in interest on that £500 purchase. So don't give in to the temptation. Try to pay off as much as you can or, better still, pay off the whole amount whenever possible.

Store cards are particularly iniquitous. Many of them charge interest rates as high as 30%, and often we don't even realise it! Our bank, credit-card and store-card statements usually show just the monthly interest rate and, let's face it, 2.21% a month doesn't look nearly as bad as the actual APR of 30% glaring out at us from the page.

Also, banks and credit card companies are so eager for your business that they'll raise your credit limit without your even having to ask. It's designed to make you feel as if you were being given free money when actually it's simply a backhanded way of persuading you to borrow even more than you already have. Their latest trick is to send you a cheque saying it's yours to spend however you like, and all that you have to do to cash it is to sign on the dotted line.

Of course, credit cards do have their good points. For example, under the Consumer Credit Act 1974, when you make a purchase with your credit for goods over £100, the credit-card company is also liable if the goods or services are faulty. So if the retailer won't replace or refund your money you can then take the matter up with your credit-card provider. Under Section 75 of the Act the credit-card company is just as liable as the trader and this can be quite useful if the shopkeeper has gone out of business. So they're not all bad. It's just exasperating when you realise all the hidden ways they try to take money off you and how expensive it can be.

Another trick of the trade comes into operation when you take out a personal loan and are persuaded to buy the insurance product that goes with it. Sometimes you can be conned into buying it because your application form requires you to decline it specifically if you don't want it and, since many people don't check the small print, they find themselves inadvertently saddled with a product they didn't necessarily want. Any bank or building society will do their level best to sell you payment-protection insurance whenever you take out a personal loan. They make a lot of money from you if you do – sometimes up to a third as much again – so the hard sell is understandable from their point of view. But the fact is you are paying your insurance premiums to the bank to protect *them* against your being unable to repay the loan. So, whilst it may be great for them, it's not necessarily in your own interests to take them up on their kind offer.

If you're taking out a loan that is secured against your home then some form of payment protection might be worth thinking about if you have no other form of insurance against loss of income. After all, you don't want to risk losing your home. In general we're not in favour of secured loans – particularly if it's to consolidate your debts – because if for whatever reason, bad luck or bad management, you can't meet the payments, you run the risk of losing your house. Taking equity out of your house to pay for your debts is also inadvisable. It's a one-card trick – once you've used up the equity in your home, that part of it is gone forever.

Many personal loans, however, are unsecured and, in these cases, people often find they're not quite as protected by insurance as they think they are.

Again, it's the small print. We don't like reading it so we don't check it properly, but it usually boils down to the fact that you'd have to be practically dying to qualify under many loan-repayment protection schemes or else be long-term unemployed. And your loan is likely to be paid off only if you actually drop dead. But they don't tell you that, of course.

For example, you'll no doubt be told that the policy will cover your monthly payments for up to a year until you find a new job. Sounds good, doesn't it? What you won't be told is that they probably won't pay up for the first couple of months of unemployment, by which time you'll either have found yourself another job or be two months behind with your payments already. The same thing will probably apply if you fall ill. Most likely you'll be well again within the non-claimable period but, unless your employer has continued to pay you your salary, again you'll find yourself behind with the payments.

You may also find if you try to repay your loan early you'll get stung by something called the Rule of 78. This is where your insurance or interest payments are 'front-loaded' at the start of the loan period. The way it works is very similar to a repayment mortgage. Your initial repayments are almost all swallowed up in interest or insurance payments, the reasoning being that at the start of the loan you have a higher balance therefore your interest or insurance payments would have to be higher to cover it. The longer you pay your loan, the lower the proportion of your repayment is taken up by interest or insurance payments and the more you pay off from the capital sum. It's something the Government plans to put an end to but until they do, you might find you're stuck. Just be sure if you take out any sort of personal loan that you check the small print thoroughly.

So watch out for these tricks of the trade!

There may be trouble ahead

What happens if the hole you've dug for yourself is far deeper than you thought? Maybe you're getting scary letters that you can barely bring yourself to open: demands for payment, final demands for payment, threatening letters from debt collectors, gas and electricity disconnection notices, eviction notices. Perhaps you're being threatened with a court summons.

If your credit record turns out to be blacker than you thought, you're turned down for either a new card or a loan or you feel you are being harassed by current creditors, then you're going to have to take a different tack when it comes to managing your debts.

It's very easy to feel overwhelmed by your debts, especially when you're receiving apparently threatening letters and phone calls. Some people become genuinely frightened and, when you're frightened, it's even harder to make yourself open those letters and respond to those phone calls. It's important that you do, though, not least because you could be digging a much deeper hole for yourself, but it's worth bearing in mind that, provided you have no savings or assets, there really isn't a huge amount your creditors can do to you – even if they're threatening you with bankruptcy. So what? It's only money and there is yet to be a law passed that permits them to squeeze blood out of a stone.

Realise, though, that there are certain payments that really should take priority when you're trying to work out which bills to pay first. Believe it or not, your Council Tax bill should be top of the list because, in certain circumstances, you can actually be sent to prison for not paying it. Once you've paid your Council Tax, your mortgage payment should be next on your list as should any loans you have that are secured on your home. If you don't make those payments, you could lose the roof over your head. Think about it this way: if you can't make that payment to Dixons for the all-singing, all-dancing widescreen TV, they can come and take the TV away. If you can't make the mortgage payment, they can come and take your home away. Which is more important?

As a first step towards dealing with any creditors you can't pay, write to them to explain that you are having problems at the moment and offer a realistic and sensible payment proposal. If you enclose your income and expenditure list, you may find they consider that you've thought out the problem and have made the best offer that you can in the circumstances.

They may even agree to freeze the interest charges if you ask nicely. It's worth knowing that creditors are nowadays expected to try to resolve matters before taking court action, so don't be frightened if they threaten it. Litigation must be a last rather than a first resort and whilst the court cannot refuse to issue proceedings (in normal circumstances), the judges do have discretion to lower payments or not to award costs. (See page 71 for a sample letter to creditors along with a follow-up version you can use if they don't initially play ball.)

> *My friend deals with debt collection and has lost count of judges sighing in exasperation at creditors refusing realistic offers from debtors. 'How do they expect you to live?' was one response a judge made to a client of hers before ordering a repayment figure of £1 a month on a £3,500 debt. He even asked her if she (the debtor) and her husband could ever afford at least one evening a month out, which he felt was very important to maintain 'spiritual and mental health at a difficult time'. Lovely!*
>
> From the Motley Fool discussion boards

The important thing is to contact them before they contact you. Most of the people you might deal with at the other end of the phone are perfectly ordinary nice individuals, and if you're straight with them about your circumstances they will be more willing to help. Ignoring their letters and phone calls is *not* the way to deal with things. Nothing winds up a debt collector more if they believe you are purposely avoiding them. It creates more administration and costs money. As one debt collector told us: 'We have all the time in the world for the 'can't pays' but none at all for the 'won't pays', and they're the ones we generally have no hesitation in taking to court.'

If any creditors continue to press you for more money, and you've already shown them that you really can't afford to pay more, then be aware that your creditors cannot harass you by law. They cannot threaten you or make abusive remarks and they're not allowed to put pressure on your family or friends to chase up your debts. And if they send bailiffs round, you do not have to let them in the house. If you feel harassed by debt collectors, you should write an official letter of complaint to them (sent by registered post) asking them to stop any further communication with you. After that they have the right to contact you further *only* if they intend to take legal action against you.

The fact is, if they issue a summons taking you to court, the judge is most likely going to make an order for you to pay them what you've offered them already – possibly even less if he thinks you're over-committing yourself. The debtor should always attend the court hearing otherwise a County Court Judgement will always be granted by default and the creditor will always ask for the Judgement to be paid forthwith. If the debtor attends the court and asks the Judge if they can pay by instalments then, unless there are exceptional circumstances, the Judge will nearly always agree to this. If not, the creditor has several ways of executing the Judgement including making you bankrupt (if the debt exceeds £750) or serving an Attachment of Earnings Order or Attachment of Property Order.

The same applies to any debts sold on to a credit agency. Sometimes lenders will get fed up with chasing you for money so, after a period of time, they may 'sell' your debt on to someone else – often for a fraction of what you owe. The new owner of your debt has an incentive to get back from you at least what they paid for it and, far from this being a bad thing for you, it can be used to your advantage. If you owed your original lender £1,000 and your debt was sold for £600 to the credit agency, then you may find that you can offer them £600 in full and final settlement of the debt and they'll accept it. At least they've got their money back, and if you offer a little more than £600 they'll have made a bit of a profit. They're not going to tell you how much they paid for your debt, of course, but you can make surprisingly low offers in full and final settlement and find they accept. Obviously you need a lump sum to pay the settlement but if you can raise the money somehow, it's well worthwhile. The point is to make an offer.

Any defaults and CCJs will stay on your credit file for six years so it will be difficult for you to borrow any more money during that period, but if you manage to pay off the CCJ you can ask the creditor about getting a 'letter of satisfaction' which you should then present to the relevant county court with the appropriate fee (£4 at the time of writing). They will issue a 'certificate of satisfaction' and will inform the Registry Trust in London which is responsible for amending the Judgement record. Although the Trust will notify the credit reference agencies, you should send them copies of the letter of satisfaction to make sure. It'll mean the CCJ is then officially marked as satisfied on the agency's database and prospective creditors may look on you a little more favourably. Ultimately, lenders are really much more interested in your current circumstances rather than any mistakes you may have made two or three years ago. It's worth rebuilding your credit file by making all payments on time so they can see that, even if you were a bad girl a couple of years previously, you've learned your lesson and might now be considered a reliable payer.

If you still feel overwhelmed about trying to sort things out, there are two organisations that will help you for free. One is your local Citizens' Advice Bureau, or CAB (look in your local telephone directory or find at www.nacab.org.uk), and the other is the Consumer Credit Counselling Service, or CCCS (phone on 0113 297 0121 or find at www.cccs.co.uk). On *no* account go to a debt management company: these organisations mostly promise you the earth and then charge you humungous amounts for services that you could easily handle yourself. The money you pay them would be better spent on clearing your debts and it only prolongs the debt nightmare. Why pay a debt management company when the CAB and the CCCS will help you for free?

Bankruptcy

If things are more serious and the word 'bankruptcy' is keeping you awake at night, then you need to consider that, while things may be pretty grim, it still isn't the end of the world. You owe people money, not your life!

The first thing to realise is that bankruptcy is a right in law. This means that if creditors are persistently pursuing you for more money than you can afford to pay, and it is unlikely that your circumstances will allow you to resolve the situation, then you have the *right* to declare yourself bankrupt. Similarly, if you persistently fail to pay or come to an acceptable arrangement with your creditors then, provided that you owe more than £750, the creditor has the right to make an application for your bankruptcy.

In times gone by bankruptcy was a *privilege* of the well-to-do. It afforded a creditor the means to retrieve his money by enforcing the sale of the debtor's assets (pretty well much the same as it means these days). However, as the vast majority of debtors were from the lower classes and owned nothing at all, it was the dear old debtor's gaol for them and so Newgate prison had a flourishing community. These days, with the exception of Crown debts, you don't get thrown into prison for owing money.

Technically, you could lose any asset that is owned or part-owned by you. This includes any savings, shares, pensions (subject to recent amendments) or equity that you have in property or a business, as well as a proportion of your salary (depending on how much you earn).

They cannot take anything that is not owned or part-owned by you. For instance, if you live with your parents they cannot take goods belonging to them. Similarly, they can't take goods belonging to your partner/husband. Where a property is involved they can only seize any equity that is yours – they cannot touch his share. Contrary to popular belief, you do not automatically lose your house when you become bankrupt. You still need to keep a roof over your head so, if there is any equity in the property, a third party (wife, brother, mother etc.) can make an offer to the Official Receiver for your share of the equity. If accepted, this has the effect of taking the property out of the bankruptcy. If this is a possibility, it should be done at the earliest opportunity as, otherwise, the Official Receiver will register a charge on the property that can be called in even 10 or 20 years down the line. Even if there is no equity, or even negative equity, in the property, it is still worth making an offer for this reason.

Similarly, they won't take things such as tools of trade that you need to perform your job – for example, a computer if it's essential for your work. And if you need your car to get to and from work, the Official Receiver can even exclude vehicles from the bankruptcy (although he is unlikely to do so if the car is a brand-new Mercedes).

If you are earning a substantial salary, the Official Receiver will ask you to make a contribution to your debts. Any contribution will be payable for as long as you remain an undischarged bankrupt. If you receive a windfall, are left money or property in a will by a relative or win the lottery, the Official Receiver will seize whatever is appropriate. Generally, unless you are earning in excess of £20–25,000 a year, it is unlikely that you will be asked to contribute to your bankruptcy and, even if you were, these contributions would cease on discharge.

At the moment, if it is your first bankruptcy and your debts are below £20,000, you will be automatically discharged after just two years. However, if it is your first bankruptcy and your debts exceed £20,000, you will be automatically discharged only after three years (provided that you have co-operated with the Official Receiver). If this isn't your first bankruptcy or you are serving multiple bankruptcies – you can be bankrupted more than once at the same time – then the bankruptcy period will be determined by the county court and you will have to make an application for discharge. Whilst you may be discharged after two or three years, the bankruptcy will remain registered against your address for six years.

Finally, whilst bankruptcy may be the only way out, make sure that you have explored every other avenue first – even telling your creditors that unless they accept what you can afford to pay, this will be the only way forward for you. In the event that you are declared bankrupt, there will be little or no pay-out at all to your creditors so it's in their interests to consider any offer you can make to them.

Individual Voluntary Arrangement

As an alternative to bankruptcy, there is a slightly less drastic route that can be taken. The Individual Voluntary Arrangement, or IVA, is an alternative to going bankrupt without actually going the whole hog. As the words imply, it's an arrangement between the debtor and the creditor which is intended to give the creditor a better return than they could expect to get from a customer who's gone bankrupt.

The good thing about an IVA is that it stops your creditors from knocking at your door and at the same time enables you to have a great deal more control over how your assets are dealt with than you would with bankruptcy. The bad thing is that it all costs money to implement and it's money that you could have used to pay off your debts.

An IVA generally lasts for between two and five years and is proposed at a meeting of creditors called by an Insolvency Practitioner at your request. If the proposal is accepted, the Insolvency Practitioner becomes your Supervisor. For the proposal to succeed it must be accepted by 75% of the creditors in number and in value of those creditors attending the meeting. (Creditors can attend in person, be represented by agent, or can vote by proxy – if they do not attend in person or by representation/proxy then they do not get a vote, regardless of how big the debt is). If they do accept, it's binding on all creditors whether they like it or not. If approved, you would then have to make the agreed monthly instalments, which includes an element to pay the Supervisor. In turn, he then makes interim payments to the creditors on your behalf.

Be warned, though, that an IVA is lodged on your credit file and if you default on your payments the Supervisor is legally obliged to bankrupt you. This happens surprisingly often, so you need to ask yourself whether you want to slog away for the next three to five years to pay back an agreed portion of your debt to the creditors when you could end the matter quickly by declaring bankruptcy. You might lose much of what you've got but you wouldn't have to pay off any of the remaining debts.

Spendthrift partners

If there's ever been one thing designed to cause arguments in a relationship, it's money. According to Relate, the marriage guidance experts, it's the biggest single cause of rows between couples and can be a direct cause of relationship breakdown. And if you think that only people *without* money have rows about it, think again. Even couples *with* money quarrel when they disagree about how to spend it.

Trying to get out of debt can be very hard if your partner is a spendthrift and refuses to accept there is a problem with his spending habits. But there are some steps you can take to help him see the light. You're going to have to do a fair bit of work by yourself and use a 'softly-softly catchee monkey' approach if you're at least going to persuade him to turn and face the same direction as you.

Before you do anything, you need to work out the numbers. There's no point in shouting about how he shouldn't have bought that new DVD player if he hasn't been given a chance to see *why* you can't afford it. Use your statement of affairs or a simple spreadsheet to work out your income, your essential outgoings and your debts so you can show him absolute proof that there is a problem. This chapter will have given you plenty of ideas for a plan of action that you can show him such as shifting the debts to credit cards with lower interest rates and changing your gas and electricity suppliers to cheaper ones.

Try to be positive rather than negative about it: 'I've been thinking about how we can afford that car/new gadget/holiday and I've been doing some numbers. Can we go over them at the weekend to see what you think?' Try and have a calm conversation, using your figures to illustrate the financial position you're both in. Use whatever tactics you know might work, after all, you know your partner better than anyone. For example:

● Play on the fact that you may not have remembered all the income and expenditure items and that you really need his input to make sure you've got the figures right. Flattery does work sometimes!

- Show him how much is going on interest payments every month. Even at a low rate, it's probably still a substantial amount. If you can point out that, say, £500 is being wasted every year just on servicing the debt and that he could get a pretty good sound system for that, it might help to gently push the point home.
- If he hates his job, point out how many hours of work he's putting in just to service your debts. 'You're busting your gut all week just to pay off the ? (insert name of toy or whatever here) that you bought three years ago and don't even use anymore.' It may annoy him just enough to want to pay it off as soon as possible.
- Try to get him to suggest ways of tackling certain debts. Show him your own plan of action, ask if he thinks it would work and what he thinks could be done to improve it.

It's important to try and sell the idea that the two of you are a team fighting the rest of the world, and that if you both work together, you *will* be able to have that new car, gadget or holiday. Not yet though, but eventually. Stress that the life changes you need to make are only temporary and that it will be worth it in the end.

If you can agree that action needs to be taken, start talking about how you're going to do it. Get him involved, even if it's just in a minor way: 'I'll sort out the application for a low-rate credit card and see if we can get a better deal on that loan. Can you sort out switching the gas company?' He'll be more likely to help if you feed him little tasks one at a time rather than overloading him with a list of phone calls to make or letters to write. Remember, if you're truly to get him on board you need to reel him in carefully. It's important to be aware that with joint loans or credit cards you are both liable for the debts. If he defaults on his share, the lender will come after you for it, so think very carefully before entering into a joint arrangement with your partner.

If your finances are really dire, you may want to consider the prospect of one or both of you getting a second job. Seriously. It's not something we tend to do so much in the UK, but in the US a second job is how a lot of people deal with financial problems as it's one of the fastest ways of getting shot of debt. While it may sound painful at first, there's almost always time in the day or night when you can find a few hours to fit in some part-time work. The extra income you bring in can make an incredible difference to your debts. Some employers won't allow you to take a second job as they may feel there is a conflict of interest, so check with your Human Resources department first.

Importantly, don't tie the noose too tightly. Work out a budget and ensure it includes some fun money. If your partner doesn't feel rewarded in some way for his efforts, he'll be more inclined to spend again. If you both plan these things into a proper budget, your partner won't feel as if you're trying to restrict him.

Above all, communicate, communicate, communicate. Show him when you've managed to pay off a credit card so he can see that both your efforts are paying off. Praise him when he's resisted the temptation to buy something he really wanted. Share all your successes and failures so you keep each other motivated.

If you can get your partner to buy into the idea of getting out of debt so you eventually have the money to do something you both really want to do, he'll be more likely to help. If it doesn't work, you haven't lost anything. If it does, you'll at least be in the position of having to find something else to argue about – because it surely won't be about money!

A final thought

We have a large empty whisky bottle and put all our coppers and 5p pieces into it. Unfortunately my 18-month-old decided it was a prime target for a ram raid with his sit-on-engine so I had to empty it out last night. It was only half full but still had in excess of £50! Pennies do indeed look after the pounds, I just can't force myself to save the £2 coins just yet, it just seems too much at one go...

From the Motley Fool discussion boards

In an ideal world, we would have no debts and we would have plenty of savings and investments to see us through our old age. We would also have enough money put by for emergencies, such as when the car suddenly breaks down, the washing machine has a hissy fit and refuses to be fixed or you suddenly get made redundant. If possible, you should strive to build up liquid funds of between three and six months' income so that, should the worst happen, you have the facility to coast for a while.

This sounds like a lot of money. You may think you could survive with the use of a credit card if you really had to, but those bills will need to be paid off at some point and you could find yourself struggling for much longer than necessary – and paying through the nose for it, too. By all means have a line of credit as a last resort, but since foresight is better than hindsight, you'd be better off with an emergency fund to start with.

Really, you should plan for the worst and hope for the best, so that means thinking about what sort of worse-case scenario could have a potentially damaging effect on your long-term finances. Ideally, you need to work out your Essential Monthly Outgoings, then multiply it by at least three (or a higher number if you feel more comfortable with it) and you've got a target figure to aim for. Don't worry if you need to start small – even a tenner a month will build up eventually.

Of course, you may think you have insurance to cover calamities such as a job loss or a boiler repair, but the money you spend on income-protection insurance possibly wouldn't be paid out until you've been unemployed for six months anyway (check the terms). The Motley Fool has always said that extended warranties are almost always a waste of money. The whole point of having an emergency fund is that you're insuring *yourself* sufficiently against particular emergencies, thus doing away with the need for certain types of insurance cover. Bear in mind that this outlay is yours forever, so, if you never have to access it, you've still got a nice lump sum to call your very own.

The important thing is not to think of your emergency fund as 'savings' – it's not. Your savings are for a long way off in the future, whereas this pot of money is for a passing crisis. So, if your clapped-out old banger goes phut-phut one day on the motorway, then don't hesitate to dip into your emergency fund to fix it. That's what it's there for. You can work on building it up again afterwards once the crisis is over.

Finally, however you set about becoming debt-free, try to see the experience as an empowering one. You are taking responsibility for your debts and that doesn't mean blaming yourself for the mess you've found yourself in. You are simply deciding to fight back, and fighting back is good for self-esteem, overall confidence and bank accounts. Sometimes you might feel you're in the middle of a rather tedious battle, but keep at it. The day will come when you suddenly realise you've won the war.

Once you've achieved your goal, remember to maintain the sensible spending habits that you've now acquired. It's no good getting out of debt, then going back to your old spending ways and constantly yo-yoing in and out of the red. It's a bit like dieting. Just as we have to change our eating habits if we want to keep the weight off, we have to change totally the way we look at our spending. We not only need to stay out of debt but also start saving for the future. After all, the plan is to end up as rich old gals rather than impoverished grannies, isn't it?

Ten easy ways to save money

It's one of those trite phrases that your mother has probably endlessly quoted at you, but never has a truer word been spoken. If you look after the pennies, the pounds will look after themselves. There are many ways of saving or making a little extra money and, added together, it can amount to a whole lot of money that will help you to fight your way out of debt. Here are a few simple ones which require minimum effort but could save you hundreds, if not thousands, of pounds each year:

- Make your own sandwiches for work instead of buying them. If you're spending a fiver a day on a sandwich, a can of Coke and a Mars Bar, then you're spending in the region of £1,200 a year. Buying in bulk from the supermarket and making your own lunch would cost you less than a tenner a week, saving you at least £720 annually. That's a pretty good holiday! And over a working life of 40 years, it's the price of a nice little Mercedes! So 'brown-bag' your lunch, as the Americans like to call it.

- Think about the services you pay for each month and look at cheaper options. You can easily switch your gas, electricity and telephone services these days. And is your mobile phone the cheapest option? The same goes for your car and house insurance. If you can save £25 a month on your outgoings, that's £300 a year of easy money. Try www.uswitch.co.uk or www.moneyextra.co.uk to compare prices.

- Consider remortgaging. Homeowners who regularly switch their mortgages for cheaper deals are called rate tarts by the industry but, if it saves you a few hundred a year, who cares about being called a tart! Make sure you do the numbers properly, because it'll cost you in fees unless you can find a bank offering to pay them for you when you switch. Otherwise, threaten to leave your current lender unless they can offer you a better deal – you never know, they might drop the rate without your having to do anything at all.

- Consider taking in a lodger if you have room. Under the Government's Rent-a-Room scheme, you are allowed to make £4,250 a year without paying tax on the income. You will need to agree this with your mortgage lender as well as your insurance company, and check how it may affect any benefits you may be receiving, but it can prove to be an effective, easy and temporary solution to immediate financial problems.

- Declutter your house and sell the pickings at a car boot sale. We often get useless birthday and Christmas presents that we can do without (that hideous vase Great-aunt Mabel gave you, for instance!). Just because you don't like something doesn't mean someone else won't. Get up early so you can get a pitch near the entrance – people often run out of money by the time they get towards the end of the route so make sure you grab them early before they've emptied their wallets.

- Never shop for groceries on an empty stomach and always take a list. Think about it. How often have you thrown things willy-nilly into the shopping trolley just because you were hungry and you liked the look of them. Making a list and eating before you go means you buy only what you really need.

- Shop at Oxfam. Yes, really! Rich people give away their clothes to charity as well as poor people and, if you look carefully you can often find good-quality items – even designer labels if you check out the charity shops in affluent areas. After all, no one's going to know unless you tell them.

- Cut the number of takeaways you have each month. An Indian meal for two can easily cost £20 or more. It soon mounts up if you're opting for a takeaway even just once a week. Instead, try to make double quantities of meals that you can freeze so you can draw on those when you're feeling too tired to cook. Cutting down on the frequency of getting takeaways can save you hundreds a year.

- Drive at a consistent speed – you use less petrol that way. Zooming off from traffic lights and revving the engine when you get impatient in traffic jams is bad for your wallet as well as your stress levels.

- Use the library to borrow books, videos and CDs. Do you *really* need to read Joanna Trollope's latest offering right this very minute? Instead of spending £16.99 on your own copy, order it from the library for free. Unless you know you are going to read and re-read a book several times, there's no point in owning it (except for this book, of course!). You won't be cluttering up your home, either!

STATEMENT OF AFFAIRS - Ms I.M. BROKE

MONTHLY INCOME

Net Monthly Salary	£1,500.00
Family Allowance	£80.00
Spouse's Net Monthly Salary	£1,215.00
Total Net Monthly Income	**£2,795.00**

ESSENTIAL MONTHLY OUTGOINGS

Mortgage	£420.00
Council Tax	£95.00
House Insurance	£58.00
Life Insurance	£30.00
Gas	£43.00
Electricity	£65.00
Water Rates	£35.00
Telephone	£20.00
TV Licence	£6.00
Food	£400.00
Clothing	£100.00
Petrol	£80.00
Car Tax	£15.00
Car Insurance	£28.00
Child Minder	£350.00
Total	**£1,745.00**
Surplus	**£1,050.00**

Creditors	Sum Outstanding	Monthly Payment
Acme Credit Card Co.	£7,000.00	£400.00
Easycash Credit Card Co.	£3,355.00	£330.00
Home Loans Inc.	£12,000.00	£395.00
Dodge E. Motors Car Loan	£14,000.00	£475.00
Furniture Emporium	£2,300.00	£260.00
Clearview Windowz	£3,700.00	£310.00
Total owed to creditors	**£42,355.00**	**£2,170.00**

Sample Letter to Creditors

Leach & Co.,
Credit Card Company,
1 Robbers View,
Right Innit, IOU 5P

Dear Sirs,

RE: Leach Credit Card – Account Number: 123456789

I write to advise that due to unemployment/redundancy/illness, I have realised that I will not be able to meet my financial commitments in full, for the immediate future.

I would like to assure you that I take my responsibilities very seriously in this respect and have given the matter considerable thought. Whilst I hope that my situation will improve in time, I feel that I will be able to satisfy my debts in full, with careful planning and a little assistance from my creditors.

I have considered approaching a debt-management company but rather than incur significant fees in this respect, I feel that if we can agree on sensible proposals, it would be better to use the money saved to pay off debts in a shorter time.

I have enclosed herewith a list of my creditors that shows the balances left to pay and the regular monthly payment to each, together with a list of my income and expenditure. You will note from the statement that I have a monthly disposable income of £?, from which I propose to deduct £? per month for emergencies, leaving a monthly balance of £? for debt repayment.

In the circumstances, I propose to divide the balance of these monies equally amongst my creditors and once some of the smaller debts are satisfied, I will increase the dividend accordingly. I would also add that in the event that my circumstances change for the better, I will increase payments as and when I am able and would propose in any event, to review the situation with you on a quarterly basis.

I would be most grateful if you would kindly consider freezing interest on this account to enable me to resolve the matter quickly.

Yours faithfully

I.M. Broke

Sample Follow-up Letter to Creditors

Leach & Co.,
Credit Card Company,
1 Robbers View,
Right Innit, IOU 5P

Dear Sirs,

RE: Leach Credit Card – Account Number: 123456789

Thank you for your letter of [date], in respect of the above matter.

I am disappointed to note, that you will not consider my proposal to satisfy my debt to you. I appreciate that this is not a wholly satisfactory state of affairs, but this is the reality of my situation.

Due to my present circumstances, I am unable to offer a better resolution and would respectfully ask that you reconsider my proposal, which was submitted in a genuine attempt to honour my commitment to you.

I understand that creditors are duty-bound to attempt to come to some form of compromise with a debtor prior to instigating court proceedings, and I am making every effort to offer you a reasonable sum that I can pay regularly to you. Other creditors have accepted my offer and payments have commenced.

I appreciate that you are not obliged to accept my proposal. However, considering that you are entitled to issue proceedings for the recovery of the balance owed to you, I would ask that you also consider that, in the event that these proceedings ensue, interest would be frozen upon judgement. I would entirely reserve the right to produce my proposal for the attention of the court and to make an application for a reduction of my previous offer to you.

This notwithstanding, I would hope that the foregoing will not be necessary and that we will be able to resolve this matter amicably. In the interim, I will forward payments to you as proposed, as a gesture of good faith.

Accordingly, I await your further comments.

Yours faithfully

I.M. Broke

Check your credit file by writing to the addresses below. You'll need to send a cheque for £2 and provide your full name, your date of birth and all addresses at which you have lived for the past six years.

Consumer Help Service   Credit File Advice Centre
Experian Ltd   Equifax Ltd
PO Box 800   PO Box 3001
Nottingham   Glasgow
NG1 5GX   G81 2DT
Tel: 0115 976 4050   Tel: 0141 951 1100
www.uk.experian.com   www.equifax.co.uk

Buying a Home

A bad husband is like a mortgage – the interest is unwelcome and the demands never end.

Anon

The nesting instinct is particularly strong in women, or so we're always being told. Think around your friends. It's quite likely that the women you know bought their own home earlier than most of the men, even though many are still on a lower wage. It just seems to be more important to us. But the fact that it's instinctive with us doesn't necessarily mean it's a good idea. We are all different, have different needs and lifestyles, and we should not do something just because everyone else is doing it. Of course, if you haven't yet bought your own home you could be forgiven for feeling waves of panic as you see house prices soar way above your salary. You may think you should buy the nearest hovel within your budget now, before they fly even further above your reach, but hold yourself back.

To buy or not to buy – that is the question.
Whether 'tis nobler in the mind to suffer
The slings and arrows of outrageous rental prices,
Or to take a loan amidst a sea of financial institutions,
And by debting, end the worry? To mortgage, to rent
No more; and by a mortgage to say we end
The payments and the thousand pounds of wasted cash
That renting is heir to? 'Tis a consummation

Devoutly to be wish'd. To mortgage, to repay.
To repay – perchance to own; ay, there's the rub!

From the Motley Fool message boards

First ask yourself some questions:

- Do I really want to tie myself into a mortgage for the foreseeable future or do my lifestyle and career choice demand more flexibility?
- Do I have the kind of earnings and the stability of income to cover these payments every month for the next few years?
- Can I afford – and do I want to pay for – all the extra costs such as legal fees, building and decorating, repairs, furnishing and the like?
- Can I afford a place that I would really like to live in now or should I work hard and save hard for the next year or two to put together a deposit for somewhere that I would genuinely be happy to live in?

Yes, buying a home can be a good investment. Certainly people who have bought in the South-East of England in the last 20 years will have seen their homes increase in value exponentially, but many of them have also spent a lot of money on their homes and in interest on mortgages and loans during that time. They may also have found themselves tied into jobs they no longer wanted to be in because 'it pays the bloody mortgage'. Do you want this?

Yes, I really do want to buy my own home

Well, that's fair enough. By and large it makes good sense, although we in the UK seem to be the only nation in Europe to think so. Almost 70% of all houses in Britain are owned by their occupants (although in many cases by their banks), whereas *sur le continent* the vast majority of people rent their homes (although there must be a substantial number of landlords as someone must own those properties). Pressure on the housing stock is increasing faster than new homes are being built, therefore in the long run the value of your property is unlikely to go down – at least for any significant amount of time. In 2000, 32% of households in Britain were single-person-occupied compared with 23% in 1979. Interestingly, in 2000, 14% of women lived alone and this is set to rise over the next few decades. So, as far as investment is concerned, buying into bricks and mortar looks pretty sensible.

So where do you buy? What do you buy? When do you buy? Well, as far as where to buy is concerned the estate agents' mantra is 'location, location, location'. If you are looking at a home purely as an investment that is certainly good advice, but if you are buying to have a roof over your head the only rules you really have to follow are to buy the nicest place (as far as you are concerned) in the most convenient and pleasant location (as far as you are concerned) at a time when *you* can best afford it. This is *your* home, it should match *your* needs and desires and, by and large, investment issues should not come into it. This is your life, you get only one shot at it and it is not a good move to spend a large part of it in a home you'd rather not be in. Unless you have completely weird tastes (and you can't have, as you're reading this book), if you have good reasons for loving the property you have bought it's highly likely that at least a few other people will think the same way when you come to sell it.

The question of *when* to buy can cause the most headaches, particularly given the extreme price rises we have seen in certain parts of the country over the last couple of decades. But again, sensible women don't pay attention to price forecasters who predict 'a rise of just 6% this year' or 'the possibility of negative equity by the summer'. Just as Fools don't try to time the short-term fluctuations of the stock market, they don't try to time the short-term fluctuations of the property market, either. Just because your property-developer friend, Denise, tells you that 'Dagenham is really going to come up in the next five years', it doesn't mean you should rush out and buy there. Similarly, if Trevor, your friendly local estate agent, says that 'prices have peaked this year', you shouldn't put off buying a place you've fallen in love with. In our experience, people who hold off from the property market because they are expecting a big crash suffer a similar fate to those who hold off from the stock market for the same reason. There are always reasons for thinking that the market might fall in the short term, just as there are always reasons for thinking that it might rise. All we can say with any degree of confidence is that, over the long term, most people investing in property find their investment has increased in value. So, when you can afford to buy a home, find the one that you want to live in and go get it girl!

If you are thinking of buying a property purely as an investment take a look at our advice on 'Buy-to-Lets' on page 100.

Whoa there! You're already talking about buying when, at these prices, I don't see how I'll ever afford to buy a hut in the middle of the road, let alone a house!

Too true. For those trying to get onto the first rung of the much-vaunted property ladder, things are looking steep. In fact, they haven't looked so steep for decades. But fear not problems are just challenges with a scary mask on, and there is always a way round if you really look.

First, go back and revisit Chapter Three – Get Out of Debt. What are your incomings and outgoings? Where can you make savings? How can you earn more? Take a good hard look at what your goals are and how you can reach them. What kind of property would you *like* to buy and, realistically, what kind of property *could* you buy? How much of a mortgage could you get and, therefore, how much do you need for a deposit? (Keep in mind that 100% mortgages are not only hard to obtain but are also much more expensive than 90% or even 95% mortgages). Set yourself a realistic time frame for saving up the necessary deposit; this could take a year or two, so be patient. You may worry that prices will go up faster than you can save, but consider the possibility of changing your job to a higher-paying one in that time too. Also consider the fact that, even if house prices do go up a lot in your area, it is still more helpful to have a wad of cash to put down as a small deposit than to have no deposit at all. Apart from anything else, you will also have to pay for solicitor's fees, surveyor's fees, mortgage-arrangement fees and possibly stamp duty, so you will need some cash to cover all of that.

Look at the various options available to help you buy affordable housing. Helpfully, it has gradually been dawning on the lumbering, Neanderthal brains of the powers that be that the lack of affordable housing, particularly in cities, is very unhealthy for communities as it pushes out key workers from city centres leaving residents unsupported by nurses, postmen, council workers and so on. Very slowly, a number of schemes have come into operation to help all kinds of people own their own home. Here is a list of possible options you could try if you think you can't afford to buy on the open market.

Housing associations – Shared Ownership

Under the shared-ownership scheme, you buy a share of a property – usually one built by a housing association – and pay a small rent on the remaining share you do not own. You can then go on to buy further shares, and eventually own your home outright. There are long waiting lists for these schemes, particularly in London, so get on one – or several – as soon as you can. They usually operate on a kind of points system, and the longer you have been on the list the more points you have. You also get extra points in some areas if you are a key worker – a teacher, nurse, social worker or the like – or if you have dependants or currently live in a home that is demonstrably bad for your health.

To find out about buying a home in stages from a housing association, and from some trusts and co-operatives, contact the Housing Corporation office covering your area (phone on 020 7292 4400 or find at www.housingcorp.gov.uk). They'll send you a list of Registered Social Landlords (RSLs) operating such schemes in your neighbourhood. Their very comprehensive website will give you all you need to know about buying or renting a home through a housing association, and show you which associations cover your area.

Housing associations – Homebuy

A somewhat more commercial option to shared ownership is the Homebuy scheme. Some RSL tenants, or those on waiting lists, can get help from this Government scheme to buy on the open market. You contribute 75% of the purchase price through a mortgage and savings and the other 25% is loaned to you, interest-free, through this scheme. You repay the interest-free loan when you sell the property, at 25% of the market value at the time of sale. Contact your local Housing Association for more details.

Ex-council properties – Right-to-Buy

Although much council housing stock has now been transferred to housing associations, about 14% of British homes are still council-owned. If you are lucky enough to get a council property, you may be eligible to buy it. Be careful, though. Some council properties – particularly those in large, poorly maintained blocks – may be very difficult to re-sell and won't hold their value. In London, the Department for Transport and the office of the Deputy Prime Minister estimates the average price of a council property is £78,000. Long-standing tenants (of at least 15 years' tenancy) may be eligible for substantial discounts of up to 70% of the property's value (capped at £22–£38,000, depending on where you live), so it can be very worthwhile. But you may have difficulty getting a mortgage on certain properties – mainly on those considered hard to re-sell – and you may have to pay a share of huge repair bills.

Ex-council properties – Rent-to-Buy

This scheme is also open to council tenants. If you are not receiving Housing Benefit – in other words, you are earning a reasonable amount each month – you may be able to convert the rent you pay to the council into mortgage payments for a share of the property. It is for tenants who want to buy their home but cannot afford to pay or borrow the entire (though discounted) price of the property in one go. This sounds like a good idea except that it is useful for only a small number of tenants:

anyone whose rent is more than 80% of the likely payments on a mortgage that would buy the flat outright is not eligible. It is mostly likely that anyone who can afford to rent a council property without Housing Benefit would be able to afford the mortgage.

The Starter Home Initiative

If you are a nurse, police officer, teacher or other key worker, you could benefit from the £250 million Starter Home Initiative brought in by the Government in October 2001. This initiative is to help people buy homes in expensive areas and has proved very useful for those who qualified. The Government has made £250 million available over the years 2001–04 in support of the scheme. Information about this scheme can be found on the Government website (find at www.housing.dtlr.gov.uk), which includes a fact sheet on the scheme and contact details for your area.

Self-build

Around 20–25,000 people build their own homes each year. This may seem a bit extreme, but you don't have to be a builder yourself, just be willing to look for land, bring in an architect and have the patience to project-manage the works while the house is being built (probably over 12–18 months). There are more and more mortgages on the market for self-build schemes and many lenders will loan up to 95%. Once it is finished, a well-run self-build project should see the final value of the home increase by 20–30% on the actual land and building costs. So, if you are prepared to wait and do the necessary hard work, you can make some sensible money with a self-build. For more information on how to go about building your own home, check out the online magazine *Build It* (find at www.selfbuild.co.uk).

Buying together

If none of the above schemes apply or appeal to you and you don't mind sharing your mortgage with someone else, you could consider buying a property with a friend, a colleague or (more dangerously) a lover. There are all kinds of possible problems with this: you may strongly disagree about the kind of place you want to live in, you may have very different ways of running a home or you could find your friendship breaks down because you live at such close quarters. But for friends or partners prepared to take the risk, buying together is one easy and affordable way onto the property ladder.

Taking on a mortgage with someone else is a serious financial commitment, one that needs to be drawn up in law. You need to draw up a legal agreement in case one of you wants to sell, or one of you loses his/her job, or you both just come to hate each other so much that the idea of breathing the same air becomes a daily torture (it can happen). These agreements can specify that if one person stops paying, they lose their rights in the property. Lenders are likely to demand 'joint and several liability', so the bank or building society can claim repayment of the full amount from either owner.

There are two recognised types of co-ownership in law: joint tenancy and tenancy in common. With a joint tenancy the co-owners own the whole of the property together, so if one dies the other automatically gets the whole property for themselves. In the case of a tenancy in common each party owns a share in the property that they can deal with as they wish, so if one dies they can leave their share to whomever they wish and it doesn't automatically go to the surviving owner. Also, the shares in the property of tenants-in-common don't have to be equal. If one side puts in 75% of the purchase price then they can reasonably demand a 75% share in the property, whilst the other side owns only 25%. All these points need to be explained clearly in the contract so that everyone knows where they stand.

If you are married, it helps to make sure both of your names are on the deeds. In the event of a divorce, you are protected by the Married Women's Property Act 1882, which gives the court the right to put the property into joint names, should they decide to do so. But why not start off on the right footing anyway? Non-married partners who are living together should definitely make sure both names are on the deeds, as they are covered by fewer laws than married couples when it comes to death or separation. Women in particular need to be very careful on this matter: far too many women have simply assumed they had a share in a property with their co-habiting partner, only to find that they lost it all when he told them to leave. Think carefully about whether you should hold the property in joint names or as tenants-in-common.

So, be good to yourself. Get the legal stuff sorted right from the start and you won't lose the roof over your head.

Looking for a home

First, decide where you want to live. Narrow it down to a few streets if you can. The most obvious way of finding homes for sale is through local estate agents. You may find the place of your dreams this way, but it's wise to try other routes as well, particularly if you want to find a bargain.

The Internet is a very good place to conduct research and to find actual properties to buy. There are hundreds of on-line property websites, but the vast majority belong to estate agents or groups of agents. Many websites are slow and the information can be out of date, but a particularly useful website for this sort of research is www.upmystreet.com. Searching the Internet will give you an idea of property prices in a particular area and will show you which agents cover your preferred area, saving you from tramping the streets.

Some websites stand out. For example, www.easier.co.uk has a free service entirely devoted to private sales. It also has a tediously long and slow registration section that you need to complete if you want to do more than browse, but it's worth it. Other websites worth looking at for their good selection of properties include www.assertahome.co.uk, www.propertylive.co.uk, www.propertyfinder.co.uk, www.findaproperty.co.uk and www.homes-on-line.com. They all work on a similar basis: some websites request more search details than others but they all tend to ask for a specific town or postcode, the minimum and maximum amount of money you are prepared to spend and the number of bedrooms you require.

Alternatively, you could look at adverts in national or local newspapers or classified ads papers, such as *Loot*. Buyers can find great bargains here, although you have to be quick off the mark. Another, more proactive, method of house-hunting is to leaflet all the houses in the area; this can often bring surprising results. Also speak to anyone you know who lives in, or near, the area who might have an idea of what's going on: parents' groups, builders, decorators, solicitors and even financial advisers. Ask around at parties or stop to chat with builders if you pass them working on a house in an area you like. Any of them could know of local homeowners who are thinking of selling but who haven't actually put their house on the market. As with anything in life, if you are buying (or selling) a property, it's all about contacts.

Once you have found a place that you would love to buy, you can often bring the price down by pointing out its defects. However much you like it, don't let the vendor or the estate agent know it. By the time you have finished rubbishing the look, location and layout of the place, the asking price won't look quite so firm. Of course, if it is really popular and you *really* want it, you may have to pay up – it's up to you whether you feel it is honestly worth that amount of money.

Looking for a mortgage

All else being equal (you have a fairly steady income and a decent deposit saved), now is a fantastically good time to get a mortgage. The competition between lenders is extremely fierce so there are some very good offers to be had. It's carnage out there in mortgage-lending land and, if we could be bothered, we would feel very sorry for the lenders – poor lambs – but somehow we just cannot find it in our hearts to grieve. They have had it too good for too long.

The argument for buying rather than renting a property is usually that, when you rent, you are effectively pouring money down the drain: despite handing over your hard-earned cash each month, you still do not actually own anything. However, the same could be said for the interest you pay on a mortgage. Although part of your monthly payments will go towards paying off the capital of your loan (except in the case of interest-only mortgages), much of it will simply be paying interest into the already swollen coffers of your lender. So, keep in mind the fact that the quicker you pay off your mortgage, the cheaper it will be. As you now know, to have a comfortable future you pay out as little interest as possible and earn as much interest as possible. The longer you take to pay off your mortgage and the higher the rate of interest you pay, the more money you are wasting – money that could be put to sensible use on a new wardrobe of Armani, that fabulous cruise round the West Indies and much, much more!

If you knew the total cost of servicing a mortgage (the total amount of interest you pay on the capital over a 25-year repayment period), you would be horrified. Interest rates fluctuate wildly from year to year, but for this example we are using a rate of 8.65% (the average for 1945–96 according to the *Compendium of Housing Finance Statistics 1997*). If that was the average interest rate on a £100,000 mortgage which you took 25 years to repay, you would pay a total of £238,038: that's the basic £100,000 loan you originally borrowed plus a staggering £138,038 in interest (a.k.a. money thrown out of your purse into the lender's 'holiday in Barbados' account). This is the joy and thrill of the Miracle of Compound Interest working against you, and we don't want that, do we?

The important thing to know about mortgages is that they are simply big loans – whopping great debts – so all the rules that apply to your approach to a personal loan or debt repayment also apply to your mortgage. In other words, go for low interest rates (but don't be taken in by short-term, low headline rates that suddenly jump up after a few months), don't borrow more than you can comfortably afford to pay off (taking into account possible rises in interest rates later on) and remember that the sooner you pay off the mortgage/debt the cheaper it will be.

Let's look again at that loan of £100,000 we just mentioned. If you had reduced your payment term to 10 years, your monthly outgoings would certainly have risen from £793 a month to £1,231, but the amount of interest you'd have had to repay would have reduced substantially to just £47,661. Impressive, huh?

That said, though, as mortgage rates *are* so cheap at the moment (way below that average of 8.65% between 1945–96), there is a strong argument for paying the minimum monthly amount into the cheapest interest-only mortgage and putting any extra money into investments. These investments will not only pay off the mortgage, but will enable you to pay it off quickly. After all, if you are on a fixed-rate mortgage of, say, 5% and you have a substantial amount of money in a tracker fund returning say, 7%, you are making a clear profit. This way you are bound to pay off that mortgage much faster than you would with a simple repayment option (find out how to do this by reading the section on interest-only mortgages on page 90).

Another, perhaps safer, way of paying off your mortgage faster without really trying too hard is to take out a current-account or offset mortgage. With this type of mortgage, all the money you earn and keep in savings is offset against the interest you would be paying on the mortgage. This mortgage option can work very well for those people who are disciplined about their spending (we go into greater detail on current-account mortgages on page 92).

Whichever type of mortgage you plump for, though, make sure that you take into account the possibility of interest rates rising either in the short term, if you have a variable-rate mortgage, or later on once your fixed-interest period finishes. If you have borrowed the absolute, outside, not-a-penny-to-spare maximum amount you could get for your mortgage, you could find that interest rates double or even triple in the next few years, giving you terrible difficulties in meeting your monthly payments. So don't borrow a frighteningly high amount of money and do try to test out the numbers to see if you could still afford the payments even if the interest rate goes up by 3% or 4%. You might be horrified at how much the repayments could jump up!

How to find a mortgage

The last thing you should do when looking for a mortgage is go to your bank, ask them what mortgage options they offer and just choose from their limited selection. Tragically, this is what a lot of people do, particularly women. These people are losing so much money this way that we'd like to grab them all gently by the neck and *shake them*! There are about 4,000 different mortgage packages on the market at the moment, and several of them could be right for you. Certainly, many of them are bound to be better than anything your own bank could offer.

When it comes to choosing a mortgage, the best way to make the most informed decision is to do a load of background research yourself. It's easy to find out what's around. The Motley Fool website, of course, has reams of general information on buying a home and more detailed advice on the specific mortgage options available. Other useful websites include www.moneysupermarket.com, www.charcolonline.co.uk and www.moneyextra.co.uk. You can also find out about the latest packages on offer by reading *What Mortgage* magazine, *Your Mortgage* magazine or pretty much any publication with 'Mortgage' in the title. The various mortgage lenders are listed at the back of these magazines with the packages they have on offer. These listings include the current interest rates and any other useful bits of information, such as whether there is a fixed period and, if so, for how long, if there are penalties attached and whether the interest is calculated daily (good) or annually (bad). *The Times* and *The Sunday Telegraph* are amongst the best weekend newspapers that offer an up-to-date 'Best Of' list that is also worth checking to see what's currently on offer.

You could also ask around your friends and relations. Ask them what sort of mortgage they have, what the interest rate is and whether they are happy with it. Particularly ask people who have re-mortgaged recently because it is likely that they have found a good deal. Don't just blindly go with the mortgage that your sister or best friend's brother has, though, as it may not be right for your circumstances and personality. Some people need to have the security of knowing exactly what they will be paying each month for a long time to come, so they like to have a mortgage with a long fixed period. Others hate to be tied down for that long and prefer the freedom of knowing that they could switch to something better without paying a penalty. They would be better off with a product that doesn't charge penalties, even though the rate may not be as good. It's horses for courses, so think about your personality as well as your financial situation when you choose the right product for you.

Importantly, though, be a rate tart. Go on, we are. Loyalty to the bank that has had your custom since you were knee-high to a grasshopper is misguided! Trust us: banks and building societies feel very little, if any, loyalty to you. They want your money, pure and simple; if they thought you were about to outlive your usefulness to them, they would happily let you go. Do the same to them. If you are looking for a new mortgage, get the best deal you possibly can. If you already have a mortgage but think it could be too expensive, by all means do your research and switch to a better one.

In fact, we think it's a good idea to be a rate tart with any financial product, whether it's a loan, mortgage, current account or savings account. Go where you get the best rates and don't feel bad about moving. Rate tarts have no loyalty, because they owe no loyalty, to any one financial institution, and that is the way to be. Don't allow yourself to get teary-eyed about any of them, no matter how sweet you think your personal banker, Kevin, is with his Marks and Spencer suit that's just that bit too big for him and his cutely vain attempts to spell your name correctly. Banks are simply money shops now and, if they think you could cost them money rather than make them money, they will dump you without a moment's hesitation. They're just not worth it. Don't be like the majority of the population who, apparently, are more likely to get divorced than change their bank during their lifetime. Shop around!

Anyway, back to the mortgages. If all this talk of doing it yourself sounds too worrying to you, by all means seek the advice of an independent financial adviser if you really must, but make sure you have done your homework first. Make sure you know what sort of a mortgage you want and what sort of a mortgage you definitely don't want, and have a fairly good idea about specific mortgage packages you are interested in so if your adviser doesn't mention them, you can bring them up in the conversation and show that you are not a pushover.

It's important to find a reputable, independent broker who charges upfront fees. Beware of all other kinds, because a broker calling himself or herself independent who doesn't charge upfront fees will make his or her money from commission and so may offer the products of only a handful of lenders who pay good money. At the start, ask your adviser if they have access to any mortgage on the market. They are legally required to let you know if they are paid commission by the companies they recommend, but it is still a good idea to ask the question yourself.

For a free guide to buying a home and mortgages, 'How to Buy a Home' or 'How to Buy a Home in Scotland', send a large stamped addressed envelope to the Council of Mortgage Lenders, BSA/CML Bookshop, 3 Savile Row, London W1X 1AF (or phone on 020 7437 0075/020 7434 3791 or find at www.cml.org.uk). The CML also produces a free leaflet on taxation and the homebuyer.

What kind of mortgage?

If you are buying a home for the first time, you could find yourself dazzled by the number of different mortgage permutations. Repayment, interest-only, tracker, variable, fixed, embossed... well, maybe not embossed, but who knows? Someone might come up with one soon. However, it's not all as confusing as it first seems. It's a bit like buying a mobile phone. With phones you first have to decide which network you want. With mortgages you first have to decide which method of payment you want to use: repayment, interest-only, or a split of both. Once you have decided that, you then need to decide whether you would like a variable, discount, fixed, tracker or capped rate of interest. At the same time, you may want to consider taking out a current-account mortgage that could be a repayment or interest-only package.

It's not about being a first-time buyer. It's about your attitude to risk. If you just want to be sure of paying the debt off one day, you want a repayment mortgage. If, on the other hand, you like a bit of risk and think that you might be able to get a better return on money you invest rather than the rate your lender is charging you, then you want an interest-only mortgage and use your 'spare' cash to fund some sort of investment. Or you could have a part-repayment/part-interest-only mortgage if your attitude to risk is somewhere in between.

From the Motley Fool discussion boards

Repayment mortgages

We like repayment mortgages a lot because they are the safest guaranteed method of buying a home. With a repayment mortgage, the borrower pays an amount on top of the monthly interest that goes towards repaying the capital. As the capital reduces every month, so does the interest. This means that although you pay the same amount each month, in the early years the majority of your payments will go towards paying off the interest as you have a large amount of capital borrowed. But in the later years, when much of the capital has been paid off, your interest bill each month will be lower, so you will be paying off larger amounts of the capital. Towards the end of the loan, the amount of capital being repaid each month sort of 'snowballs'. Be aware that halfway through a repayment mortgage, much less than half of the capital will have been repaid, which can make your mortgage statement depressing reading.

Interest-only mortgages

With the interest-only option, the monthly payments to your lender go towards paying off only the interest on the loan and none of the capital. You then have to set up an investment vehicle to repay the capital at the end of the mortgage term. Some interest-only mortgages will insist on a certain type of investment, such as an ISA mortgage or an endowment mortgage. Whatever vehicle you use, though, there is an element of risk involved as the appropriate investment vehicles are almost always linked to the stock market.

With endowment mortgages, the amount you invest is set from the start at such a level that it should cover the cost of the capital at the end of the mortgage term, but only if it performs the way the policy provider projects. These projections aren't guarantees; recently many endowment policy-holders have found significant shortfalls between the level their invest-ment has reached and the amount of capital to pay. It's up to you to moni-tor how well your investment is doing and to make additional monthly repayments if necessary. ISA mortgages involve investing in equities within an ISA (up to your annual tax-free ISA allowance) and using the accumulated lump sum to pay off your capital at the end of the term.

One further option is a pension mortgage, where your mortgage and personal pension plan are linked. At the end of the term, you take the tax-free lump sum from your pension and use that to pay off the outstanding capital. This way you get to use the income tax credits of a pension, as well as those on the interest of your loan. However, this also means that the amount you have left for your retirement is reduced. Because you are paying only interest each month, these mortgages are the cheapest in the short term. If you are clever and you have made sure that you have a mortgage that allows you to pay off lumps of the capital without penal-ties, the low interest rate will mean that you have brought the costs down. However, you really have to be very sure that you have a large enough pension, and enough other investments for your retirement, to cover your mortgage payment as well as your retirement needs. If you pay off the capital as you go this need not be a concern, but if you decide to pay off the full amount with your pension at the end of the term then you could severely cut into your retirement savings. Given that women are particularly poorly provided for in pensions and investments for retirement, this is probably not the best option for most of us.

There's a lot of debate over whether repayment or interest-only mort-gages are better (just look at the Motley Fool discussion board on mort-gages under Managing Your Finances at http://boards.fool.co.uk/

Messages.asp?bid=50067), but it really depends on your attitude to money and risk as to which one you go for. You have to ask yourself if you are happy and able to take on the extra risk of an interest-only mortgage and then decide if you expect your investment return to beat the interest you're paying. If you are sanguine about your investment returns and you don't mind taking the risk, go for the interest-only option. If you are the kind of person who likes to know that, whatever happens, if you keep up your repayments you will eventually pay off the whole of your mortgage, go for the repayment type.

Current-account and offset mortgages

One of the most sensible mortgage options around is the relatively new current-account mortgage. This is where your mortgage, your current account and your savings are all lumped together in one pot so that any money you have in your current account or savings is automatically set against your mortgage. Effectively your mortgage becomes one big overdraft that is eaten away by your monthly mortgage payments and your savings. This way, instead of making small amounts of interest on your savings and current account, you save a lot more interest on your mortgage and therefore pay it off earlier. Also, whereas you have to pay tax on the miserly amounts of interest you make on your savings, here you pay no tax because the Inland Revenue doesn't count it as interest earned, merely interest saved. Basically, a win–win situation.

With this type of mortgage, you can also have some cash stashed away for rainy days *and* use it to cut down the interest payments on your mortgage, thereby avoiding the problem of how to maximise your back-up savings. After you have paid off some of your mortgage, you can have rainy-day cash in the bank without even saving because the mortgage includes the facility to borrow back some of the money if you want to. For example, if you bought a £100,000 property with a mortgage of £90,000 and a deposit of £10,000, you would start off with a mortgage/overdraft of £90,000 on which you'd pay a typical mortgage rate of interest. Each month your salary goes into the account, expenditure goes out again and anything left in the middle will go to reducing your mortgage/overdraft. If you can manage to reduce your mortgage/overdraft to, say, £80,000 you will still have a borrowing limit of around £90,000 so, in effect, you will have a £10,000 stash of rainy-day cash without actually having to have the money there.

There are only a couple of problems with this kind of mortgage. First, as we are writing this, there are only a few companies that offer them, including the Woolwich, Intelligent Finance, First Direct and Virgin. The choice of lender is rather limited and so the interest rates are probably not as competitive as they would be in a larger market, although this should improve as more companies decide to offer them. Secondly, they are not the best type of mortgage to have if you lack the discipline to pay off your mortgage quickly. If you use the borrowing-back facility more than the overpaying one, you may never have that emergency reserve and never actually pay off the mortgage. If this sounds like you, go for a straight-forward repayment mortgage that will force you to pay the money back.

There are also many flexible mortgages on the market that are not attached to a current account. They come in many guises, but in most cases they allow you to make extra lump-sum or monthly payments, borrow back money, take payment holidays and make underpayments. Also, they all calculate your interest on a daily basis. This is important: you should never go for a mortgage that calculates interest annually because any payments you have made during the year will be wasted in terms of interest saved. When interest is calculated daily, any payment you make into your mortgage reduces the capital still owed and therefore reduces the amount of interest you should be paying. But with a mort-gage where the interest is calculated annually, you have to pay the same amount of interest all year, however much you have paid in. So even if you pay in a lump sum of £10,000 in January, you won't get the benefit of the reduced interest payments for a solid twelve months. Such a rip-off!

Be honest with yourself about how much you would overpay, though. Many people who take out a flexible loan at the start do not use the over-payment facility, often because they have so much to pay out for in the first year or two. If you are not very likely to overpay, a flexible mortgage is probably not for you. Ordinary mortgages with no early-repayment penalties often allow you to pay back a certain amount extra per year and charge lower APRs than their flexible counterparts. In fact, for the first couple of years after buying your place, you will probably have very little money, if any, to overpay into your mortgage. In this case, it may be worth considering taking out a cheap repayment or interest only mortgage that is fixed for a year or two and then, once the penalty period is out and you start to have a bit of cash to spare, switch to a flexible one.

Mortgage rates and other joys

Fixed rate

The advantage of a fixed-rate mortgage is that it will not change during the specified term, which can be anything from two to five years, or even more. Many people like the security of a fixed rate as they can manage the household budget knowing that their biggest monthly outgoing is not about to increase suddenly. However, if interest rates fall greatly – as they have done in the last couple of years – you could find yourself lumbered with an expensive mortgage, often with penalties for moving.

Capped rate

With a capped rate your mortgage will never rise higher than a fixed ceiling price, and if interest rates fall, you will pay less than this. Basically, you get the best of both worlds. But capped rates are usually higher than the cheapest fixed rates.

Discounted rate

These mortgages have a fixed period during which your rate is reduced, after this time the mortgage will revert to the lender's standard variable rate. Sometimes the lender includes a penalty period after the fixed rate has ended to stop you taking our advice and being a rate tart when the discount ends.

Variable rate

The variable rate moves up and down according to any changes in the bank's base rate. It is often higher than the special offers available on fixed, capped and discounted rates. The variable rate can often be quite high as mortgage companies make most of their profit here, although it can't charge too much or all its borrowers will simply move elsewhere.

Tracker

This is similar to a variable rate, except where the variable rate more or less follows fluctuations in the bank's base rate (depending on how the lender is feeling), with a tracker you know you will pay a fixed percentage above the Bank of England's base rate at all times.

Redemption penalties

Fixed, capped and discounted mortgages are likely to carry penalties for stopping the loan in the middle of its term. This charge may be as much as six months' interest payments. These redemption penalties can stretch beyond the life of the special period. For example, a five-year fixed-rate mortgage may require you to borrow for a further two years at the lender's standard variable rate before you are free to move without penalty.

Questions to ask about your mortgage

As your mortgage is probably the biggest loan you are going to take out in your life (unless you set up a huge business), it is imperative that you get the best deal you can. A new code of practice for mortgage lending, introduced in 1997, was supposed to make sure that you get the best deal, but you cannot rely on it. Do as much research as you can before going to see a lender or a broker, and *ask questions*!

Here are some questions you should ask of your lender:

● Are there any penalties for overpayment of the mortgage?

● Are there any penalties for paying off the mortgage completely before the end of the mortgage term?

● Is the interest on the mortgage calculated daily, monthly or annually?

● If the Bank of England base rate goes down, will my mortgage go down with it?

● What are the charges (surveyor's fees, legal fees etc.) for setting up the mortgage?

● If the interest rate is fixed for a specified period, will there be any penalties for overpaying or switching the mortgage at the end of that time?

● Can I have payment holidays or borrow back money I have paid in from the mortgage?

Likely costs

Buying a house or flat can be costly. Make sure you have some money set aside for all the extras, such as:

● Solicitor's fees. These can vary enormously, so you should shop around for the best quotes. As a rough guide, expect to pay somewhere between 0.5% and 1.5% of the value of the property.

● Search fees. You will have to pay for searches at the Land Registry to check who owns the property you're buying and at your local council to check there are no plans for developments, such as a bypass running through your back garden. These can cost £25–75.

● Lender's legal costs. This depends on your mortgage lender, but you could be paying £100–400.

● Survey costs. This amount will vary depending on the kind of survey you want. A basic survey costs around £200 and a full structural survey will probably set you back £400–500, depending on where you live.

● Deposit. You will need to pay a deposit of around 10% of the value of the property when contracts are exchanged.

- Stamp duty. If the property costs over £60,000, you will have to pay a stamp duty of 1% of the total value of the property. If it costs over £250,000, you have to pay 3%. Over £500,000, you have to pay a whopping 4%. What is this payment for, you ask? Nothing. It's just a tax. We have to live with it.
- Hidden costs. These include the costs of furniture removal (which vary enormously depending on how much stuff you have to move and where you are moving to), buying new furniture, redecorating etc.

Mortgage Indemnity Guarantee (MIG) and life assurance

Another unsuspected joy for potential buyers to be aware of is what is known as the Mortgage Indemnity Guarantee premium, or MIG. It's a nasty little addition made by some (although not all) lenders to mortgages that are over 75% of the property price. Their reasoning is that, statistically, loans of this size are more likely to be defaulted on so they want to be covered for this eventuality. Note the point that *they* want to be covered. Not us. Oh no! The MIG doesn't cover *you* if you encounter a problem paying your mortgage: it covers the mortgage company.

This means that if you do default on your mortgage they will still repossess the property, you will still lose your home and they'll still sell it on for whatever they can get (probably more than the mortgage is worth). Nevertheless, they still want *you* to insure them against this terrible thing that might happen to them and it could cost you £1,500 or more! In fact, there has been such an outcry against this obviously biased and expensive move that many mortgage companies have ditched it, but there are still a few who are trying it on. The Council of Mortgage Lenders points out that if MIG didn't exist then a number of lenders wouldn't consider giving mortgages to certain people, and that is why it hasn't yet been abolished. Our advice to you, though, is that if your potential lender insists on it, simply look elsewhere. You just don't need it.

Another thing you don't need is special life assurance to go with your mortgage. In fact, if you keep your mortgage down to 75% or so, there's a good chance the mortgage company won't require you to have any (although they may still try to sell it to you because sales of life assurance carry impressive commission levels). If you have no dependants, you almost certainly don't need it. If your mortgage outlasts you, the lender will get its money back when the house is sold. Even if you do have dependeants, you still might not need *more* life assurance. If you already have life assurance (and you probably do if you have dependants), you don't necessarily need to add another policy or increase your payments just because you have taken on a mortgage. You may need to, depending on your circumstances and the size of your mortgage, but you may not. Don't let anyone force you into it. By avoiding unnecessary life assurance, you can save yourself sizeable sums that can be added to your savings or paid into your mortgage, which are both far better places for your money.

Getting someone else to pay your mortgage

If you can bear to share your personal space with another human being, having a lodger renting a room in your home can be a pretty painless way of earning money and paying the mortgage. As a move to lift the burden of demand on affordable housing, a few years ago the Government introduced a tax incentive to prospective landlords allowing them a certain level of tax-free earnings per year. Currently landlords can be paid up to £4,250 gross per year tax-free, although that also includes a share of utility bills, like gas and electricity, if you charge for that too. As this comes to just over £354 per month, you can see how this would substantially increase your monthly income and, in some cases, cover your entire monthly mortgage payments. Financially, it's well worth considering.

The problem with having a lodger – apart from the obvious one of losing your freedom to jump naked round the house bopping to *Dancing Queen* any time you like – is the possibility of being lumbered with the tenant from hell. Imagine a lodger who floods your bathroom, farts like a buffalo and steals your boyfriend – and he's a bloke! If you're not lucky enough to be able to rent to a good friend or someone recommended by a good friend, you will need to advertise for a lodger, interview prospective candidates and check their references thoroughly. When you meet someone you feel you could possibly live with, ask him to supply at least two written character references (which you should then phone yourself to check they are genuine) as well as a reference from his employer and his bank manager to prove that he is earning money and he does pay his bills. There are now a number of agencies that will check prospective lodgers for you, including Maras (phone on 020 8882 6161) and Homelet (phone on 01522 524212).

When a new lodger moves in make sure you get an upfront deposit of one month's rent and one month's rent in advance. It's also useful to have a contract that you both sign which states what the rent will be, when it should be paid, how it should be paid and how much notice either side should give if they want to leave or you want to get rid of them. It should also cover what is unacceptable behaviour from either party. If you feel happier joining a lettings agency to find a lodger for you, they will be able to provide you with the relevant contract.

House insurance

Your home is likely to be the biggest single possession you will ever have, so it's important to have it insured inside and out. When you buy a property you will be asked to consider taking out all kinds of insurance, some of which will be relevant, some not.

The insurance of the actual building – whether it's a house or flat – is something that most lenders will rightly insist on. As the building is the only security the lender has if the borrower defaults, the property needs to be maintained in good condition throughout the term of the mortgage. However much they try to make you, you should not be cajoled into taking out buildings or contents insurance through your mortgage lender. It's illegal for a lender to make taking out their insurance a condition of receiving a mortgage from them, so if they sound a bit too persuasive just drop that fact into the conversation. That'll shut them up.

If you are buying a flat in a block of several, you may find that the buildings insurance is paid from your annual service charge. If so, you will need to get written details of the insurance company and the amount insured from the managing agents.

If you do have to arrange your own buildings insurance you can easily do it on-line. Once you have filled in your details, there are a number of websites that will search all the insurance companies for you and come up with the cheapest quote around. Go to www.find.co.uk for a selection of these websites. You can also obtain a free factsheet on mortgage-protection insurance, buildings insurance and contents insurance from the Association of British Insurers by writing to ABI, 51 Gresham Street, London EC2V 7HQ (or phone on 020 7600 333 or look at www.abi.org.uk).

Buy-to-Let – property as an investment

So you've already got your own home, you're paying your mortgage without too much trouble and you have some money you would like to invest. You have a pension, you are already investing in a tracker fund or individual shares, but you really like the idea of investing some cash in property, raising a mortgage for the rest and then letting someone else pay it off. After all, property prices have been rising at a rate of knots over the last 20 years, so you should get on that bandwagon fast before it leaves without you. Or should you?

Well, certainly a lot of other people in this country think so. In 2001 the whole buy-to-let market rose by about 60% and is now worth more than £10 billion in mortgage debt. Around 90% of landlords have just one buy-to-let property, so we're not only talking about the big property-developer types! It just shows how many people are putting their money into bricks and mortar. Also, it has become easier and cheaper to raise a mortgage for a rental property as more lenders have come into the market and are now offering rates that, in many cases, are cheaper than ordinary residential mortgages. Unlike standard mortgages, which are calculated on your salary or ability to repay, these loans are calculated on the basis of the rental yield of your property and rate of interest. However, should you opt for a short-term mortgage, you must satisfy the lender that the rental income is sufficient to service the final mortgage rate.

The pros

- People will always need somewhere to live and, as the number of single households is predicted to rise in the future, so the demand on the housing stock is likely to increase faster than dwellings can (or will) be built. In the medium term, at least, the demand for accommodation to rent should continue or even increase.
- Unlike shares or pensions, property is something you can physically see and feel. You know it is there and, unless it is blown up or burnt down (and naturally you would have it insured against those eventualities), it is unlikely to crash or dwindle away.
- You can feel rather more in control of property than you might with shares, and certainly than you would with a pension. It's up to you to keep it up, monitor the tenants and set the rent.
- If you get the right property in the right area at the right time, you could find it rocketing in value over five or ten years.

The cons

- Property is an inflexible investment. It has the potential to produce good returns but those looking to make a quick buck should think again. If you want to buy a second property for investment purposes, you should be thinking about investing for the long term. Also, when you come to sell the property, bear in mind that it could take months to get your hands on the money.

- You can't guarantee 100% occupancy. Your property only needs to be vacant for a month of two for your annual return to be knocked down significantly. In extreme cases, your property may be empty for long periods and that can cause major problems.
- Tenants who don't pay the rent can be very expensive. Not only can you lose rental income but getting them evicted can cost money too. If it happens to you and you're really unlucky, you may have to figure on writing off a whole year's rent.
- Even decent tenants will cause wear and tear to parts of the house and furniture. After a few years of ordinary, understandable wear and tear you will have to foot the bill for repairing and redecorating. This will severely cut into your income. Rectifying damage after a tenant has moved out takes time too: time when you're not getting any rent. You also have legal responsibilities in relation to safety of the building, the furniture and the gas and electricity supplies.
- Unless you pay a management company to deal with any problems your tenants have with the property, you may have the hassle of midnight phone calls about the boiler or Sunday-morning calls to a plumber to fix the drains.
- A buy-to-let mortgage is a debt, and debts have to be paid. When you take out a mortgage, be sure to stay well within your means. What will you do if (for any of the above reasons) you don't get any rent for six months, or a year, or more? The answer is to be sure you can cover the repayments from your own income. You may have net outflows each month or, in the worst cases, have to sell the property.
- You still have the growing asset value of the house too, and that keeps on going up, doesn't it? Well, house prices can't keep growing faster than earnings forever and the rises we've seen in recent years won't continue indefinitely. When you do sell your property, you'll have to pay Capital Gains Tax if you make a profit. Any decent profit is likely to put you in the 40% tax bracket, if you're not already there. Unlike shares, you can't put a house into your ISA.
- You also have to pay tax on any rent you receive, less deductions for

interest payments, letting fees, wear and tear and any other expenses you think you can get away with.

● You can reduce your risk by letting more than one property, allowing you to ride out periods when you don't have tenants in one, for example. Obviously, this means taking on more debt and it will take some time, possibly several years, to find and buy a small portfolio of properties.

How to go about it

If you are still determined to invest in a buy-to-let property, the important thing to remember when looking for a house or flat is that it is an investment and not somewhere that you want to live. Try to keep emotions out of it. This is business, not comfort.

As with buying your own home, location is everything. First, look for areas where there is likely to be high rental demand. A property close to transport links in an area with good amenities will be easier to let and is more likely to appreciate in value too. But of course this means that there can be a lot of competition for the 'best' properties. However, if you want to save money and manage the property yourself, you should make sure you buy in an area that is easily accessible from where you live.

Speak to local letting agents about the kinds of properties that let best. Generally flats and small houses seem to be the most popular, particularly in cities. Also ask the local agents whether furnished, unfurnished or part-furnished properties let most readily and follow their advice.

Once you have bought somewhere, decide whether you want to use a local agent to let it or whether you want to save the monthly charge by doing it yourself. To start with, it may be wise to let an agent find and check your tenants and collect the rent. Once you have worked out how it is done, you should be able to do it yourself using the services of credit checkers and basic contracts from your local newsagents. You can get lots more information by joining the Residential Landlords Association (find at http://www.rla.org.uk).

Conclusion

Considering all the things that can go wrong during the process, buying a house can be very stressful. The average time it takes is reckoned to be somewhere between three to five months, as the laws governing home-buying in this country are somewhat outdated. It's rather strange when you consider that more of us own our own home in the UK than in almost any other developed country. There have been recent moves to streamline the process, but for the moment we are stuck with the current, cumber-some system.

When you own your own home, you own a real asset. 'Real' as in it's actually there: bricks and mortar. Not only is your home very likely to grow in value as the years go by, but when you make the last payment on your mortgage, you will be sitting on (and in!) a house that belongs entirely to you. You don't get any of that by renting.

The hard part of buying a house is finding the money to pay for it. The great advantage in all this mortgage madness, however, is that at the end of your 25-year term, you will own your very own piece of capital. Of course, your home is primarily a place to live rather than an investment, but property has produced some excellent returns in recent years. It is, however, a long-term investment, so make sure you do your sums before taking the plunge and don't overstretch yourself.

Invest for your Future

I don't know much about being a millionaire, but I'll bet I'd be darling at it.

Dorothy Parker

So, you've got yourself out of debt, you have set (and are keeping to) a budget, the mists are clearing and you are moving out of the fungal fog of debt and uncertainty into the serene sunshine of solvency and 'having a bit left over'. Well done! Now you can get into the fun stuff.

Investing *is* fun. Who doesn't enjoy getting others to work for them, and for nothing? Effectively that is just what you're doing when you invest money – you get your money to work for you. If you put your money in the stock market it can *really* work for you and earn more without your having to lift a finger. That's our idea of working for a living.

Now, before you run screaming from the room at the very idea of making investment decisions yourself (particularly in the stock market), let's get one thing straight. The possession of red braces, facial hair and other accoutrements of masculinity are not necessary for you to make sound and profitable investment decisions. In fact, as we mention in Chapter One, the possession of any of these features can be an actual hindrance. You may be surprised by this, but to become a seriously hot investor and stock-market doyenne, you don't even need a university education, let alone a job in a large, overfed City firm with hot-and-cold running receptionists called Arabella or Tamara. You just need to be you: you with a bit of money to invest, a willingness to learn and some time to wait.

Before you invest in anything, though, make sure you really are out of all non-mortgage debt (re-read Chapter Three if you want to remind yourself how). We can safely say it's the best investment you will ever make. Also as we have already said, have some spare cash set aside for a rainy day, ideally enough to live off for at least three months. All the top billionaire investors advise this and, hey, they must know.

You need to be prepared to invest your money for a minimum of five years, but preferably a lot longer, without touching it. Although you can expect to get more by investing than saving, the value of your capital will fluctuate all the time. If you need to get at your cash in a hurry, then you may not get a good price. If you want to use your money to put down a deposit on a property or buy a new car in the next year or two, then investing in the stock market is not the best thing to do with it. If you need to be able to access your money quickly within less than five years then a high-interest savings account or flexible mortgage are the most sensible option.

Saving or investing?

On the face of it, saving and investing are the same thing. They're both things we do with our spare money. But actually, saving is almost an unconscious act where we put money into deposit accounts, or even a biscuit tin under the bed, so that we have something for that proverbial rainy day. It's a way of giving us a bit of security so that we don't find ourselves strapped for cash at any point. Investing, on the other hand, is more of a conscious decision. It's about making plans for the future so that we know we can cope with expensive events like weddings or retirement. It's also about making money, and then some more, so that the money invested is worth more in the future. If you just save money over a long period of time, the amount you can buy with each individual pound will reduce as prices go up. If you *invest* it, though, your pounds will be worth the same, or more, when it comes to spending them.

So, which would you prefer? Investing so that your money is worth less when you come to spend it, or investing so that you are as rich as, or richer than, you are now? Ooh, tricky question. Can't imagine which one you'll choose. All right, so the next question is, what do you invest in to be richer later on?

Different vehicles in which to invest

We are all different and all have varying attitudes to risk and reward, so, given the same information, none of us will behave in the same way. That's why it's important that you do your research, find out the facts and then make up your own mind as to what you want to invest your money in. No one else really knows (or cares) as much as you do about your money and how you see your future. So consider the following different options – and do more research elsewhere if you like – and then put your money in one or several of them.

Cash

Safe, dependable cash. You know where you are with it, don't you? For most of us, saving cash is the closest we've ever got to 'investing'. Perhaps your mum and dad opened a building society account for you when you were a kid, then, when you've been feeling sensible, you've put some money in here and there and got a bit excited once a year when the extra few quid earned in interest has been printed on the annual statement. So why not carry on with that? It's safe, it's guaranteed to bring a bit of money in and you can't lose? Well, actually, in real terms over time you most certainly can.

In the long term, building society returns only just about match the long-term rate of inflation so, once you've taken tax into account and considered the average earnings growth, cash really is a loser. This means that even if you keep re-investing the interest you get each year, over time the real spending power of your little pot of money will actually decrease. Currently you can get a return of around 4% (before tax) on the highest-paying accounts, which is better than a smack in the face with a wet kipper, but only really worth having for accumulating reasonable amounts of money over the short term to put in better-paying vehicles later on. If we're thinking long term (and we are, aren't we?), keeping your money in banks or building societies is only slightly better than sticking it under the mattress.

Bonds

All right. We're going up in the investment food chain here, but not very far. Like cash, bonds are a nice, relatively safe place to put your money. You do get a better return than with cash, but it's still not great. That's the trade-off, you see: safety costs and absolute safety *really* costs.

Bonds are essentially loans that can be bought and sold on a market. The most common are Government loans, or gilts (see below), but you can also trade corporate bonds, which are loans to large companies. Essentially, you are lending the company a sum of money to use as they see fit. They then agree to pay the money back to you at a specified date in the future, plus an annual amount of interest. Bonds have different safety ratings depending on the risk, but mostly they're pretty safe if you stick to big, solid companies. If you wait until the bond's term is up before cashing it in, and if you bought at the right price to begin with, you should get your money back in full. However, if you try to sell it on in the meantime, its value will vary depending on the current yields on bonds and the time remaining to the redemption date.

The capital value of bonds moves up and down in relation to interest rates, so they are not absolutely as safe as houses. They do tend to be popular with many investors and IFAs, however, as they give a half-decent yield with very little risk.

Gilts

These are a kind of bonds subset. They are also known as Government Bonds, as they are basically loans to the Government. As we are living in a stable country with a relatively stable, democratic government (rather than in one of those places where the leader has a special salute and a predilection for tight uniforms, although give it time…), lending money to the Government is generally considered to be a pretty safe bet. After all, the Government does print the stuff! It's certainly safer than lending to companies. So, though nice and secure, the return on gilts, is even smaller than that on company bonds. Hmmm. Worth bothering with as long-term investment? Not unless you're afraid of your own shadow.

With-profits bonds and endowment policies

These products have come in for a lot of criticism in recent years, and rightly so. They are highly inflexible beasts that require you to commit to investing a regular amount over a long time. That's no bad thing in itself, but if you don't manage to keep up the regular payments you end up being charged heavy penalties. Worse than that, they tend to have high charges, which means they are inefficient and give you a poor return for your money. The way they are designed – particularly the endowment policies – means that it's often hard for the investor to work out what the charges are and, therefore, how much they are losing, so they often don't find out until it's too late. What delightful little animals they are!

With-profit bonds attempt to smooth out the return of the stock market by awarding annual bonuses that cannot be taken away. But the largest bonus is kept right until the end, and many people don't get that far. A further problem is that over long periods the stock market tends to rise, so these 'guaranteed' annual bonuses offer little value anyway. You pay a lot in charges for something that probably won't be necessary. And as if that weren't enough, the guarantees often turn out to be less than rock-solid – remember Equitable Life!.

The National Lottery or Lotto

Investment? You've got to be kidding! You'll do yourself more of a favour by spending the money on a couple of Kit-Kats each week. Don't waste your time.

Equities

Ah! Now you're talking. Numerous studies have been done on the rates of return that each of the main types of investment have made down the years. Over and over again they've shown that equities, or shares, give significantly better returns than cash, bonds or gilts. In the UK, for example, a study by Credit Suisse First Boston investment bank came up with the following figures for the period 1869–2001. The rates shown are the annual rate of return after accounting for inflation, otherwise known as the real return. It's the 'real' return because it represents the real value of your money, in other words, your spending power now versus your spending power in the future.

Cash	1.8%
Gilts	1.7%
Equities	6.4%

The numbers may look small but you need to consider the joy and wonder of compounding. Let's consider what would happen to £10,000 invested over 20 years at the above rates, again in real terms.

Cash	£14,287
Bonds	£14,009
Equities	£34,581

Also, remember charges. All else being equal, the lower the charges you pay, the higher you can expect your eventual return to be. As you can see from the list above, even small percentage changes can make a huge difference to the final amount. Unfortunately, here in the UK we have a financial services industry that has a talent for both charging high rates and hiding the fact that it is doing so. Always read the small print as all investment products have to lay out their charges in what is known as a Key Features document. The industry is moving towards a clearer and fairer charging structure, but we've still got a long way to go.

Why the stock market is not as scary, volatile or risky as you think

Honestly, if you are looking to invest in the stock market over a long period of time (five years or more), it is not the risky, frightening place that the media, and possibly your friends and family, picture it to be. Certainly in the short term (anything under five years), the stock market can go all over the place. Look at the serious dip we've had over the last couple of years. If you were one of those people looking to make a fast buck by investing short-term in technology companies or biotechs, then you will more than likely have had your fingers burnt.

But short-termism is not Foolish behaviour. When we talk about investing in the stock market, we really mean *investing* and all that that word entails. The dictionary defines investing as 'to commit (money) in order to earn a financial return', or 'to make use of for future benefits or advantages'. So, investing involves committing money for the long term, seriously thinking about it, researching it and deciding to leave the money where you committed it until some future date. Frankly, if you put money into anything for the short term or without any real thought and consideration, you're not investing, you're gambling. And that's just silly!

So, if you are serious about making your money work for you and letting it grow over the years to provide a comfortable retirement, overall the stock market is a pretty safe place to invest it in. All right, we can't promise you hand-on-our-hearts, that the stock market will keep on going up and up over the next few decades, just as we can't promise you that the Government will keep on taxing you. Judging by past performance, however, we can say that it is highly likely that both these things will continue in the future, barring a nuclear holocaust or a worldwide ban on Viagra.

If you look at the performance of the stock market over the last 30, 50 or even 100 years, it has climbed steadily. Certainly there have been dips, sometimes quite substantial, such as the infamous 1929 crash and the Great Depression that followed, together with World War II, Black Monday in October 1987 and the Asian Crisis of 1998. There was a dip in 1973–4, when, overall, shares lost 65% of their value, but then the very next year they rose by 149%. Between 2000 and mid-2002, UK shares fell by around 40%, but the point is that the *general trend* over the years has been upwards and, for those who invested for the long term, those bumps got smoothed out and made relatively little difference in the long run.

Even if you had invested your life savings in the stock market in 1972, for example, only to see them decimated in the next two years, as a serious investor you would not have considered jumping out of a window because you would have known that, in this business, what goes down must come up. By sitting tight for just five years you would have seen your investment not only return to its former level, but also start to grow. Another five years on and it would have grown by rather a lot – even doubled – and by now you would have been doing very nicely, thank you. Take a look at the graph below. You can see that, even though there are all sorts of little peaks and troughs, the general trend for the stock market has been upwards for the last century, and we have no reason for supposing that trend will change in the future.

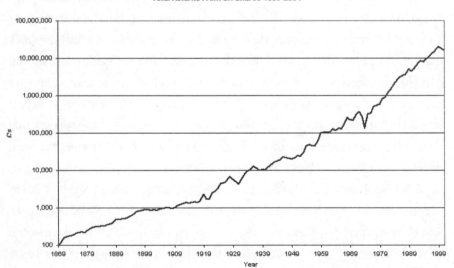

Total Returns From UK Shares 1869-2001

Source: CSFB Equity Gilt Study

How to invest

'That's all well and good, girls,' we hear you chime, 'but how *do* you invest in the stock market in the first place?' Good question. From the outside, the stock market seems like an horrendously complex animal full of dangers for the unwary. When you get to know a bit about it, however, you find that, in fact, it is… an horrendously complex animal full of dangers for the unwary. Well, maybe it's not quite that bad, but if you don't want to spend days, weeks and months learning about the ins and outs of companies, share movements, brokers and economics generally, then there are certain aspects of the stock market that you should avoid.

There are ways of investing in the stock market, however, that involve a minimum of effort and worry for a substantial return. The prime way in which you can invest directly into the stock market, make some sensible money and not have to give it more than an hour or so of thought *per year* is to invest in a tracker fund. Keep that word '**tracker**' in your mind as you read on.

Funds tend to invest in part or all of various world markets. There are thousands of funds in the UK alone, some specialising in particular areas such as technology or health or in companies that match predetermined ethical criteria. Others just invest in geographical areas: British or European companies, or American or Asian firms only. There are two basic types of funds. There are active, or 'managed', funds where highly paid fund managers pick and choose shares they want to invest in (with varying degrees of success), and there are passive, or 'tracker', funds which simply buy into the whole stock market, or a part of it, according to preset criteria logged into a computer.

It's the managed funds that you will probably have heard the most about. They are the ones that have serious advertising and marketing budgets. You will probably have seen posters or newspaper advertisements for them, often emblazoned with pictures of their not-too-attractive star fund managers. Now, you would think that with all the money and marketing thrown at them, these managed funds would be absolutely the best-performing investment vehicles on the market. Oh no. Not so.

The truth is that the vast majority of managed funds underperform the humble computer-led tracker funds. And when we say vast majority, we mean 75% or more! The main reason is the lower charges that you pay on trackers. A typical tracker fund charges around 0.5% a year in management fees and the majority do not have an initial charge. Managed funds, on the other hand, tend to charge at least 1.5% a year *plus*, in many cases, an initial charge of 3–5% for the privilege of buying one. Over the years, the difference of 1% in annual charges can really eat into your investment. Also, many fund managers spend a lot of their time trying to second-guess each other and worrying about their short-term performance rather than looking at the long-term. This means that they trade more than they should which, in turn, means they, or rather you, incur a lot more in transaction charges. All in all, it's a tricky and expensive business.

I came to the conclusion some time ago that there was no way on earth that I could tell if a fund run by Jupiter or M&G or Uncle Tom Cobbly would provide me with index-beating performance ten, twenty or whatever years down the line. All I had to go on was the publicity pushed out by the companies in question highlighting past performance and some positive spin telling me why I shouldn't wait a moment longer. And there, tucked away discreetly was the disclaimer that investments can go down as well as up. *When you come to think of it, buying investments and financial products is a uniquely ambiguous state of affairs. After all, how would we feel if after having bought a car the paperwork came with the disclaimer: 'This car may or may not work!' Or having bought airline tickets: 'Thank you for flying with British Airways we will do our best to get you to your destination although this cannot be guaranteed!' I'm sure you get my drift.*

From the Motley Fool discussion boards

Trackers just get on with doing their job of following the overall market nice and cheaply. (Well, computers don't generally need a new

Porsche Boxter each year and they don't demand obscene Christmas bonuses, either!) They are also a lot simpler and less time-consuming to invest in, and you don't have to read the financial pages of the quality Sunday papers each week to check if your star fund manager has been poached by another company.

They are known as index trackers because they attempt simply to track an index – nothing cleverer than that. An index measures the over-all performance of a group of companies. In the UK, the best known is the FTSE 100, or Footsie, which consists of the 100 largest companies on the London Stock Exchange. There's also the FTSE All Share, which tracks the fortunes of around 700 of the UK's largest companies, giving you even more diversity. You can also get funds that track all the companies in a particular sector, such as technology or pharmaceuticals, in markets all over the world. That's a bit more risky but the charges are still much lower than sector-specific managed funds.

Basically, tracker funds try to match the performance of a particular index by investing proportionately in all of the companies in it, depending on the size and value of those companies. There are various clever calculations involved in these investments which we won't go into here because we think they're a bit dull, but if you'd like to know just how they work have a look at *The Motley Fool UK Investment Guide* (3rd Edition) for a full explanation. Suffice to say that they *do* it and all *you* need to do is consider whether to invest in them and, if so, which one to grace with your hard-earned cash.

How to invest in tracker funds

First, you will need to decide which index you want to be exposed to (ooh err, missus!). If you live in the UK, you are likely to want to invest in a UK index (although feel free to invest in the US, Europe or any other part of the world if you would prefer). In the UK you have a choice between the FTSE 100 and the FTSE All Share. There's not a great deal to choose between them as far as returns are concerned. Long-term history gives the FTSE All Share a bit of an edge, but in the last ten years or so the FTSE 100 has done rather better. If you can't decide between the two, you could invest in one type this year, then in the other next year. Hedge your bets, spread your risk and other investing clichés. It might be interesting to see which does better than the other.

There are a few companies that offer tracker funds (see pages 128–30 for a list, together with contact details) and it can be hard to work out which is the best. Frankly, there's not too much difference between them and, as tracker funds are a relatively new product, it's hard to judge which have the best track record because none of them has been going that long. So, when trying to decide between them, go for the ones with the lowest charges (certainly, there should be no initial charge) and a name you know and trust. There is something called 'tracking error' which can affect the performance of a fund but, again, it's a rather dull issue and, in the long-run, is not really worth looking into unless you like that kind of maths (see *The Motley Fool UK Investment Guide* again for an explanation of that). At this stage, if you just go for the lowest charges and the most trustworthy names, you should be fine. Certainly, over the long term, whichever tracker fund you go for, its performance is going to be better than the vast majority of actively managed funds – so don't get in a sweat over it!

Once you have decided on a company and the fund you like, give them a ring or apply online and either set up a monthly direct debit or stick in a lump sum. Most have minimum lump-sum or monthly investments that they allow, although some, like the Virgin one, can be as low as a humble £1.

Do it in an ISA

The first £7,000 of any money you plan to invest each year should be done through an ISA. If you want to invest up to that amount in a tracker fund then you should do so in a Maxi ISA. If you want to spread your investments between cash and equities, then you can invest up to £3,000 in a tracker fund through an ISA. Happily, most tracker funds come prewrapped in an ISA, so that cuts out some of the work (and potential cost) for you.

As you will discover in Chapter Six, the main benefit of an ISA is the tax relief. These days the income tax relief you get on any dividends paid out is nothing to write home about and it will disappear completely in April 2004. As far as equity investments are concerned, the key attraction of an ISA is that it protects you from Capital Gains Tax (CGT). You only pay CGT on gains over a certain amount – £7,700 for the 2002/03 tax year. That may sound a lot if you are only investing £25 a month, but, if you intend to invest for the long term, it's something you need to consider as your investments grow exponentially year on year (we hope). It's surprising how the gains add up over the years. Taking out an ISA is almost like insurance against paying CGT. You may not need it, but it's nice to have it just in case.

The benefits of regular investment

Plumping for an index tracker takes a lot of the worry and stress out of investing, but you may still be concerned that you're investing at the 'wrong' time – for example, when the market hits a temporary peak or when it is in one of its troughs. In fact, troughs are good because you're buying more for your money, but the trouble is that you never know what the stock market will do next. Countless column inches are devoted to predicting the short-term direction of the market, but it's all pure speculation. No one knows which direction the market is heading, but everyone has an opinion. The best thing to do is ignore them all.

The fact is, the long-term direction of the market is upwards. You can't time your entry to perfection – no one has a crystal ball – so the most important thing is simply taking part. There's an old investment saying: 'it's time not timing'; you should remind yourself of it if you are tempted to wait for a better moment to invest. You are never going to buy at the very bottom and sell at the very top – at least, not unless you are extremely fortunate or you have a time machine. However, if you leave your money in long enough you will make money in the end, even if you bought just before a massive crash and had to wait a couple of years for the market to struggle back up again. The general trend is upwards, so just put your money in, then weather the storms as well as the sunshine.

An excellent way of pacing your investments is by a regular contribution of say £50 or £100 a month – or more if you can afford it – into an index tracker. Every fund has a regular savings scheme set up these days and usually the costs are extremely low. Setting up a regular investment is also a good discipline as you effectively force yourself to invest every month. It's a good habit to get into. Set up a direct debit or standing order and then you won't have to think about it again.

Likewise, when you cash in your investment the reverse strategy makes sense. Rather than take all your money out in one go, you can sell gradually. Of course, you may decide that shares are the best place for your money in perpetuity and that you intend to let your capital grow whilst living off the income from those shares (the dividends). By the time you come to retire, you could stop re-investing your dividends and start having them paid directly to you. It's up to you, but whatever happens you will at least have more control over your savings and your income than you would if you had all the money in a managed pension scheme.

Going beyond trackers

Although we are very fond of index trackers at the Motley Fool, they do have their limits. For many people regular investment in an index-tracking ISA is all they will ever need (and if you do that alone, you will still be streets ahead of the vast majority of the country, who never invest in anything more lucrative than a local building society account). If you want to do better than the index, however, you have to be prepared to get your hands grubby. We won't go into too much detail here about other ways of investing in the stock market because, to do it properly, we would have to write another book. However, *The Motley Fool UK Investment Guide* and

The Motley Fool UK Investment Workbook both contain pages and pages devoted to this topic and the Motley Fool website (www.fool.co.uk) has a whole 'Strategies and Ideas' section, so check those out if you want to know more. In the meantime, though, here are a few ideas on where you could go next in your stock market investment odyssey.

Buying managed funds

The first way to beat the index is by investing in managed funds, but as we saw earlier, it's an uphill struggle as only a quarter of managed funds, if that, actually do better than trackers. You may decide to take the risk, however, in order to gain a few extra percent on your returns. You may fancy investing in technology or biotech shares, for example, but don't feel comfortable or have sufficient funds to choose them yourself. In that case a specialist fund could be the way to go, but remember, charges on managed funds tend to be very high compared with index trackers. Some managed funds charge up to 5% in entry fees and 1.5% or more in annual charges, so look carefully at those.

Of course, there will always be some funds that do better than trackers. The only trouble is identifying them in advance. Some people claim they can, although research has shown that the past performance of a fund is no guide to its future performance, which doesn't help you much. Also, beware of clever marketing ploys because most specialist funds appear *after* that particular sector has done very well so that they can be sold using some impressive 'look at what you could have got' figures. Quite often, by the time the specialist fund appears that sector has peaked and the only way is down, so make sure you don't let excitement rule your investment decision. Witness the surge in Far East funds a few years ago and the splurge of technology funds in March 2000, and learn from their mistakes.

If you *are* thinking of buying into managed funds, however, the cheapest way is probably through one of the ever-increasing fund supermarkets that offer a pretty decent range of funds at cut-price initial charges.

You will still get stung with the annual charges – which are what count in the long run – but it's definitely worth cutting initial costs if you can.

There are a number of companies that run fund supermarkets, including AMP, Fidelity, Charcolonline, Egg, FundsDirect and Charles Schwab. If you have the time and the inclination, you can trawl through them all to see who offers what and who offers the best deals on certain funds. Charges do vary from company to company, so it's worth checking out at least two to compare prices. If you're serious about buying managed funds, take a look at what's on offer on their websites (www.ample.com, www.fundsdirect.com, www.schwabfundselect.com, www.egg.com, www.fidelity.com and www.charcolonline.co.uk).

Unit trusts, investment trusts and OEICS

Managed funds can be unit trusts, investment trusts or Open-ended Investment Companies, or OEICSs (pronounced 'Oiks'). With a unit trust your money is invested along with thousands of others in one pooled fund. Presiding over the fund is a manager, or managers, responsible for achieving the fund's stated investment objective. Many people like unit trusts because they invest in lots of different companies and so are considered to be a lot less risky than individual shares. However, most unit trusts underperform the index and have high charges. They are beginning to be replaced by OEICs. An OEIC has a company structure, so, when you invest in one, you hold shares in that company. Like unit trusts, OEICs are 'open-ended', which means that the fund can get larger or smaller, depending on the number of investors who wish to buy and sell shares. Many investment funds in the US and Europe have a similar legal structure.

In fact, most tracker funds are sold as unit trusts, so if you get the forms for your first tracker and think 'Help! I've bought a stupid product,' fear not. Some unit trusts (ie: trackers) are acceptable.

Investment trusts, on the other hand, are public limited companies that make investments into a variety of other companies. Like unit trusts, they are pooled stock market investment funds, but they are actual companies that are listed on the London Stock Exchange with a fixed number of shares quoted. Unlike unit trusts, they are 'closed', so their own share prices go up and down depending on how popular they are with investors. That price may be more or less than the value of the underlying assets in the fund and you need to take this into account when deciding which trust to buy, particularly when you know that they can take on debt if they want. However, charges on investment trusts tend to be lower than managed unit trusts, especially for the larger ones, because they have to act in the interests of their investors. For these reasons, while investment funds are seen as a riskier bet than unit trusts, the rewards, obviously, can be much greater.

If you want to know more about these managed funds you can contact the Investment Management Association (IMA). IMA provides a wide range of information on investment funds whether you are a beginner or experienced investor. It has also produced a factsheet on ethical investment, which can be found in the Investing Literature section of its website (www.investmentfunds.org.uk). Which brings us neatly to...

Ethical investment

One of the problems with tracker funds – of which we are so fond here at the Fool – is that you don't get a choice of companies in which to invest. As we have explained above, tracker funds are run by computers and computers have no ethics (as you may have noticed when yours repeatedly refused to hand back all the wonderful work you spent the entire day doing before it decided to crash). Many companies produce goods or services, or have business practices, that at least some people find unacceptable. So, if you strongly object to investing in companies that produce cigarettes, or that experiment on animals, or have their goods made by five-year-olds in Asian sweatshops, then you may need to avoid catch-all tracker funds.

It is still possible to invest ethically in the stock market, though. One way to do this is through any of the increasing number of ethical funds, usually in the form of unit trusts. Ethical investment is big business these days, and growing fast. At least £5 billion is currently invested in specially branded unit trusts that shun shareholdings in companies trading in arms, alcohol or tobacco. Others go further and rule out holdings in companies that are considered to damage the environment or exploit their employees.

For all the press interest they've received over the past few years, ethical investment funds, which are also 'managed' funds (as you know, we're really not keen on those), have not done particularly well (surprise, surprise). In fact, over the last *five* years, the average return from funds in this sector has been even lower than the average for unit trusts of all kinds (which in turn is lower than the average return for tracker funds). Apart from the high charges, of course, one explanation for their poor performance is that ethical funds tend to exclude many larger companies so they have a higher proportion of assets in smaller companies. Overall, smaller companies tend not to produce such an impressive return, particularly when the economy is inclement. That said, though, only one of the 43 ethical funds that currently exist (there may be more by the time you read this) lost money for its investors and six performed better than the unit trust average. The question remains, though, as to how you choose a good performer for the future.

Worry not! There are alternatives for the diligent investor. One possible way to go is to invest in individual companies. When you invest in companies directly, you will need to research them yourself – according to the information you can get from the Motley Fool investment books and on our website (www.fool.co.uk/lrninvint.htm) – and one of the aspects of a company you can look into is its ethics. Helpfully, there is a website that has done much of that ethical research for you already. It is the website of EIRIS (www.eiris.org), a charity that was set up in 1983 by representatives from various churches and charities that wanted to know they were investing their funds in companies that met their ethical criteria. Anyone can use EIRIS's services, which cost from £60 for ethical company reports.

Another, much easier, way is to invest in a tracker. Yes, we know we said they weren't the best method for the ethical investor. However, as of 2001, there are now ethical trackers thanks to FTSE4Good, a family of indices for socially responsible investment designed by the index provider FTSE. FTSE4Good's marketing blurb states that it 'aims to facilitate investment in companies which meet certain eligibility criteria in the area of corporate social responsibility'. You can find out about their trackers on their FTSE4Good website (www.FTSE4Good.com).

One company that offers a tracker fund based on the FTSE4Good Index is Close Fund Managers. They charge an annual fee of 1% and, annoyingly, an initial charge of 4% (which you could reduce or lose entirely if you go through a fund supermarket or a discount broker). The bid/offer spread is 4% and it has minimum investments of £1,000 lump sum or £100 per month. If you're interested contact Close Fund Managers to discuss it further (phone on 0800 269824 or look at www.CloseFM.com).

Becoming a stock picker

Ha ha! Now we're coming to it. This is where you get *really* scared! Visions of sweaty young men in shirtsleeves and red braces standing at their desks shouting 'Buy! Buy! Sell! Sell!' down the phone come to mind. Well, take a deep breath and relax. You don't *have* to invest in individual shares – ever, if you don't want to. If you only ever put your money into trackers and leave it there, you will be doing very nicely, thank you. However, if you do want to invest in individual shares at some point, we recommend that you spend some time studying the animal that is the stock market and learning about how to invest wisely before you actually commit your cash to individual companies.

Of course, you may be one of those lucky people who have had windfalls of shares from their building society or pension company, or perhaps your employers are offering you share options in the company you work for. Without intending to, you may already have become a shareholder and you may be wondering what to do with the shares you have in your hot little hand right now.

There are no easy answers to the question of whether you should keep your free shares or cash them in. However, if you are willing to do the research, you can work out for yourself whether you think this company is a goer and likely to do well in the future (in which case, you should keep hold of your shares and possibly buy more) or whether it's not (if so, then you should cash your shares in now). If you don't want to mug up on the company, you will probably be best just selling the shares and putting the money into a tracker fund. At least that way you will know that, in the long term, your money is in a comparatively safe place and it will still be earning more for you than if it were left in a bank account.

If you're serious about going down the do-it-yourself stock-picking route, then you'll need to put a share selection strategy in place, because, if there's one certainty on the stock market, it's the certainty of losing money by haphazardly buying and selling individual shares on a whim. However, if you spend some time and effort deciding on a stock-picking principle, you will have a fine chance of choosing good shares on a regular basis.

This is quite a big subject, so we're not going to go on about it here, but there are a few basic rules that you should keep in mind when you start thinking about investing directly into companies:

● Only consider investing for the long term. Stories of fortunes made and lost in day trading (buying and selling shares within the same day) are fun tales for those who like gambling, but, as we said before, gambling is not Foolish behaviour. This is about investment and the long-term acquisition of wealth, not short-term hopes.

● Do your own homework. If you are considering investing in a company, find out about it yourself. In order to find out *what* you need to find out about, go through the Fool School on the Motley Fool website (find at www.fool.co.uk) and read the Motley Fool books on investing first.

- Don't take any notice of media tipsters. There is the usual handful of tips in various newspapers and financial programmes each week; they are completely pointless. For a start, if those tipsters *really* knew what they were talking about, they would be sticking all their own ill-gotten gains in these companies and would make enough not to have to bother with journalism. So naturally the question arises, 'How come they're still there if they know so much?' Forget all about tips. Blindly acting upon them will lose you money. At very best, they'll provide a springboard for you to conduct further research. The Motley Fool advocates: 'Develop your own strategy to become your own tipster.'

- Invest in what you know about. And we mean really *know* about. Too many people invest because they *believe*, not because of what they actually *know*. There's a difference! It can sometimes help to research and invest in companies from the sector in which you work because you will already have some knowledge about what makes that sector tick and, therefore, what makes a good company in that area. Make sure you still do your business homework on the company beforehand, though, and don't just let nostalgia or emotions rule your investment decisions.

- Make sure you have a good spread of shares but don't diversify too much. You have to have a balance. Unless you are very sure of yourself (and you probably shouldn't be too sure of yourself), you should settle for around 10–15 good, solid, individual holdings that you are happy to keep an eye on over the years.

- You will make more money in the long run if you thoroughly research, and keep abreast of, a few companies, investing in them regularly, than if you scatter your funds across lots of businesses.

- Don't rush into it. All right, you may miss out on some good opportunities by not investing in Allied Moneymakers right now, but you could also be avoiding a major loss of good money by waiting until you have learnt about the company. Have a go at virtual investing on the Motley Fool website to get the hang of share trading before putting your hard-earned cash where your beliefs are.

Doing your homework

We keep banging on about 'doing your research', so how do you do it? There are books aplenty about the stock market, investing, investors and so on, most of which are dull to the point of screaming, but some are very helpful and actually interesting. If you are really interested, do take a look in the investing section in your local library or bookshop and, if nothing else, make sure you read *The Motley Fool UK Investment Guide*. Read the money and finance pages of your favourite broadsheet, too. Journalists don't always know what they're talking about (and we should know, we're journalists), but occasionally you may find some nugget of information that points you in the right direction.

The Internet is a fabulous resource full of excellent websites. Obviously, the number one site that no one should be without is www.fool.co.uk, giving you all you need to know about personal finance, investing and recipes for flaky pastry (yes, really!). On our site you can find out how to sort out your finances, learn how to invest and talk to literally thousands of other members about anything from pensions news to your favourite film. We strongly suggest you start there (well, we would, wouldn't we?).

Other very useful sites to find out the breaking news and the latest financial and company information are www.reuters.com, www.bloomberg.co.uk and www.bbc.co.uk. If you really get into this stock-picking and investing lark, check out www.financial-freebies.com, which provides free copies of magazines, software and bulletins. Do be prepared, however, to get more junk mail than you bargained for if you do offer up your details to one of the companies there. Once you're on their database, they've got you! You can also look at www.carol.co.uk if you want to check out company reports online before deciding whether to invest in them; www.barbican.co.uk has a lot of data on unit trusts that can be useful if you have one; www.dismalscience.com gives more detailed comment on economic issues and is a site with a rare, but welcome, display of humility from economists; and www.londonstock-exchange.co.uk has general information on the stock market.

If you are a normal human being who speaks English but has some difficulty with financial and technical jargon (how strange that you couldn't instantly understand all those wonderful words and phrases!), look them up on the Motley Fool website at www.fool.co.uk/school/glossary/glossary1.htm, or check out www.plainenglish.co.uk/finance or www.investorword.com. If you get tied up in all the technical jargon of some of the technology companies, then go to www.whatis.com for an explanation.

Finally, our three top tips for investing are:

- Consider a low-cost index tracker. You'll have realised by now that consistently beating the stock market over many years can be very difficult. If we use history as our guide, over the long term an index tracker will outperform all other forms of investment, the majority of managed funds and (quite probably) most other private investors too. Best of all, the tracker requires the absolute minimum time, skill and worrying over long-term underperformance. On an effort-to-reward basis, the index tracker certainly outshines all other alternatives hands down.
- If you want to invest in individual shares then form a strategy. The basis of your investment homework should form an investment strategy based on your own personal circumstances. Having an overall investment strategy leads to clearer thinking and reduces the stock market distractions.
- Be patient. Regardless of whether the stock market is racing ahead or plummeting like a stone, don't panic. See, the stock market will still be around next year and the year after that. You wouldn't fork out thousands of pounds to build your own conservatory just using your intuition, would you? Yet many novices spend similar amounts of money buying shares on a whim and then selling them in a panic. Needless to say, there's no quicker route to a financial headache than 'gut feelings', so don't be sucked in.

Major UK Index Trackers

(Information correct as of April 2002)

None of the following tracker funds levies an initial charge:

Dresdner RCM UK Index
Index: FTSE All Share
Annual charges: 0.6% (0.5% management plus 0.1% trustee fees etc.)
Bid/offer spread: 0.5%
Minimum investments: £500 lump sum or £25 per month
Website: www.dresdnerrcm.co.uk
Tel: 0800 317573

Edinburgh UK Tracker Trust
Index: FTSE All Share
Annual charges: 0.25%
Bid/offer spread: 1.3% (estimated)
Minimum investments: £250 lump sum or £30 per month
Website: www.edfd.com
Tel: 0131 313 1000

Fidelity Moneybuilder
Index: FTSE All Share
Annual charges: 0.72% (0.5% management charge plus 0.22%)
Bid/offer spread: 0%
Minimum investments: £500 lump sum or £50 per month
Website: www.fidelity.co.uk
Tel: 0800 414161

Gartmore UK Index
Index: FTSE All Share
Annual charges: 0.75%
Bid/offer spread: 0.5% (estimated)
Minimum investments: £1,000 lump sum or £100 per month
Website: www.gartmore.co.uk
Tel: 0800 289336

HSBC FTSE All Share Fund
Index: FTSE All Share
Annual charges: 0.5%
Bid/offer spread: 0%
Minimum investments: £500 lump sum or £25 per month
Website: www.hsbc.co.uk
Tel: 0800 289505

Legal & General UK Index
Index: FTSE All Share
Annual charges: 0.53% (0.5% management plus custodian and
    registrar fee)
Bid/offer spread: 0%
Minimum investments: £500 lump sum or £25 per month
Website: www.legalandgeneral.com
Tel: 0800 0920092

M&G Index Tracker
Index: FTSE All Share
Annual charges: 0.439% (0.3% management plus custodian and
    registrar fees)
Bid/offer spread: none
Minimum investments: £500 lump sum or £10 per month
Website: www.mandg.co.uk
Tel: 0800 390390

Scottish Widows UK Tracker
Index: FTSE 100
Annual charges: 0.5%
Bid/offer spread: 0%
Minimum investments: £500 lump sum or £50 per month
Website: www.scottishwidows.co.uk
Tel: 08457 678910

Virgin UK Index Tracker
Index: FTSE All Share
Annual charges: 1%
Bid/offer spread: 0%
Minimum investments: £1 lump sum or £1 per month
Website: www.virginmoney.com
Tel: 08456 101020

The Taxman Cometh

A fine is a tax for doing wrong. A tax is a fine for doing well.

Anon

One of the easiest ways of making the most of your money is not to pay tax. Gasp! Shock horror! We need reporting to the fraud squad!

Of course, we don't mean tax evasion (which is illegal), but tax avoidance (which is perfectly legal). In its efforts to persuade us to save, the Government has handed us the latter option on a plate with the Individual Savings Account (ISA). It's such an important aspect of your financial future that we're going to devote much of this chapter to the subject, not least because some people think you're better off saving for your retirement via an ISA rather than a pension scheme.

First, it's worth outlining how certain elements of the current tax system work so you have an understanding of why there is such a huge discrepancy between your gross and your net income from earnings.

Income Tax

The Inland Revenue allows you to earn a certain amount before you start getting taxed on your income. It's called a Personal Allowance and usually goes up a little each year to keep pace with inflation. In the 2002/03 tax year, it's been set at £4,615, so if your income is below this you will not pay tax. (Depending on their age, pensioners may get a slightly higher Personal Allowance.)

Once your income exceeds the tax-free Personal Allowance figure, a series of tax bands then come into play; it depends how much you earn over and above the Personal Allowance as to which tax band you fall into. The tax bands are essentially 10%, 22% and 40% of your gross income and it works like a tier system as follows:

The first £4,615 of your earnings is tax-free (Personal Allowance).
The next £1,920 is taxed at 10% (Starting Rate)
The next £27,979 is taxed at 22% (Basic Rate)
Anything over that is taxed at 40% (Higher Rate).

If you do the sums (ugh!), you'll realise that you need to earn £34,514 a year before you start getting taxed at the high rate as £4,615 + £1,920 + £27,979 = £34,514.

Note that the tax rates are marginal. That is, they apply only to the band of income concerned and do not apply to the whole income. So, if you were to earn £34,515 (just one pound more), the tax rate would be at the higher rate of 40% on that extra pound alone. It does not bring the whole of the income into the higher rate band.

Remember that you will also be taxed on your investment income, which is usually the interest you earn from your savings or the dividends you receive from holding shares. With dividend income there's a complicated system of tax credits involved which we won't go into here – suffice to say, the tax rate for a basic-rate taxpayer works out at 20% rather than 22%. (Even though a person's income is in the 22% rate band, say from employment plus the interest itself, they are not liable to pay the additional 2%. The Inland Revenue lets you off that 2%, lovely people that they are!)

National Insurance

National Insurance (NI), which was referred to in the olden days as the 'stamp', is paid both by employees and employers. This is because your employer literally had to buy special stamps to stick on each employee's card. The system's not so antiquated these days, so the only thing you'll probably know about it is that whopping great sums of money get taken out of your salary every month before you see a penny of it.

Much as governments like to deny it, National Insurance is really a type of income tax. Broadly speaking, the principal difference between income tax and NI is that the former applies to income of all types whereas the latter applies only to what might loosely be termed earned income. It is mind-numbingly complex and theoretically is used to pay for certain social security benefits such as sick pay, maternity pay and your State Pension. In April 2002, the Government announced that it would be increasing NI contributions across the board by 1% to pay for extra funding for the National Health Service.

There are four 'classes' of National Insurance Contributions (NICs) and it depends on how you are employed as to what type you'll pay. Roughly speaking, it amounts to 10% on any earnings over and above £89 a week (rising to 11% after April 2003).

The single most important thing that NICs pay for is the State Pension. At the moment, your NICs are mostly being used to pay for the meagre pension that is being doled out to our current pensioners. Similarly, your State Pension will be paid for by your children and grandchildren. The fact that we're having fewer and fewer kids these days is mainly why the Government keeps trying to persuade us to save up for our own pension; there won't be too many youngsters around to pay for our old age when the time comes!

You will be entitled to the basic State Pension only if you've made full NICs throughout your working life. The Government expects you to work for 44 years to qualify for the full pension, which, in the 2002/03 tax year, amounts to £75.50 a week for a single person. It's a long time to work for not a lot at the end of it, isn't it? If you haven't worked for the full 44 years, your pension is reduced proportionately. And if you've worked for less than 11 years, you get zilch! (The rules are currently slightly different for women but are being changed to bring them in line with the rules for men.)

There are obviously certain times in your life when you're not working for a good reason and the Government will let you off in those instances. For example, you'll be credited as if you've paid full NICs if you're sick or you're raising a child. But if you haven't paid enough into the pot because you've spent half your life back-packing around the world, you are allowed to make extra contributions later if you need to.

Not many people make their own provision for old age, so it's important to check that you're up to date with your NICs to ensure that you'll get at least something when you hit retirement age. You can do this by asking for a pension forecast. Write to Benefits Agency, Retirement Pension Forecasting and Advice, Pensions and Overseas Benefits Directorate, Newcastle upon Tyne, NE98 1BA, or fill in the form on-line (www.dss.gov.uk). It takes a few weeks to come through but it'll tell you if you ought to pay a bit extra to catch up.

Capital Gains Tax

If you are in the fortunate position of being able to pay the maximum permitted amount into your ISA each year and you're in a position to save and invest even more, then how can you do it without being clobbered for tax on the profits you make? It makes sense to consider paying into a pension scheme, of course, because of the tax relief, but you may want to invest your surplus money in other ways without committing it to a pension fund. For example, if you wanted to buy a residential property to rent out as an investment, you can't do this via an ISA anyway, nor can you do it within a pension scheme.

The answer is to use your annual Capital Gains Tax allowance to alleviate the pain of paying money to the taxman. If you splash out on a buy-to-let property or shares (whether in the form of individual shares, an index tracker or a managed fund) and you sell later for a profit, the

Government likes to get its mitts on some of that gain. Par for the course really, isn't it? However, it does let you keep some of it before taxing you on the rest.

Capital Gains Tax is, remarkably, a tax on the gains you have made. The specific rules and regulations are complicated and if you end up with an extensive property and/or share portfolio, then you definitely need an accountant to sort out your tax liabilities. However, it's worth explaining the basics so you've got some idea of how it works.

First of all, each one of us – man, woman and child – is allowed to make a specified annual profit – £7,700 in the 2002/03 tax year – on our capital assets before the Inland Revenue takes its cut. Let's say you bought some shares for £5,000 and they've shot up in value to £15,000. Your profit is a fantastic £10,000, so how much are you going to get taxed if you sell them? Yes, you've got it. You deduct your £7,700 allowance, leaving £2,300 of taxable profit. The level at which you are taxed depends on whether you fall into the Standard Rate or Higher Rate tax bracket. If your profits take you into the higher range then you're looking at 40% of your taxable £2,300 going into the Inland Revenue's coffers! So how do you get around it?

Well, in the case of shares, the solution is to sell them while your profits are still within your CGT allowance and then buy them back again thus 're-basing' their value and enabling you to start afresh. Let's take our £5,000 worth of shares again. This time you sell them when they're worth £10,000, so you've made £5,000 over and above your initial investment. You have 'realised' your gains and, since you are well within your £7,700 allowance, you have no tax to pay. You then buy those same shares back for £10,000, at which point the Inland Revenue allows you to start counting afresh (in other words, you start at £10,000 and can make profits of £7,700 on top of that before you have to worry about tax).

In the old days, you could sell your shares and buy them back the very next day to use up your CGT allowance and thus 're-base' the cost of the shares. If you sold them at 4pm on a Tuesday and bought them back at

9am the next day, the chances of the share price changing much was minimal: this was known as 'Bed & Breakfasting'. People did this on an annual basis just to use up their exemption entitlement. However, the Government now has a rule that prevents you from using this defensive method if you buy back your shares within 30 days. Of course, the risk of the shares going up in price by the time the month is up is now much higher. You might sell them for £10,000 on the 1st of the month only to find that by the 31st they have shot up to £15,000.

What you can do as an alternative, though, is to sell your shares and use the money to buy *different* shares (or a different index tracker or managed fund) the next day (or the same day in fact); this way you're safe. As long as you're not buying back the same shares, you can realise your gains and get around the anti-'Bed & Breakfast' rules. (Note that the 30-day rule is irrelevant if the shares are held within an ISA.)

Men also have their uses when it comes to ownership of shares that have made a profit. If you have a partner, you can use each other's CGT exemption to get around the problem of excessive gains. How this works depends on whether you are married or not, since the Government lets married couples transfer property and shares between each other without incurring any tax liabilities at all.

If your husband's own allowance isn't needed for personal purposes, consider transferring some or all of your shares to him. That way, when the time comes to sell, you'll be using up his CGT exemption instead of, or as well as, your own. As a spouse he'll be treated just as if he had bought them himself for the original cost, so you will not have used any of your own CGT allowance in making the transfer.

For unmarried couples the transfer will be deemed a gift to your partner made at current market value, so you will be regarded as having realised any gains the moment you hand them over to him. However, if you do some forward thinking then you can protect yourself from subsequent gains in the following year, as he will be holding the shares and not you.

There's also a 'Bed & Breakfast' style of using your partner's CGT allowance, although again this is different for the married and unmarried. If you're married, you can sell the shares, use up your CGT exemption and then get your spouse to buy them back immediately. After 30 days, he can transfer them back to you at the new price with no tax liability. Those who are unmarried can simply transfer the shares back and forth to each other every year, leaving a 30-day gap in between, thus rebasing the price of the shares each time. As long as you don't realise gains of more than both of your allowances each year, you won't have to pay any CGT at all.

For both married and unmarried couples, an easier way would be to hold all shares in your joint names in a nominee account with a broker. The double exemption would apply and you wouldn't have to think about how and when to transfer all the time.

When it comes to property, though, it's not really feasible (and would be much too expensive) to buy and sell a buy-to-let property every year, so the easiest way of protecting yourself from paying too much CGT is to put the property into joint names with your husband or partner. Since he gets an annual allowance, you'll be able to make a profit of £15,400 before either of you faces a CGT liability. That's only if you're sure you want him owning half your property, though! (By the way, the home you live in is classed as your principle residence and you don't have to pay CGT when you sell.)

ISAs

An ISA protects your savings from tax. It's a bit like a fortress, which even the Chancellor of the Exchequer can't invade, so everything you keep inside your fortress is all yours! We couldn't put it any better than one of the Motley Fool contributors (thanks, dpickard!), which is to think of your ISA as a shark cage.

Get into the shark cage and, as long as you stay in there, no matter how dangerous it gets outside, you are safe and snug inside. Get out of your shark cage for just one second and you are lunch. ISAs are the same. Put your annual entitlement into an ISA and it is safe from the taxman. Buy the shares of your choice, inside the ISA, and they are safe. Sell those shares, and they turn into money: but your ISA manager keeps the money inside the ISA for as long as it takes to use that money to buy other shares: and those shares stay inside the ISA. So they are still safe from the taxman. It doesn't matter how much those shares grow or diminish. It doesn't matter how much they are worth. The limit comes on putting money in, not on churning existing assets inside the ISA.

From the Motley Fool discussion boards

There are other ways of getting around paying tax on our savings and investments, but they usually involve having to learn about various tax regulations, such as those relating to capital gains, and filling in nasty tax returns. If you keep your money in an ISA, however, you don't have to think about such boring things. The interest on your cash savings will be tax-free and any profits made from your stock market investments will be free of Capital Gains Tax. Simple, isn't it?

Well, not quite. ISAs are actually a bit of a challenge because the rules and regulations governing them are jolly confusing, in fact, irritatingly so. For example, you're allowed to have several ISAs and yet you're only allowed to operate only one. Eh? Yes, the ISA is a beauty when it comes to Government bureaucracy!

Some basics

To start with, there are two types of ISA: The Maxi and the Mini. It's pretty important to distinguish between the two because each year you are allowed to invest in only one of the two types.

The Maxi

This is made up of three components:

- Cash
- Stocks and Shares (equities)
- Insurance

Think of the Maxi ISA like a big teapot with three different types of teabag in it. These are teabags of varying strengths and tastes that you can choose according to your fancy, more or less, but they all go into one single teapot. You will appreciate that if you put all three types into one teapot, you can have only one person be Mother. In other words, only one financial organisation can run your Maxi ISA for you.

The Mini

This is made up of the same three components:

- Cash
- Stocks and Shares (equities)
- Insurance

This time, think of three little teapots, each with its own teabag. This, of course, means that you can choose three different people to be Mother with whatever type of teabag you fancy. So, if one company's offering great interest rates on its Cash Mini ISA but you don't like the charges on its Shares Mini ISA, that's okay. Open their Cash Mini ISA and go to someone else for your Shares Mini ISA.

At present you're allowed to invest a maximum of £7,000 a year, although there are provisos about how much you can invest in each component. In an effort to encourage the financial whizzes in the City to offer us punters a good deal, some ISAs have been allocated a CAT standard. The CAT standard is a bit like the Kite mark: it represents good value for money. So, if an ISA has a CAT mark then you'll know that there are restrictions on how much those moneymen can charge you for looking after your money and where they can invest it. More details later but, suffice to say, a CAT-standard ISA is supposed to reassure us when we're worrying about where to put our hard-earned dosh (and, indeed, it does!).

Of course, not all ISAs are CAT-marked and those that aren't are likely to incur higher charges, fewer guarantees about the potential profits and less easy access. On the positive side, though, you will have more freedom to invest in areas of your choice, particularly in the global market: potentially higher returns for higher risks.

As for where you can get them, well, practically anyone who's anyone is offering ISAs nowadays! Banks, building societies, insurance companies, unit and investment trust companies and, of course, ever anxious to get in on the act, supermarkets.

We all know that governments like to chop and change their ideas every now and then, but we have been promised that ISAs will run until at least 2009. The rules are simple: you have to be ordinarily resident in the UK for tax purposes, and you have to be at least 18 to invest in the Shares and Insurance components or at least 16 and over to invest in the Cash component.

Now for the nitty-gritty! (This may be the moment to fix yourself something a little stronger than a cup of tea.)

A few details

The ISA is, of course, designed to persuade us to save. The incentive to do it through an ISA is that you don't have to pay tax at all on the profits. By 'profits' we mean the interest or dividends that will (hopefully) accrue throughout the term of the ISA, and the capital gains you will (hopefully) make when you buy and sell investments within the ISA.

Remember, you are allowed to take out only one type of ISA each year. So if you open a Maxi ISA this year, then you can't suddenly decide you want one of those cute little Mini ISAs as well. Or, if you open just one of the cute little Mini ISAs then you can't decide you want a Maxi ISA too. It's one or the other, at least until the next financial year when you have the grand opportunity of making the wrong decision all over again! However, now that you're thinking sensibly, that's not going to happen, is it?

For the Maxi ISA or the three Mini ISAs combined, the maximum *contributions* permitted are £7,000 per tax year. This amount will apply until at least 2006, at which point the Chancellor will review it.

The components of an ISA are (repeat after us) Cash, Stocks and Shares, and Insurance. This is how they work:

Cash

The Cash component operates in exactly the same way as if you were putting money into a building society savings account that pays interest (only this time, you don't pay tax on the interest, remember?). So, whether you've gone for a Mini Cash ISA (one little teapot) *or* you've decided to save some cash inside a Maxi ISA (a teabag in a big teapot), the Cash component works in exactly the same way. You simply get interest on your money. The limit for *contributions* to a Cash Mini ISA or to the Cash component of a Maxi ISA is £3,000 per year.

The word *contributions* is in italics because the rule is that your *contributions* must not exceed the annual allowance. Let's say Great-Aunt Vera pops her clogs and leaves you the handy sum of £3,000. You put it all into a Mini Cash ISA whilst you happily make arrangements for that little back-packing trip up the Andes you've been wanting to do since you were 12 years old. A few months later, you come back from your trip and – miracle of miracles – you find you didn't need quite as much money as you thought and you've managed to return with £500 in your pocket. Can you put it back into your now empty Mini Cash ISA account?

Nope! It's the paying-in slips that count, not the withdrawals. While you are free to take out your money, tax-free, and use it for whatever you want, you aren't allowed to top it back up again *within the same tax year.*

Obviously, what you are looking for in a Mini Cash ISA is the best interest rate possible at the time of opening the ISA, but bear in mind that the rate will fluctuate. After all, you know how the banks have a habit of attracting you with pretty rates in big newspaper adverts and then quietly cutting them by sending you a boring letter that you throw in the bin because you think it's a circular! Beware of companies which offer a higher rate for a guaranteed period after which it plummets like a stone! If you don't fancy moving your money around every few months, you might be better off going for a company that doesn't pay the highest interest rate, but is, at least, fairly consistent. Anyway, once you've picked the best of the bunch, you don't have to do anything. You just sit back and watch your little pile of money get bigger.

Should the interest rate fall, or fail to rise in line with others on the market, you can switch your Mini Cash ISA to a company that offers a better rate. However, it is vital that you follow the correct procedure when moving your ISA, otherwise you could scupper yourself. More on this later!

Stocks and Shares

The Stocks and Shares component enables you to invest your money into the stock market, rather than just saving it. You can either take out a Mini Equity ISA (your second little teapot, if you like) *or* incorporate your investments within a Maxi ISA (your second teabag in the big teapot) alongside your Cash component, if you have one.

There are now no restrictions on where you can make your investments as long as they are in recognised stock exchanges worldwide. You can find a Shares ISA that simply tracks one or more of the indices: this could include the FTSE 100, the FTSE All Share Index, a European tracker, the American Nasdaq or even a mix of global equities including gilts, OEICs and bonds. Otherwise, you can leave everything up to the particular fund manager you've chosen and hope that he/she does better than you could do. As you read in Chapter 5, this is probably an idiotic thing to do considering index trackers tend to outperform managed funds over the long term.

You can even choose your own individual shares. You can opt for this last vehicle via a Self-Select ISA and you can get them from stockbrokers.

Inside a Self-Select ISA you can buy and sell as often as you want as long as your actual *contributions* from *outside* the ISA do not exceed the annual allowance. Once your shares are inside the ISA, you can chop and change your portfolio as often as you like with no tax penalties as long as the shares, or cash from the sale of the shares, never actually leave the ISA. Some Self-Select ISA managers will even allow you to hold individual shares *and* unit or investment trusts side by side within your ISA.

Remember that on top of the normal dealing costs from running your investments yourself there will be a charge by whoever is administering the ISA. Also, if you put a unit or investment trust alongside your individual shares in your Self-Select ISA, then you will most likely be charged twice, once by the fund manager and once by the company running the Self-Select ISA. If you want a unit or investment trust inside an ISA (whether an index tracker or a managed fund), it will almost always be best to have the same company do the fund management and provide the ISA. Anyway, make sure you do your sums carefully.

As far as dividends are concerned, at the moment the Government allows you to reclaim a 10% tax credit on your gross dividends provided they are paid on shares within an ISA. However, this only applies until 2004, when the reclaimable tax credit will disappear, so, at that stage, you will lose this small benefit altogether.

There is also, of course, the ubiquitous 0.5% stamp duty, which is still payable on all share purchases even within an ISA.

Unlike the Cash component, the rules on how much you can invest in a Mini Shares ISA and the Shares component of a Maxi ISA differ quite a bit, so pay attention. Repeat: 'PAY ATTENTION!' (We're not trying to bore you. Honest!)

The Mini Stocks and Shares ISA
The contribution limit is £3,000 per tax year (out of the combined total of £7,000).

The Maxi Stocks and Shares ISA

The Government seems to favour equities, so, if you want, you can put your *entire* allowance into shares. Yep! The whole damn lot if you want to. Therefore, it follows that the contribution limit for a Maxi ISA is £7,000 per tax year (out of the combined total of £7,000).

Can I put the share options I've been offered by my employer into an ISA?

Shares maturing from some Inland Revenue-approved company share schemes can be transferred into an ISA within 90 days of being exercised and you will not be regarded as having realised a capital gain. These include some of the Save as You Earn schemes and some of the Profit Sharing schemes. You will need to check with your employer to find out if your particular share saving scheme is ISA-ble and then you must bear in mind a number of points.

You may first have to pay income tax on the 'profits' you have made (under the 'benefit in kind' system) from being able to buy a share at a lower-than-market-value price in the first place. So, if your company's shares are worth £2 on the open market but you've had to pay only £1 for them because of the share-option scheme, you may still have to pay income tax on the £1 profit. You will not have to pay income tax if certain conditions are met. Following that, the amount you can then put into the ISA will be based on the current market value of the shares after you have exercised the option. So, in the above example, you will be able to put in 3,500 shares (priced at £2), which will make up your maximum £7,000 contribution.

Insurance

The Insurance component is almost not worth talking about since there are very few financial organisations offering them. In fact, if you do try to find a company offering them, you'll be hard pushed. There is a limit on what you can invest in the Insurance component of an ISA: it is £1,000 per tax year (out of the combined total of £7,000). This is probably the main reason for their unpopularity: you can't invest much in them. They're more expensive to run so the charges are usually higher even with a CAT-marked Insurance ISA. There is a life-cover aspect and some offer things like a 'with -profits' element, but, frankly, they're incomprehensible and you can probably get the same benefits elsewhere. It's up to you if you bother with them, but we wouldn't.

ISA transfers

You can transfer your ISA to a different company whenever you like, but only into the same type of component. For example, you cannot switch a Cash ISA with one company to a Stocks and Shares ISA with another – the money must go into another Cash ISA.

Simply approach the new company that you want to switch your ISA to and they will arrange the transfer of your savings and/or investments for you. *Leave it to them to sort out!* On no account do you close down your ISA, withdraw the money and try to put it into a new ISA. As you've already learnt, there is a limit to how much you can *contribute* each year – it's a one-off shot – so the money you've saved always needs to be *transferred* to the new ISA and *not withdrawn*.

Some fund managers may charge a heavy penalty for the privilege of leaving them, so double-check before you make the decision to move. In fact, you should check this before opening the ISA in the first place. Either way, if you want to move, the thing to do is to start by contacting the company you have decided to move to. They should be able to take it from there.

As an aside, you might be wondering whether you should invest via the Mini system or via the Maxi. It really depends on how much you've got to invest. Mini ISAs are probably better if you have only small or fluctuating amounts to spare throughout the tax year. Maxi ISAs are advisable for people who have larger sums to invest, who have some knowledge of the stock market and who would rather put their full contribution allowance into investments.

What happens at the end of the financial year?
Can I continue with my ISA or do I have to start a new one?
That's entirely up to you. You can continue contributing to the one you have already chosen if you want to – it just rolls over to the next tax year. If you pay into your original ISA, it continues to be active and you can't open a new one. If you stop paying into your original ISA (before the new tax year starts), you're then allowed to start a different one.

As long as you cut off the cash supply to the old one at the right time, it will simply freeze (just like Windows does) and the interest or dividends will continue to accrue behind the scenes. It only freezes in the sense that you can't put any more money into it, so if you have a Self-Select ISA, you can continue to buy and sell using whatever funds you already have within that Self-Select ISA.

Starting a new ISA each year with a different company can be quite an effective strategy, as you're spreading your risk across a range of providers each year – like making a pot of tea and leaving it to brew while you get on with making the next pot. There are always all sorts of ISA goodies on offer from the Wise, so it's worth keeping an eye out for them just in case they're better than the one you've already got.

One very important thing to remember is that, if you decide you want to start a new ISA at the beginning of the new tax year, it is vital to remember to cancel your direct debit (if you have one) into your original ISA. If you make any payment into your original ISA once the new tax year has started, you'll have to stick with it. You mustn't break the rules about having only one active ISA each year.

So now we know what ISAs are, let's have a look at the system introduced by the Government to make sure that the good ones get noticed. It's all about CATs, but we're not talking about the feline variety here.

CAT marks

The CAT mark is purely voluntary. You will often find that an ISA provider will offer two similar products: one that has the CAT mark and one that doesn't. These initials refer to Charges, Access and Terms; any fund manager offering a CAT-marked ISA is required to be clear and upfront about what they're offering. The Government use the term 'fair' when discussing how fund managers should behave, which is a bit odd since it must mean they accept (and even allow) that fund managers are often 'unfair' in the way they treat individual investors!

Do bear in mind, however, that ISAs *without* the CAT mark do not have to follow these rules, so watch out for hidden charges. You should also realise that CAT-marked ISAs do result in restrictions for you, the investor.

So, the CAT-marked ISA means:

Charges

Cash ISA	no charges allowed at all
Stocks and Shares ISA	no more than 1% a year in charges of net asset value (and some are charging even less than that)
Insurance ISA	no more than 3% a year in charges

Access

Customers must be able to get access to their money within seven working days.

Terms

Interest rates for the cash element are never allowed to be more than 2% below the base rate

ISA fund managers are not allowed to set an investment level higher than a £500 lump sum or £50 per month. So, if you want to put lump sums into a CAT-marked ISA as and when you have the money, you will never have to find more than £500 (and, in fact, some funds require far less). Likewise, if you want to pay by monthly instalments, you will never have to pay more than £50 per month (again, some funds require even less).

Well, that's about it for ISAs. The next section is for those who still have any interest in PEPS and TESSAs so you can skip it if you've never heard of either!

PEPS and TESSAs

Surprise, surprise! You didn't really think PEPs and TESSAs were extinct, did you? That they'd gone the way of Brontosaurus? Of course not! As it happens, the rules for PEPs were changed in April 2001 to bring them more into line with ISAs, so if you've got one and you're not sure how they work these days, then keep reading. If you've got a TESSA, you might have some vague recollection of a time limit on your decision-making when it matures.

First of all, let's run through a few basics about PEPs. If you've got one or more of them, you'll know that they were the forerunner to the Shares component of the ISA (in other words, a method of investing money in stocks and shares without having to pay tax on the capital or the income). They were scrapped in April 1999 to make way for the more flexible ISA, so you can't open a new PEP any more. If you already have a PEP, though, you continue to benefit from the tax-free status, but you can't put any more new money into it.

Until 5 April 2001, PEPs came in two varieties: Single and General. An individual could buy one of each in any tax year up to 1999. The two types of PEP had slightly different rules on what they could invest in, so brokers and fund managers had to hold them in separate accounts. A single-company PEP could hold shares in only one company (duh!) and it was limited to an initial investment of £3,000. Such a modest capital sum meant the economics of running these accounts were not attractive for managers or investors. Even so, 3 million PEPs were sold in total. General PEPs could contain a number of different shares and you could invest £6,000 a year into those.

Since April 2001, the distinction between Single PEPs and General PEPs has been abolished. This brings two advantages. The first is that Single PEPs can be combined into one (or, more officially, 'amalgamated') and then, if appropriate, amalgamated with a General PEP. At a stroke that reduces the amount of paperwork a manager has to do and so ought to be reflected in lower costs for the investor. PEP fees are varied but are usually based on a percentage of the funds under management. The second benefit of the change is increased flexibility. If it happened to do well, being limited to one share in a Single PEP was a constraint as it became a very large part of a portfolio. Under the old rules you either had to live with that or sell it and buy another share. Now it is possible to hold more than one investment.

At the same time as these changes were made, the Government simplified life even more by extending the rules on ISAs to PEPs. This has widened the range of corporate and Government bonds that can be held in PEPs as well as the geographic spread of equities. PEP investors are no longer confined to Europe.

Apart from the restrictions on the sort of investments you could put into both types of PEPs, there were also other limitations (some of which are still in place). For example, while you can withdraw income from investments and the interest from cash deposits within your PEP, there are conditions regarding the interest on any cash deposits you may have. You cannot draw out more than £180 of the interest from any cash deposits in a single tax year otherwise all the interest becomes taxable.

As with ISAs, you can take some of your capital out of your PEP or close it down completely, but you cannot later replace any of the money, so be aware that you will lose any tax-free benefits permanently. Holding a PEP doesn't affect your entitlement to an ISA, so you can simply run the two tax-protected vehicles alongside each other.

The changes to the rules make it much easier to switch the investment mix of a PEP portfolio, particularly in the international markets. If you're unhappy with current performance or lack of investment choice, you can now transfer to a new PEP manager (or managers) with much more simplicity. The fact that you can also now transfer part of your PEP investments means that, if you've ended up with a series of PEPs in a 'bundled' account, you'll be able to hive off part of the fund if you choose to do so.

Finally, don't forget that, while you may want to switch everything to one provider so you can keep track of things, diversification can be a good thing.

TESSAs

TESSAs were the precursor to the cash component of an ISA. The acronym stands for Tax Exempt Special Savings Account. Unlike PEPs and ISAs, you can only have one TESSA account open at a time. Since April 1999, you can no longer open a new TESSA, but as they are five-year savings vehicles, there are still plenty of them around.

If you have a TESSA, you'll know that you can save a limited amount each year in a tax-free savings account, as long as your contributions are locked in for five years. The maximum you can save over the five-year period is £9,000 in capital and, if you're still paying into your existing TESSA, you'll know that you can still do so under the usual rules until it matures (five years from the date of starting it). If you want to switch your current TESSA to another manager before it matures, perhaps because of better rates, you can do so, but you may be required to pay hefty penalties for an early transfer. Check the potential costs before you make the move as some of the exit fees can be as much as six months' interest!

Whatever you do with your TESSA, it doesn't affect your entitlement to open an ISA. Effectively, you're allowed to run two tax-protected vehicles alongside each other.

Lots of these TESSAs are now maturing. The five-year period is coming to an end and, if you've got one, you may be wondering what you'll be allowed to do with the accumulated funds other than just saunter off with your pile of dosh.

When your TESSA matures you have six months to decide what to do with the money. If you've already used up your full annual ISA allowance, but you want to continue to protect the TESSA money from tax, you have three options:

● Transfer the capital into a special TESSA-Only ISA, which will pay interest in the usual way (but see below).
● Transfer the capital into your Cash Mini ISA.
● Transfer the capital into the Cash component of your Maxi ISA.

Note that you are allowed to transfer only the *capital* – that is, up to the maximum of £9,000. You aren't allowed to include all the interest you have accrued throughout the term of the TESSA. If you want to put the interest somewhere safe from tax then it'll have to go into the Cash ISA, where it will count as part of your annual ISA entitlement.

Some fund managers will try to tell you that you cannot transfer your TESSA capital into the Cash component of your Maxi ISA or Mini ISA, but, in theory, you *are* allowed to do this. However, since ISA managers are not forced to permit it, you'll be hard pushed to find many that will let you merge your TESSA money with your ISA money They will usually insist on keeping the two funds separate by directing the former into a TESSA-Only ISA. After all, if they keep the TESSA-Only ISA separate from the cash ISA, then it allows them to charge different interest rates for both, doesn't it?

A final word

Finally, if you really, really, really want to know even more about ISAs, then have a go at reading the Inland Revenue's extensive guidance notes for ISA managers. You can download it from the Inland Revenue's website (www.inlandrevenue.gov.uk/isa/isagn.htm). There are 17 chapters and 8 appendices, but there's the odd one-liner in there that might answer some of the more obscure questions you may have! Also check out the ISA discussion board on www.fool.co.uk. There's no doubt that the current tax system is horrendously complicated and incredibly dull. Luckily, there are accountants out there who are positively thrilled at the idea of filling in your tax return. So if you're not sure whether you're making the best use of your ISA and Capital Gains Tax allowances, don't be afraid to plonk your paperwork in front of a tax expert.

7

Ugh! Pensions

Retirement means twice as much husband for half as much money.

Anonymous

Oh, the glamorous world of pensions! What could be more thrilling than sifting through the complex twists and turns of these delightful products with their annuities, their SIPPS, their SERPS, their defined contributions and their AVCs? Mmm... don't you just want dive into all that right now? No? Well we don't blame you. Pensions are not exciting. In fact, they are positively off-putting, mainly because pension documents, and the laws that govern them, are written by people whose first language is Klingon. Also, the very word 'pensions' conjures up images of wrinkles and support tights, blue rinses and an intense interest in the price of butter which cool chicks like us cannot bear to consider. Let's face it, most of us would rather undergo exploratory surgery without an anaesthetic than investigate pensions in any great depth.

However, as part of a retirement fund (together with investments in the stock market, ISAs, PEPs, some cash and, perhaps, property) pensions can be useful. They are not right for everyone, and certainly we don't advise that you rely solely on a pension to keep you in Scholl sandals and cat food in your golden years. In fact, depending on your circumstances, you may find it makes sense not to have a pension at all in your retirement fund because you have other options. As you may have heard in recent times, pensions, even cushy company ones, have been giving increasingly poor value and there are no signs of them improving greatly in the future. They are also even less helpful for women as our annuity rate (the amount we'll get when we buy an annual income with our pension pot) is even lower than that for men. Mind you, that's because we live longer so it's not all bad news.

Having said that, pensions do have benefits for most of us. For a start there is the issue of deferred taxation (payments into a pension fund generate tax relief before you retire although you have to pay tax on the money you receive once you've retired). This is very useful if you are in the happy position of having to pay higher rate tax as the Government effectively chips in an extra 40% of any contributions you make to a pension fund. Also, there is the fact that you cannot get your hands on any of the money in your pension fund until you're at least 50. If you are the sort of person who doesn't have the discipline not to dip into your retirement fund in times of crisis (or overspending) then you should definitely have a decent-sized pension fund on the go at all times. Spouses, can get their hands on them, even if you divorce, which is great if your partner has a nice fat pension but not so fab if you're the one with the years of savings.

Certainly we *have* to have some sort of a retirement fund, possibly including a pension, to keep us going in our old age. We can't expect anyone else to look after us. The current derisory State Pension to which we are all entitled (if we have paid enough National Insurance contributions) is set to dwindle further. People are living longer, and with the birth-rate falling in this country, there is no longer enough money coming in to provide the money that has to go out.

Is it true that women typically get annuities that are significantly smaller on a week-to-week basis than men's due to their longer life expectancy? Arithmetically I can see how it would make sense, but it is simultaneously completely outrageous. The whole thing gives another reason to make as much use of other tax-sheltered investments than pension schemes, seeing as it looks like we'll get a poor deal whatever type of individual pension we go for!

From The Motley Fool discussion boards

As women, we have ourselves to blame for being so healthy and living so long. Average life expectancy has increased by more than 10 years since the 1950's. Men retiring at 65 can now expect to live for another 15 years, while women are likely to live for another 20 years (Hurrah for us!). Of course this is 'a good thing', except when it comes to paying for ourselves for that length of time. The way our pensions fund us is that we buy an annuity from the pot of money we have saved over the years, and that gives us a monthly income until we die. Annuity rates, being based on life expectancy, are particularly low for women – less than 7% for a 60-year-old at the moment. Annuity rates for both men and women could go even lower in years to come, if we keep living longer and longer, which is why Jane, as a 40-a-day smoker, should be applauded for unilaterally trying to bring down the national average.

So although the title of this chapter is 'Pensions', we will be looking at your retirement fund as a whole – how much you will need to save up for your retirement, which are the best ways in which to do it and how to make the most of it once you retire.

How much will I need?

That is a big question but it's an important one because, if you're anything like us, having some sort of a figure to aim for can really concentrate the mind and give your saving activity more impetus. There is no hard and fast figure that we should all aim for because we are all different, our needs and wants are different and so are our sources of income. Sorry about this, but you are going to have to work out a figure to aim for yourself because we don't know you and so we can't work it out for you.

We can give you a rough guide to aim for, however, and help your thought processes. It's a good idea to start by thinking about how much you spend per week or month now, and what you spend it on. How much money do you need to be comfortable now? Naturally, some of that money will be spent on your mortgage and on savings plans and pension payments. By the time you retire, these should not be necessary any more. Also, you might not want to go out clubbing every weekend when you retire (although we hope you do) and you are unlikely to want the very latest gadgets every year either. So all-in-all, your general outgoings should be less than they are now. Against that, though, you may want to factor in extra care, medical bills and general help which are things you probably don't need at the moment. So when you are working out how much you might have to save for your future, don't underestimate your needs.

At the moment, according to the Office of National Statistics, the average family spends about £386 a week on general, every day living. That is the average, of course, and yours might be much less or much more. What you spend it on could be very different from the average too. If your mortgage is huge then a large proportion of your weekly spend will be on that. By the time you retire, you would hope to have paid that off so you wouldn't need so much money. The charity Help the Aged says that the bare minimum that an elderly person should be expected to live on is just over £5,000 a year. But that is really the absolute minimum, just covering food, heating and basic clothing and living. There's nothing else. To have a half-decent way of life, you will need at least £20,000 a year in today's money, we consider, and frankly both of us hope to have an income greater than that when we retire.

But what you need to do is to sit down with a pencil and paper, or a computer with a spreadsheet programme, and list your expenses today next to what you think they may be when you retire. Put down your essential expenses, your conveniences like a car, TV licence etc and then your luxuries including holidays, hobbies, clubs and so on. Be generous with yourself, though, because you might as well have a really comfortable retirement, rather than a limited and scrimping one.

Hopefully you will come up with a pretty realistic figure that you would like to aim for. As we don't know you, we are going to stick to our fairly reasonable figure of £20,000 as an example, so that you can get an idea of how much you will have to have in your retirement pot to fund a good annual income. You will perhaps be surprised or even horrified to know that even to bring in this (to our minds) pretty modest income you will need to have savings of at least £400,000 by the time you come to retire. Yup. Sobering thought, huh? You have to save all of that just to give yourself a basic income.

How did we work that one out? Well, remember, neither of us is a maths genius (or even competent, frankly) but we can understand the basic concept. That figure is arrived at by assuming that once we have our pot of money we will invest it sensibly to give us an annual investment income of around 5%. This is not a definite figure but it's a pretty realistic – if conservative - forecast, given that none of us knows what will happen in the future and it's best to assume a low figure rather than a high one. Then we can take that 5% out of our pot of money each year and the pot should still maintain its real value. We then have the following sum:

Pot x 5% = £20,000

Remember back to your maths lessons in the dim and distant past when Miss Axton droned on and on about simple equations and you struggled to get it? Well, here it is again. We can rearrange that equation by dividing both sides by 5% to give:

Pot = £20,000 / 5%
As 5% is the same as 0.05, we have
Pot = £20,000 / 0.05 = £400,000.

See? Easy!

Of course, if the State Pension still exists once you retire you could add that on which would be a help but don't bank on it. Whatever amount you have worked out you need, keep that as your goal and any other money that comes in when you retire will be a nice surprise!

When it comes to how to save this enormous-seeming amount of

Overall 29% of men compared to only 18% of women have occupational pensions. Partly this is because marital status has a significant impact on pension ownership for women in a way that it doesn't for men. Being part of a couple suppressed pension ownership among women, with less than one in three married or cohabiting women having a pension, compared to one half of cohabiting and two-fifths of married men. Women with dependent children were half as likely to have a pension as men in the same circumstances." ('Women and Personal Finance' study, FSA, 2001)

money you should keep in mind that as with any form of investing, the earlier you start saving for your retirement fund, the better. And, because of the joy and wonder of 'compounding', even small amounts of money invested early on will more than match quite large contributions that you make later in life. So even if you are a low earner in your twenties and thirties, it is still worth putting away as much as you can afford each month. And even if you are a low earner and in your forties or fifties, don't let it stop you. A small amount saved each month is miles better than nothing saved at all.

What you put that money into, though, should be decided by you. Your retirement fund, as we've already said, will probably include various different savings plans including a pension, ISAs, cash, perhaps some property and even valuable collections. *How* you make up that retirement fund is up to you. Just make sure that you *do* do it.

Your Retirement Fund

So, you've realised the importance of saving for your retirement but you're just not sure how to do it. Should you take out a personal pension? Will your company pension do? Should you buy property or shares? Or should you just put everything into your classic Barbie collection and watch that increase in value? Good questions, but you won't be able to make an informed decision without actual information. So here are your various retirement fund options from which you can make a selection. First off, let's find out what kind of pension (if any) you should have in your pot.

So What Exactly Is A Pension

A pension is basically a savings plan. That's it. You sign up for a 'pension' and stuff money in it for forty years or so while that money is invested mostly in the stock market for you. When you reach 50 years old or later you are left with a pot of money with which you can fund your retirement. The general theory goes that in return for its fees the pensions company will have invested your money sensibly, so with a bit of luck your pension fund may have done better than average. Hmmm, maybe.

A pension can be provided through an employer (that's a 'company' or 'occupational' pension), or through a private company (a 'personal pension') but whatever type of pension you have, it is still simply part of your retirement plan. Unlike other parts of your retirement fund, though, such as shares, property etc, you can't do what you want with all of the final lump sum. The best way to think of it is as a kind of insurance plan for your old age. You will be forced to buy an annuity with most of the money you save in your pension fund which will guarantee you a certain amount of money each year until you die. The Pickering Report on Company Pension Schemes, commissioned by the Government, has suggested changes to annuities to make them more flexible. But it's still in the consultation phase.

Your pension contributions for personal or company pensions come out of your gross income – in other words you are not taxed on it. This is quite an important point because it means that if you contribute to a pension *the Government gives you money!* Yes, this is an aspect of pensions that seems to have been forgotten in all the criticism of the poor-performance of pension funds. If you are a basic-rate tax-payer, every taxable £100 you earn has £22 taken away by the Treasury in Income Tax. But some of that money is given back to you if you invest in a pension. So for every £78 you pay into a pension, the Government also puts in £22. If you are a higher-rate tax-payer it is even more generous. For you, with every £60 you put into your pension, the Government gives back the £40 it would have taken out of your earnings. It's not to be sniffed at.

The downside is that the money you get from it once you retire, through an annuity, *will* be taxed. As it's more likely that you will have an income below the higher rate tax band at that stage, though, it is very much worth your while contributing now if you have to pay 40% tax. In the long-term your pension pot will be much bigger.

The amount you are allowed to put into your pension scheme each year depends on how much you earn and how old you are. The Government has set limits as percentages of your earnings which go like this:

Age 35 or less	17.5%
36 – 45	20%
46 – 50	25%
51 – 55	30%
56 – 60	35%
61 or more	40%

There is also an earnings limit as far as these percentages are concerned. For the tax year 2002/3 it is £97,200. So if you are 40 and you earn £100,000 (lucky you) you can still only put in 20% of £97,200 into your pension fund.

While 6% of men and 4% of women under 20 have occupational pensions, for women between 35-44 the difference has grown to 44% of men and only 28% of women, and the figure for personal pensions is 17% for men and only 8% for women." ('Women and Personal Finance' study, FSA, 2001)

Pensions for All

As far as pensions go, your retirement income starts (and only *starts*) with the Basic Retirement ('State') Pension. You will only get this if you have paid enough National Insurance Contributions (NICs) over your working life.

Just to depress you, the current Basic Retirement Pension for a single person is a pathetic £75.50 a week. A "widow's" weekly pension (where your late husband paid full contributions but you have none) is £40.40. Hardly enough to pay for your weekly visits to The Ivy and the skiing holidays in Val d'Isere we think.

Anyone whose only income is the State Pension is currently topped up to nearly £100 a week by the Minimum Income Guarantee. And from April 2003 onwards a new Pensions Credit will be introduced to ensure that anyone with extra income from his or her own savings or pensions will be allowed to keep more of it before being taxed. It will amount to £135 a week for a single person and £200 a week for a married couple. Up to two thirds of those who benefit will be women.

The State Second Pension

You may have heard of SERPS – the State Earnings-Related Pension – a kind of top-up to the basic pension and, remarkably, related to the amount you earn. Well now, it has been replaced (sort of) by the State Second Pension. This new type of pension has widened the net and provides a more generous additional state pension for low and moderate earners, and to certain carers and people with a long-term illness or disability. It was introduced because the Government realised that this section of the public was being unfairly penalised for being poor or being unable to earn.

If you are earning, you'll be interested to know that employees earning up to about £24,600 a year (at 2002/03 levels) will be eligible for the State Second Pension. The most help goes to those on the lowest earnings (up to around £10,800 a year at 2002/03 levels). So, if you earn less than

£10,800 but you earn more than the Lower Earnings Limit (£3,900 in 2002/03) the State Second Pension rules will treat you as if you had earnings of £10,800.

If you are not in paid employment (or you are working part time and are earning less than about £3,900 a year in 2002/03) because you are a carer – either looking after a child under the age of six or a person with a long-term illness or disability - you may also be able to build up a State Second Pension. This will be because you get Home Responsibilities Protection (HRP). If you qualify, you will build up about £1 a week of State Second Pension for each year you are a carer.

If you are not in paid employment because you yourself are ill or disabled, you may build up State Second Pension for each tax year that you are entitled to long-term Incapacity Benefit or Severe Disablement Allowance (for a full tax year). If you qualify, you will also build up about £1 a week State Second Pension for each year you are ill or disabled.

By the way, if you've kept hearing about SERPS and wondered what on earth it was – suspecting that it was a nasty-sounding, communicable disease – worry not, because it has now been phased out and has been replaced by the State Second Pension. It was originally introduced to top-up the basic state pension for certain earners, but it didn't cover nearly as many people as the State Second Pension will.

In fact, although the State Second Pension is a nice idea, you may find that it's not worth bothering with at all as it is subject to means-testing. This means that if you are only able to save a smallish amount in this secondary pension you could lose out later on because if you didn't have anything in it you would get social security benefit payments anyway. It is only worth it if you are going to save a large amount – larger than the benefits threshold. Frankly, it's all a bit of a mess, no one really knows what's going on – including the Treasury – so it may be better to save any money you are going to save in an ISA or other savings vehicle rather than trust your luck to the vagaries of the pensions fairies.

Personal Pensions and Stakeholders

Personal Pensions give self-employed people, or those working for businesses without occupational schemes, a crack of the pensions whip. They are not nearly as good as company pensions because all of the money that goes into them has to come from you. But they are better than nothing. They are known as 'defined contribution' or 'money purchase' schemes and the holder pays a percentage of her salary into an investment fund with the Government effectively chipping in an extra 22% or 40% in the form of tax relief. It's this pot that you use to buy your annuity when you finally retire.

Up until 2001 when the Government introduced the concept of Stakeholder Pensions, we at the Fool were thoroughly underwhelmed by private pensions. They were very expensive and difficult to comprehend. Now that the Stakeholder has been introduced things are rather different. The idea behind it is that, while the Stakeholder may not necessarily be the *best* personal pension on the market at any given time, (though it usually is) it should be a flexible product of reasonable value that is easily understood by the consumer. All Stakeholder schemes must accept contributions of as little as £20, which you can pay each week, each month or at less regular intervals. Pension managers are restricted to charging a maximum of 1% in annual charges. You can stop and start your payments whenever you like over the years. It's portable so that if you have a Company Stakeholder Pension you can take it from job to job and you can switch it to a different provider whenever you want. It's also available to all – including children. If it's a Stakeholder then it has a sort of Government seal of approval rather like CAT standards for ISA's and other financial products.

Another crucial change is that before the Stakeholder arrived you were only allowed to contribute to a pension scheme if you actually earned an income. But now the tax relief applies even if you aren't working or don't earn enough to pay tax. This is particularly useful for people going through career breaks as it means they can keep their pension contributions going if they have the money to do so. So, if you are, say, taking a break from work to look after children and you are lucky enough to have a generous partner, he can make contributions on your behalf. We strongly suggest that you persuade him to do this if you possibly can. However, there is a limit to how much you can contribute as a non-earner and it amounts to £2,808 a year with the Government topping it up by 22% to a total of £3,600.

These factors make the Stakeholder the most Foolish type of personal pension scheme in existence – particularly if you make sure your contributions are invested in a simple index tracker, rather than a managed fund. It'll be invested for a very long time, remember and the evidence is that, over the long-term, index trackers perform much better than managed funds

As far as we are concerned, this new type of pension, which caps the charges fund managers can claw from you, is 'a very good thing'. As we have said before, the lower the annual charges on your financial products, the more money you will make in the long run. In our view, if you are going to take out a personal pension, you should take out a stakeholder one. You will still have to choose a good one based on trustworthiness of the name and their customer service record, but the one thing you will know, if it is a stakeholder, is that the charges will be kept at a minimum which, in the long term, will mean that your fund should grow faster. Some stakeholders charge less than others so look at the lower charging ones first.

If you are employed, your employer must provide you with access to a stakeholder pension scheme unless they have fewer than five employees or they already offer an occupational pension scheme for all their employees to join within one year of them starting work. This can be useful for employees but it is nowhere near as good as a traditional company pension because the employer is not likely to contribute to the pot.

Unless you're earning less than £10,000 a year, a Stakeholder Pension is worth considering if you don't have any form of pension scheme at all, or are reviewing your current provisions. The only reason not to bother is if you're in a great company scheme, which offers benefits such as added contributions - or if you feel you've made adequate provision via an ISA and can trust yourself not to help yourself to the funds between now and retirement.

If you've got money to spare, and a non-working partner, then consider paying into a Stakeholder on their behalf. If nothing else it'll reduce the chances of your partner being able to get his or her hands on your own pension scheme if you get divorced! And, since you can pay into one for your kids (and if you don't want them to be lumbered with a big Inheritance Tax bill when you pop your clogs), then it's a way of passing on some money to them without them being able to fritter it away on frivolities – at least not until retirement anyway!

Company Pension Schemes

Company schemes are usually a 'good' thing because the company will make a contribution to the fund on your behalf. Some company schemes, known as defined benefit or final salary schemes, pay you an income based upon the amount you were earning just before you retired. Other company schemes operate similarly to a personal pension in that you convert the final lump sum into an annuity. These are referred to as defined contribution schemes.

In theory, you should be able to take your pension with you when you move jobs but in practice they've tended not to be very portable unlike Stakeholders. Since you are unlikely, these days, to be spending the whole forty years of your career at Scrimping and Scrooge - the average person changes job five times in his or her working life - this could leave you with a number of small pensions, each paying out not very much. If it is portable, you're still likely to lose out to some extent on the 'transfer value'. This is basically an exit charge where the pension fund retains a percentage of your accumulated savings in return for letting you take your money elsewhere.

However, given that a company pension involves someone else (your employer) putting money in as well as you, generally speaking they are 'a good thing'. But pensions exist in a world where all men (and certainly all women) are not equal and, yet again, there are complications in company pensions – some, those called Defined Benefit pensions are generally better than others, namely 'Defined Contribution' pensions.

If you have a Defined Benefit pension, more commonly known as a 'Final Salary' scheme, this means that the monthly income you'll get when you retire is guaranteed and will be based on your, um, final salary. These are generally considered to be the better option, and are also becoming rarer than honest politicians due to the risks they represent to employers.

If you have a company pension however, you are most likely to have a Defined Contribution pension, which means that the amount you pay in is defined (like, you know that if you pay in £100 per month, then you've paid in £100 per month...), but how much you get when you retire depends heavily on the performance of the fund's investments, the level of charges, the whims of the pension fairies and so on. On top of that, your monthly income in retirement is determined by the annuity rates when you retire.

As with other pensions, how much you can pay into your company pension depends on how old you are and how much you earn. If you are a member of a company pension scheme you could top it up yourself with *Additional Voluntary Contributions* (AVCs). Your employer's pensions department will be able to give you a form to fill in to do this. However, we at the Fool have generally found that AVC's are expensive and are generally poor investment vehicles. In our opinion you would be better off putting the extra money in an ISA.

Fringe Benefits

Some company pension schemes include "*death-in-service*" benefits. It's worth taking a good look at these, as they may save you having to pay life assurance premiums. Check the small print regarding spouses and children. Should you or your partner die, what will the survivor get? If you die just after retirement, what will your surviving widower get? How long will these payments be made for? If you are relying on your husband's company pension, what will happen if he predeceases you? Do you need an extra fund? If you are not married, can an unmarried partner benefit? What if your partner's another woman?

What Happens When You Change Jobs?

Under an occupational scheme, if you have worked for an employer for two years you get to keep the value of any pensions benefits that have built up if you change jobs. Either you can keep the 'preserved benefits' in the old scheme, or you can get the old scheme to transfer enough money (called the 'transfer value') to the new scheme to give you the same benefits that you had already built up in the old scheme.

Whether you are better to keep your 'preserved benefit' or 'transfer' to a new scheme is always a tricky question. In theory there should be no difference as you should be able to invest the transfer value elsewhere and get the same final pension pot. But it's very difficult to check if this is the case. The trouble with transferring is that it often costs you money to do it and that would make the transfer value less than what you'd have if you left the preserved benefits alone. So decide for yourself whether you would make more money in another vehicle and if so, go for it!

With people changing jobs more frequently these days, some are ending up with lots of little pension policies scattered around. That makes it even more difficult to keep track of them all, and work out how much you need to continue adding to your pension. Many people prefer to lump them all together in a personal pension. A Stakeholder pension is well suited to this. If you have worked for less than two years with an employer, you basically just get back any contributions that you've put in.

In fact, it's been estimated that more than £3 billion is languishing in forgotten pension funds. So if you have flitted between a number of jobs and think you may have bits of pensions sitting around unclaimed, you can search them out through one of a few pension-finding services. Try The Unclaimed Assets Register (0870 241 1713) or The Pension Schemes Registry (0191 225 6393) or The AMP Pension Find Service (0800 068 5456). You might as well – there could be some very helpful extra bits of money just lying around, waiting for you to use them.

SIPPs

Another type of personal pension is the Self-Invested Personal Pension or 'SIPP'. These have the advantages of other types of pensions, but you have much more control over what you invest in. In the past, SIPPs have been prohibitively expensive for most but the advent of the online SIPP (with charges similar to online brokers) has changed that. If you like to do your investments yourself, they're certainly worth a look. However, they are very much an advanced option – only really a good idea for people who are very experienced and confident in investing, and who have the time and energy to research the options. Statistically men are more likely than women to take out a SIPP (note the word 'confident' above), which may or may not be a good thing depending on how good they really are at investing (as opposed to how good they *think* they are).

Essentially SIPPs are like ISAs in that they are just wrappers within which you can put one or more different investments and, like ISAs, there is no Capital Gains Tax to pay on profits. The difference, of course, is that SIPPs are basically subject to the same rules as personal pensions. They have the same limits on contributions, the same 25% restriction on the tax-free lump sum on retirement and the same requirement to buy an annuity by the time you reach 75.

However, they can also be useful to gather together any frozen pension schemes that you may have left behind from previous jobs - if it makes sense to do so, of course. The cash from these can then be used to buy the investments of your choice.

The range of investments you're allowed to have in a SIPP include stocks and shares on the world's major stock exchanges (and a few of the minor ones too, including those quoted on AIM), investment trusts, unit trusts (such as an index tracker), OEICS, gilts and even commercial property. The commercial property thing is quite interesting because the SIPP is actually allowed to take a mortgage of up to 75% of the property's value. You can then lease the property to a business which you own (on commercial terms), or to a third party. If you're a business owner, this can be tax-efficient since the rent comes out of the business's pre-tax income and comes into the SIPP as tax-free investment income. Fun huh?

WHAT SHOULD I BE THINKING ABOUT BEFORE I TAKE OUT A PENSION?

A pension is a *long-term* investment - you can't get at the money you put into a pension until retirement age.

● what age do you want to retire?
● what level of income do you want for your retirement?
● can you afford the premiums you will need to put into the fund to give you that level of income?
● can you afford to pay additional contributions to give you maximum benefits?
● do you have any pensions which you are no longer paying into?
● do you have any other savings or investments that will be available for your retirement?
● would you like the flexibility to stop your premiums for a while if necessary?
● how much risk are you willing to take with your pension fund?

Is my pension any good?

Damn good question and one that is quite difficult to answer simply. However, we'll have a go.

As we've already mentioned, it is pretty much against your average pension fund managers' religion actually to tell you in clear and understandable language how your pension is doing, how much is in the fund and how much they are really charging you for the joy and thrill of giving them your money. However, if you have the time, energy and emotional strength to deal with it, it is pretty important to keep abreast of how your fund is progressing (or not) each year so that you can decide whether to keep contributing to it or move it or simply to freeze it and set up something else that will deliver more money.

When you get your delightful annual review of your pension you will thrill at the obscure and befuddling prose, the strange terminology and even stranger figures. However, do your best to scour the pages to find out just how much you are being charged each year for the management of your fund. If it is higher than 1% (and if you can't see it in the literature, phone the company up and nag them until they tell you) then it's probably time you froze this particular product and set up something better-performing somewhere else.

Also, have a look at the bottom line – how much you actually have in your pension pot right now. Have a look at last year's figure, and the year before that, and ten years before that. Has it been keeping up with the stock market (or, ideally, beating the market) or would you have done better putting the money in your local building society? If it has been under-performing the stock market for the last decade then it may be time for a change of direction.

However, we don't advise you to chop and change funds on a regular basis. Ideally you should research a pension fund first, put your money in it and keep doing so unless something really drastic (like the Equitable Life disaster) makes you change your mind. Changing investment vehicles nearly always incurs charges and pensions are one of the worst for penalising you for leaving them. Besides, how many times do we have to mention that index trackers are the cheapest and easiest way of investing your money in the stock market – and they're more likely to do better than an actively managed fund.

It's really not too easy to tell if you have a good pension fund, other than checking the charges and the actual amount by which your fund is growing each year, but at least those two things will give you an idea of where you're at and whether it is all worth it. With a company pension you should, again, check the amount you are being charged each year and also check that your company is paying into it too. If they're not and the charges are higher than 1% then switch. Generally, though, company pensions – even money purchase ones – will be worthwhile because many companies will pay something into it for you and hey, that's free money! We like that.

To keep a proper check on how your fund is doing for your future you can order a pension forecast from your fund managers. In a roundabout, confusing and long-winded way they will let you know what sort of amount of money you can look forward to having when you retire if you continue to contribute the same amount each month until that date. They'll give you two figures – the actual amount of money they expect you to have and the 'real' value of that money. That is, how much that money will actually buy you in real terms, taking inflation into account. Obviously the second figure is the important one because we want around £400,000 in 'real' terms, not just in numbers. Add that to the other money you have invested and you'll get an idea of how much you will have once you hang up your briefcase for the last time.

How to spend it

The Government - and you won't be surprised to hear this - doesn't trust us a great deal. It doesn't trust us not to blow the entire amount of our retirement fund on Pretty Boy in the 3.30 at Sandown or on our own pretty boy who will spend all our cash on his own lavish lifestyle then move onto the next sugar-mummy when it has all run out.

If the Government did trust us not to do any of these things and we let them down, then they would end up having to feed and house us and that's why they make us buy an annuity with the money we have accrued in our pension fund. Annuities are a kind of insurance policy that pays out every month for the rest of our lives. The company takes your lump sum and in return pays out this annuity. We can shop around for the highest rate possible. Naturally, they don't want to lose money so the longer they *think* you will live, the less they want to pay each month because the longer you live, the more they will end up shelling out. This is why, as we've already said, women's annuity rates are generally lower than men because we tend to live longer. Also, the older you are when you retire, the better your annuity rate, for the same reason.

Under *current* personal pension legislation, you can take up to 25 % of your cash pot as a one-off lump sum. This accounts for around 90% of the shiny Rover 400s you see driving very slowly down the middle lane of the motorway with a tartan travel blanket over the parcel shelf. The rest *must* be used to buy an annuity whether you like it or not.

The amount you receive does *not* increase with inflation, unless you opt for an 'index-linked' annuity, and that will have a substantially reduced initial annuity income. Your spouse may get nothing when you die, unless, again, you opt for a 'joint life' annuity and, you've guessed it, that will mean a substantially reduced initial annuity income. Finally, you and your spouse are both dead and the annuity company keeps the money – or rather they use it to fund the next lot of people who are drawing a pension. That's it. It's like a regular insurance payment – when you no longer need the money, that's the end of it.

One of the problems with annuities is that these days we are living too long for them. With the basic annuity, an insurance company effectively takes your money and uses it to buy some low-risk assets such as gilts. It has to do that because it has to guarantee your income (and be confident of making a profit itself). But you may be looking at twenty, thirty or even more years of retirement (let's hope so), and that sort of investment tends to be awful over that long a period as we saw in Chapter 5.

However, if you've built up a big enough pension pot, then at least you can buy the security of an inflation-proofed income and you can choose various ways of doing it.

Income Drawdown

An alternative option on retirement - at least until you reach the age of 75 - is to use what's known as income drawdown, or income withdrawal. The concept was introduced in 1995 and if your pension scheme permits it, it enables income to be paid to you directly from the fund, rather than by purchasing an annuity. The amount you can take out each year is subject to a maximum based upon annuity rates provided by the Government Actuary's Department. The minimum amount of income that must be withdrawn each year is 35% of the maximum. These limits are calculated when you retire and are reviewed every three years.

The advantage of income drawdown is that you're able to take the income you require (subject to the limits) while maintaining your fund's exposure to the stock market which tends to be the best home for your money over the long term. When you reach 75, however, you have to buy the annuity.

Phased Retirement

One other thing worth mentioning, while we're on this fiddly stuff, is 'phased retirement'. This is not to be confused with income drawdown, although the effects are kind of similar. If you have a money-purchase scheme that allows for something called 'segmentation', then it means that the scheme is, in fact, lots of little schemes rolled into one. Each small bit of the scheme is its own discrete pension, and you can take the benefits from each of them when you like, between the ages of 50 and 65. So you could, perhaps, take one bit of your pension every month from the age of 55 to 60. That way you gradually phase in your retirement benefits.

Phased retirement can be used in conjunction with income drawdown and is particularly useful for the self-employed or, indeed, anyone who wishes to wind down their workload (and income) gradually over several years. As ever, though, watch out for the costs associated with taking this type of option.

Help, My Pension Company are a Bunch of ****'s

So, your pension company is sticking your money in the Bolton Instant Access Cash Account, and charging you 15% per year for the privilege. It's time you moved. Luckily, you can actually transfer a pension, just like you can transfer a PEP or ISA. But you may be charged for it.

If you are a member of the company pension scheme, provided you've been paying into it for more than two years, you can leave the pension fund 'frozen' and start paying into a new one. This new scheme could be a private personal pension or the company scheme with your new employer if you've just changed jobs. If you've been paying into the company scheme for less than two years, you'll get your contributions back, minus tax and National Insurance. If you 'freeze' your pension, you'll get your retirement benefits when you retire, as usual. You can also transfer your company pension fund into a private pension, although you must look into it very carefully as there are many ways in which you can lose money this way. If you do a transfer, then the values should be worked out so that the benefits of the new scheme will equal the benefits of the old scheme (less the costs of transfer of course). If it's a final salary scheme becoming a money purchase scheme, then it changes your risks, but you should make sure that expected benefits are same.

You can also transfer a private personal pension fund from one pension scheme to another. There are charges associated with this, surprise, surprise, but if your pension is really awful it may be worthwhile. Bear in mind that when you transfer money from a pension scheme, the money cannot go into your own bank account and sit there for six months while you make up your mind about what to do next. Funds withdrawn from a pension fund will be subject to full income tax and you'll lose all those national insurance rebates forever.

Moving pension providers can be complicated and costly and in this case it may be worth seeking professional advice. Bear in mind all the usual pitfalls of dealing with the city types and make sure you go to an Independent Financial Advisor who charges for advice, not one who will make their money from commission. If your pension has some sort of death-in-service benefit included, you may need to make alternative life assurance provision if you leave the scheme. Unless you have an absolute dog of a pension scheme (very poor performance and/or exorbitant charges), freeze this pension and make a fresh start with a more sensible alternative.

Whatever you do with pensions there will be charges – it's just a given. The charge for moving could be around 10-15%. If you simply freeze the pension – i.e. you stop putting any more money into it and invest somewhere else each month – you will still get the annual charges for managing your fund. If you have a final salary pension the charges will not make any difference as you are guaranteed a certain amount when you retire. For defined contribution pensions, however, the charges will make a difference and you will need to work out (with the aid of a calculator, the Fool site and a glass of something comforting) whether you would be best, in the long-term, to stay with your current fund, freeze it or move, depending on their general charges and performance. Sorry, that's pensions!

Divorcing a Pension

New rules and regulations just brought in by the Government have made it much easier to get a good chunk of your spouse's pension if you divorce. Of course it works both ways so he should have access to your pension as well as you getting some of his, but for most couples, the benefit should be greater for the ex-wife as men, on average, still have better pension savings than women.

You'll find much more information on divorcing a pension – how to do it and how to get the best deal - in Chapter Ten on Divorce.

Not just Pensions but also...

Right, so you've trawled through all that information on pensions (or just skipped the pages – go on, admit it, we don't mind) and by now you should realise why pensions are only partly useful vehicles for saving for your retirement. In fact, if you are self-employed, or not employed at all, the pensions open to you are not likely to create enough wealth for you both in terms of how much your money will grow and how much you can get from it once you retire (annuities, don'tcha love 'em?). So really, although pensions have their uses in terms of saving a bit of tax and providing a safety net if everything else goes pear-shaped, you probably shouldn't rely on them alone to create a nice fat wad of money for you to live on later in life.

However, there is nothing to stop you having a pension together with one or more other investment vehicles which you can mix and match to provide a (more than) decent retirement income. Here are some to choose from.

ISAs

In February 2002, the independent financial advisor (IFA) Bates Investment Services (http://www.batesonline.com/) published some research which found that, in spite of the tax relief available on pension contributions, the tax-free income produced by ISAs was likely to be more than the same sums could produce from a pension.

Now, before you rush off to cancel your pension contributions, there is a 'but' to this research and it's a big one. The reference to 'the same sums' is significant.

As you know, if you contribute to a pension scheme, the Government will add an extra 22% or 40% to your contributions depending on your tax rate. That means more money will be going into your pension fund in the first place. So if you opt to save your retirement fund in an ISA rather than a pension, then you need to put in an equivalent amount if you're to end up with the same lump sum on retirement. The benefits of saving some of your retirement fund in an ISA though are obvious. The money is entirely yours. You don't pay tax on anything that comes out of it and when you die, you can leave the contents of your ISA to anyone you like, even your dog.

However, if you lost your job, you'd have to use up most of your non-pension savings before you qualified for any welfare benefits. Your funds aren't protected if you are made bankrupt and, of course, you are restricted on how much you can invest each year. In truth, it's probably better to have both a pension and an ISA if you can afford it.

Property

"Don't bother with a pension. Put your money in property. That's the best bet for your future." This is what everyone seems to be saying at the moment. And you can understand it given the poor performance of the stock market in the last couple of years, the dire warnings on pensions from everyone from employers to the FSA, the destructive ripples from the Equitable Life scandal and the phenomenal rises in the price of property in certain parts of the country in the last thirty years. *But...*buying property is not a sensible alternative to a pension for most people. Certainly, if you know what you are doing and are happy to take the responsibilities and costs associated with taking on buy-to-let property, then it can be a useful *addition* to your retirement portfolio. You really *do* need to know what you are doing, though, and have to be very businesslike about it to benefit. (See our advice on page 100 on how to invest in property and the pro's and cons of it.)

As far as using property to help fund your retirement is concerned, the pro's are that you should get growth and, increasingly as you pay off the mortgage, income from your house purchase. You buy some property now, with a mortgage, rent it out to pay the mortgage off and by the time that has been paid off you can enjoy the full income each month from the rent. Assuming you have bought a good property in a good area which continues to be a des res for renters, and the rental market doesn't go through the floor, you should end up with a nice, regular, safe(ish) income from a solid investment that you can pass on to your descendants later on.

However, the problems with property as an income source for your retirement are many. For a start, you really have to invest in the right property from the start because although prices are at least likely to keep up with inflation, if not more, some areas and some properties undoubtedly grow faster and higher than others. Also, you can never guarantee constant occupancy of your property, even in a popular area. All sorts of things outside of your control can affect the rental price you can ask for and unforeseen problems that arise in the area you buy in could have devastating effects on your investment. Also, some properties can cost you quite a lot in terms of repairs, service charges and other outgoings. It can cost you time, effort and annoyance to put them right, unless you hire a management company to oversee things which would, in turn, cost you even more money.

Once you retire, you may not want the hassle or worry of collecting rent and mending leaking pipes or dodgy boilers and, again, you can never guarantee that your property will be occupied every month. If that is your only income source when you are retired you could find yourself having a lot of sleepless nights worrying about where your next tenant is coming from and whether they will be a good one. Not only that, but property experts are predicting a glut of rental properties in the not too distant future which will mean that rental prices will go down and those who are depending on the income could find themselves out of pocket.

So all-in-all, you cannot rely on property alone to keep you in clover in your sunset years. Certainly consider it as part of your portfolio, but be careful!

Investing un-protected from tax

So, good girl, you have saved the maximum you can this year in your pension and your ISA and you still have money left over. Good on you. It's up to you how you save it. If you are paying off a mortgage you might like to put some or all of it into that. At least you know you are saving on interest payments that way and it is a nice feeling to get rid of some of that debt burden. But if you want to make better money then why not continue to invest in the stock market? Granted you won't have the advantage of tax savings that you have through an ISA but you will still have the growth, even if you just put it in a tracker fund, and you can always use your capital gains allowance to soak up some of the tax implications. Generally-speaking, mortgage interest rates are lower than the rate you could make on a tracker fund or on individually-picked, *good* shares. At the moment, for example, mortgages are around 5-6% whereas you'd hope to get around 6-7% from a tracker fund over the long term. Think about it. Investing in the stock market can be fun.

Other investments

Fine art, wine, diamonds, pop memorabilia, BMX bikes – whatever is your passion, it is sometimes worth investing in it for the future. The advantage of collecting as an investment is that not only are you putting money into something that will (hopefully) increase in value over the years, but also you are owning something that you love and enjoy looking at/playing with/using while you have it. The disadvantages are that there is no guarantee that what you are collecting really will increase in value (celebrity navel fluff, for example, may not be as interesting to others as it is to you) and even if it does, can you honestly say that you would be willing to sell it when you come to need the money? Not only that, but many collections can cost a lot to keep up, particularly in insurance costs which can really cut into the item's projected growth.

When to spend it

The next question is: when is the best time to retire? This depends largely on the state of your finances and how you feel about your job. Some people can't wait to throw in the job and go fishing, others can't imagine a life without the hustle and bustle of at least part-time employment.

Either way, if you are employed, your employer may not be interested in giving you any choice in the matter. Some organisations force employees to retire at 65, even though they may still be perfectly capable of doing their jobs. There is currently no law to prevent this discrimination. Other companies may have an unwritten rule of 'weeding out' employees above any arbitrary age through 'voluntary' redundancy. So really, you could argue that pensions, and your other investments, need to be almost infinitely flexible to take account of all these changing circumstances. Unfortunately, pensions are not. Another good reason to have lots of other investments to keep you going.

It may be worth calculating an 'insurance' buffer into your retirement fund to take account of any early exit from the job market. You may be made redundant and unable to find another job; you may have to give up work through ill health or to look after a relative. Either way, if you start early enough you can aim to reach your retirement target by 50 or 55. If you carry on working after this age (and there are proposals to raise the statutory retirement age to 67 or 70), then you can do so through choice and enjoyment, rather than through necessity.

Future uncertainty

The trouble with the structure of the UK savings industry, particularly pensions, is that it has served consumers very poorly in the past. Too often, we end up with inflexible products that overcharge and underperform. In addition, countless products have been sold that do more for the financial companies and salesmen than they do for the consumer. For example, if you wanted to invest in a unit trust or the OEIC equivalent, would you know which one to invest in and why? And would you know how to compare charges to ensure you weren't paying through the nose? And would you be any good at sniffing out the hidden costs?

The answer is probably no, and it's not surprising because there are some 1,600 of them to choose from, they vary hugely in terms of performance and cost and they're all rather complicated. What you'd probably do is go to an Independent Financial Adviser but, even then, how would you know whether you were being given sound advice and getting value for money?

The publication in July 2002 of the Sandler Review, an independent report on the retail savings and investment industry, has pointed to all of the above questions as the main reason we're not saving enough for our future.

It's no wonder we're reluctant to save for the long term – we don't know how to do it ourselves because there are too many complicated products on offer and we don't particularly trust anyone else to do it for us. As the author of the report Ron Sandler himself says:

"It is of fundamental, and growing, public importance that Britain should have a savings industry that is both efficient and widely trusted. The long-term welfare of millions of people depends on it, as does the effective operation of our capital markets. The industry has achieved considerable success in many respects. But there are also grounds for concern."

These concerns are the key to the recommendations that Sandler makes in his report which has largely been welcomed by the government and the Financial Services Authority.

There should be a selection of products available that are transparent and easily understood by the consumer and which are sufficiently regulated so they can be bought without the need for financial advice. This would entail using regulations similar to the Stakeholder Pension and the CAT standard that currently applies to certain types of ISA — both of which have ensured cheaper products because there are no initial charges and annual management and surrender charges are strictly regulated.

Products that involve a 'with profits' element have come in for particular stick. They're so unintelligible that they might as well be written in Sanskrit. Worse than that, if it makes much difference, information about performance and costs is quite often simply unavailable. We don't know how they work and yet we're pouring money into these policies year after year after year. All we know is that they're supposed to 'smooth out' investment returns so the volatility of the market doesn't affect our investment over the longer term.

Sandler reckons that smoothing is a good idea in principle, but he's recommended a new model for consideration which should enable us to compare performance and costs more easily. Among other things, he suggests that funds should publish an annual report setting out the current state of the fund, its performance and costs, as well as providing clearer information about payout rights to policyholders.

Interestingly Sandler was rather puzzled about why consumers invest so much in actively-managed funds when he's discovered that they tend to underperform the market by an average of 2.5% a year. As you've already read the same thing has been puzzling us for some time! It is, of course, mainly because of high charges but also because of 'unsuccessful active management', ie: consumers who pay more don't usually get more for their money.

Financial advisers also come under scrutiny with the suggestion that the products they recommend should not be commission-driven. (The industry watchdog, the Financial Services Authority has also been reviewing this part of the industry and they found 'statistically significant evidence' that advisers recommend one product over another because it pays a higher commission).

Instead, Sandler recommends that the price of advice should be negotiated between the adviser and the consumer, without any input from the product provider. This would provide more transparency so the consumer knows how much he is paying for advice. In fact, when The Motley Fool responded to Sandler's initial review in Autumn 2001, we suggested that financial advisers should not be able to style themselves 'independent' if they worked on a commission basis. This idea has cropped up in the Review. Sandler suggests that only if advisers are fee-paid should they be permitted to call themselves 'independent' or, indeed, 'advisers'. He suggests that those who are paid by commission should adopt the term 'Financial Product Distributor' which is a more accurate description of what they actually do.

The Review goes a long way in its recommendations towards protecting the consumer from the vagaries of the industry and encouraging the introduction of cheaper, more comprehensible products. It's to be hoped that the Government, the FSA and the industry move quickly to start implementing them.

As it is pension legislation is being re-written at a faster and faster rate at the moment. It's generally assumed that most of these changes are for the benefit of the public, but sometimes the government has its own budget-balancing agenda. All in all, there have been literally dozens of changes to pension legislation since the war, and many of them have only served to complicate matters and put even more people off investing in one. How many more will there be before *you* retire? Is it worth giving your money to a bunch of expensive 'professionals' over 40 years where the terms and conditions can be messed about with at any time and you can't get a refund if you don't like it? Worth thinking about when you decide where you put your money each month and year.

...but don't panic!

The point of writing this book is to help you sort your finances out and also to give you all a kick in the butt to make you do it. But, don't let all of this panic you. Life is full of surprises – many of them good ones – and if you don't see how in the world you are ever going to save up enough to have a survivable retirement, let alone a comfortable one, don't despair. J.K.Rowling couldn't have imagined in her wildest dreams how much fame and fortune her children's book idea could have brought and we're sure Noddy Holder didn't write 'Merry Christmas' in order to fund his retirement – although that's exactly what it's likely to do. Saving money and investing it well is just part of the story. Money in the bank (or savings scheme) is not the only source of supply so always keep an open mind and a sense of expectancy and you'll be surprised what turns up. Perhaps you have an idea for a great book or business. Take some time out and really work on it. Who knows where it could lead!

Also, retirement is not necessarily the best answer for everyone. For many people, being forced to work, to go out into the world and deal with the challenges and rewards of earning a living can bring them much more happiness and fulfilment than they would get spending the year doing Mediterranean cruises. Contrary to what you may think *we* think – given the subject matter of this book – we don't believe that money is the answer. It's just a useful support to the rest of your life. So don't panic – where one door closes, another will always open...if you kick hard enough!

Useful (though sometimes dull) websites

www.annuity-bureau.co.uk/rates.html - takes you through the joys of annuities.

www.pensionguide.gov.uk - pretty obvious really

www.stakeholder.opra.gov.uk - everything you ever wanted to know about stakeholders and just couldn't be bothered to ask

www.stakeholderhelpline.org.uk - does exactly what it says on the tin.

www.cappa.org.uk - this is the website for the Compulsory Annuity Purchase Protest Alliance. If you don't like the fact that the Government forces us to buy an annuity, check out this site.

www.dss.gov.uk/index.htm - this allows you to check the whole range of benefits you might be entitled to

www.inlandrevenue.gov.uk - this is the Inland Revenue site which offers help with your income tax.

www.open.gov.uk - gives a very comprehensive overview if you really aren't sure which bit of the government you want (as if you'd want any of it anyway, but hey, you never know!)

www.opas.org.uk - go here if you have a query about your occupational pension

8

Two's Company

The boy with cold hard cash is always Mr. Right...
Only boys who save their pennies make my rainy day.

Madonna, *Material Girl*

It may seem strange to start a chapter about beginning a new life with your soul mate with a negative comment, but there's good reason for it. So, here goes: The brutal truth is that there's a fair chance your relationship will fail at some point.

This chapter is not about the fabulousness of falling in love. We all know how glorious it is – it goes without saying that it's one of the best bits of life. If it's good, if it works, if you're perfect together and you go on to live happily ever after, then great. Congratulations. But we're willing to bet that at some point so far you've had a failed relationship, even if you only kissed little Jonny from next door when you were 12 and then wondered why he wouldn't speak to you for three months.

Love does strange things to us and for the most part it's truly wonderful. But when our emotions take over, cold hard logic has a rather skittish habit of flying out of the window! If you've just opened your mouth to point out that, if a relationship is to work, surely there should be complete and total trust, just close it for a moment! Remember that 4 in 10 marriages end in divorce and an even higher number of cohabiting couples split up, and then read Chapter Ten if you want to know what can happen when it all goes wrong.

We're neither being unfair to men nor being unromantic. Honest! It's just that we know how hard it is when you've fallen passionately for someone and have the feeling in your bones that this is *it*. Reaching through that fug of love to get at the bit of your brain that houses your common sense isn't easy. Just keep at the back of your mind that there's the *possibility* of the relationship failing at some point and you'll realise there can be some advantages to protecting your position from the start. You don't need to be mercenary about it – you just need to think sensibly, difficult though it is when you're going through that phase of walking on air.

> *I used to work in a Women's Centre. We saw a lot of cases where men were financially taking advantage of women because the women acted on trust and hope instead of financial savvy. Philosophically speaking, I think the more Vulcan you can be about it the better. No one melds finances with the expectation of relationship dissolution, but it happens. Whatever you decide, please, please, please protect yourself.*
>
> From the Motley Fool discussion board

Remember that looking out for your own interests can also be very good for your *partner*: after all, if you're clearly in control of your money and your life, then he might rather like some of your special magic formula to rub off on him. If nothing else, your soul mate will know that you can afford to live without him if you need to and that's bound to keep him on his toes! If you protect your financial position then it means you could even help him out, should he prove to be less than competent with money. If the relationship is a success, then, logically you will *both* be richer for it, financially and emotionally.

Start as you mean to go on. Who should manage the money in a relationship? Should you discuss right from the beginning what might happen financially if everything ends in tears? Should you pool your resources from the get-go, regardless of who is earning what, or should you contribute to the household finances in proportion to your respective incomes? What happens if one of you owns a house and the other doesn't?

There are no easy answers to any of these questions: the simple response would be, 'Whatever works for you both', and to a great extent that's true. But if it's not working, then it makes sense to tackle the issue. In fact, whether you are just embarking on a new relationship, whether you've already acquired your 1.7 children or whether your kids have already flown the nest, it's never too late to greet the love of your life with the immortal words, 'Darling? I've been thinking...' (Actually, those words are probably on a par with, 'What are you thinking?' – a phrase designed to make any man break out in a cold sweat. Perhaps you might want to think of a different approach!)

The important thing is never ever to assume that it'll all work out in the end; if you haven't properly talked about your financial future, do it now! If you need more convincing, read Chapter Ten on what happens if you split up. If you need some motivation, then nip down to your local video shop and rent *The War of the Roses*, starring Michael Douglas and Kathleen Turner. Be alternately amused and horrified at this film, and then decide you are never going down *that* route!

Do pre-nups work?

Speaking of Michael Douglas, you'll perhaps recall the rumours that abounded in the press about the pre-nuptial agreement he allegedly signed before he married the Welsh lovely, Catherine Zeta Jones. In case you need reminding, our Catherine apparently managed to negotiate a rather jolly $3 million for every year that she stays married to her ageing paramour. She'll obviously have to divorce him eventually to get that money, but it must be some compensation to know, if things are going badly, that you've only got to hang in there for a mere decade in order to walk off with a cool $30 million!

The lovely Catherine does have a few million quid herself, of course, but it's peanuts in comparison with his supposed $200 million fortune. However, considering Mr Douglas is 25 years older than she is, he's had a bit of a head start. To be honest, why *should* she be entitled to dip into the money he was earning on *The Streets of San Francisco* when she was still at primary school? She's known him for a mere smidgen of his long and eventful life, after all.

Putting to one side the notion that most of us girls prefer to think about our relationships as true lurve and soppy suppers by candlelight (not to mention his going down on bended knee when he pops the question), this Hollywood habit of drawing up such an agreement does pose an important question. Is a pre-marital agreement a good thing for us 'commoners' before we take the plunge? As ever, the rules are different for couples who plan to marry than for those who intend simply to live together.

Pre-marital agreements

A pre-marital agreement is probably worth it only when there are substantial assets involved at the start – but it also depends on whether you're the one with the money! To an extent, it's almost academic anyway because pre-marital agreements aren't officially recognised by our UK courts. That's not to say that a judge will automatically throw it out, though. There have been hints from the Government over the last couple of years that such agreements should be given more credence, not least because of the potential cut in the Legal Aid bill, as well as the number of messy divorce cases that are currently clogging up the system.

At the moment, in this country, a 'pre-nup' will sometimes prove persuasive to a court when divorcing couples are arguing about who promised what to whom, but it's usually only when the marriage has been comparatively short and there are no children involved. It would certainly be struck out if it were considered in any way unfair to either of the parties, or if it appeared to have been signed under duress.

There are already divorce laws in place governing the division of property, maintenance and the residence of any offspring, which would override much of what might be set out in a pre-marital agreement. Currently, the court's first priority is to look at each partner's income and assets at the time of the divorce, the length of the marriage, their ages, standard of living and the reasonable requirements of the 'poorer' party. The terms of a pre-marital agreement come way down the list of considerations, particularly if it was drawn up a long time before the divorce and circumstances have since changed. If there are children involved, it may well be ignored altogether.

If you are the wealthier partner in the relationship, however, it still might be worth thinking about before you take that walk down the aisle. Indeed, it may be essential if you are about to enter a second marriage and want to safeguard inherited family money, your business or your children from a previous relationship. After all, if your partner agrees to abandon future claims to a moderate amount of the incoming assets, he can hardly demand the agreement be set aside at a later date without good reason. (It goes without saying that if you're the poorer partner and you're not being offered much, don't sign!)

Cohabitation agreements

What if you don't want to get married? Perhaps you think marriage is an outdated institution and you plan to share a future together without the benefit (or not) of a piece of paper that binds you together legally.

The rules for unmarried couples are quite different. There is no such thing as a 'common-law wife' in terms of legal recognition of a relationship. You're not entitled to anything while you're in the relationship (and neither is he, for that matter). If the relationship ends, you can't use the protection of the law unless you've got children or have some sort of interest in the family home. Whether or not you want a ring on your finger is irrelevant: just be aware that your rights as an unmarried woman are different from those as a married woman. However, cohabitation agreements are wholly enforceable by the courts, if they choose, because they're seen as binding contracts between unrelated parties. Couples who aren't married have no legal right to each other's money, regardless of how long they've lived together. So, if a couple is committed but simply doesn't believe in marriage, a cohabitation agreement might be a good solution. In cases where one partner has substantial wealth and the other does not, they can prove rather useful in setting out who owns what and where it should go in the event of a breakdown in the relationship. It would certainly provide a measure of security for the less wealthy partner if he/she could negotiate a decent deal.

Property ownership

The biggest asset either of you may have, of course, is a home of your own or rather any equity in it. If you're setting up home in his house or flat, do you expect a piece of it? And if you're the property owner and he's moving in with you, do you want him to have some of it?

Time for a little anecdote! Several years ago there was a young couple who'd been seeing each other for about a year and decided to get married. She was just completing her studies at university and had a little part-time job whereas he worked full-time for the family business. At about the same time as they announced their engagement, his parents sold the family business and gave him a deliciously large sum of money – enough to buy the soon-to-be marital home without a mortgage, at any rate. Jolly decent of them. Whilst sitting in their solicitor's office discussing the house purchase, they were asked whether the property was to be in his name alone or in joint names. Being a generous sort of chap, the answer was that it was to be in joint names.

Shortly afterwards the couple moved into their lovely new home and, you've guessed it, did *not* live happily ever after. He came home from work one day, told her he didn't want to marry her after all and gave her a week to get out of 'his' house. Since she had no money of her own, she asked him for a little financial help – enough to pay for the deposit and a month's rent on a tiny flat – so she would have a little time to sort herself out. He refused. She was distraught.

That was until a friend who was a law student reminded her that he had *given* her half the house. Her name was on the deeds and, if she felt like it, she could go to court, force the sale of the property and disappear into the sunset with some £50,000 in her pocket! Now, being a nice girl, she wouldn't have dreamt of walking off with half of his money, seeing that she'd set up home with him only a few months before. But, oh, she *did* enjoy pointing out to him that she could if she wanted to. Guess what. He coughed up the tiny amount she had asked for and she merrily moved on with her life, knowing that she had left behind a gibbering idiot who was unlikely to want to put his home into joint names ever again!

The fact is, your or his entitlement to anything in the event of a break-up depends entirely on whether your home is in joint names or, if not, whether you or he can establish that some entitlement to those assets has been acquired (by contributing to the mortgage, for example). If you can show that you have contributed *directly* to buying your home or to improving it in some substantial way, you may be able to show that you have acquired an interest even though legal ownership belongs entirely to him. For example, if you paid the deposit or have contributed directly towards the mortgage instalments, this would constitute a beneficial interest. You've actually 'bought' a little bit of the house even though the title deeds don't say you have.

Difficulties can arise, however, if your partner has been paying the mortgage and you've merely been paying all the other household bills. It may just have been the method you were both happy with at the time, but you would somehow have to prove that this arrangement was based on an understanding or agreement that you were effectively making contributions towards the purchase of the house itself by freeing up his income.

There's more information on this in Chapter Ten, but for the time being, just be aware that prevention is better than cure. The more cynical amongst you will already have realised a couple of things. If you move into your partner's house, make sure that you have a joint account for the household bills – including the mortgage – and that you keep your bank statements as evidence of your contributions. It goes without saying that if someone moves into your home then make sure you do exactly the opposite: on no account let him anywhere near the mortgage payments!

Nevertheless, if you both decide that you want to co-own your home then you need to think about how you want to divide it up in legal terms. To that end, it's worth knowing the two ways you can do it: either jointly or on the basis of 'half each'.

As we have already pointed out in Chapter Four, in legal terms, you can own a house with someone else either as *joint tenants* or as *tenants-in-common*: it's a very important distinction. To ensure we don't confuse the issue by bandying the word 'tenant' around too much, we'll refer to joint tenants as joint owners. So let's look at the difference and remind you of some of the pros and cons, because there are several implications that need explaining.

Joint owners

In this instance, two people simply own the whole house between them. There is no technical division of the property and, if one dies, ownership of the house passes automatically to the surviving partner regardless of whether there's a will. Essentially, it means you cannot 'gift' your share of the property to anyone else.

This also applies to people who are not part of a couple. Three siblings could jointly own a house, for example, and, if one dies, owner-ship automatically passes to the remaining two.

Usually when couples buy a home together they do it as joint owners, regardless of who is actually paying the mortgage. It's so common that solicitors handling the purchase sometimes even forget to suggest the alternative option! Because lots of people don't bother to make a will, this at least covers the problem of dying intestate since there'll be no arguments about who subsequently owns the whole house – often the main asset in a relationship.

Tenants-in-common

Here the couple own half each of the house. It's obviously a technical 'half each' but it does mean that each tenant-in-common can leave their share of the house to anyone they like. It gives each partner an element of control and can be a useful mechanism should you have enough assets between you at a later date to be concerned about Inheritance Tax. (See Chapter Eleven for more details on Inheritance Tax.)

A tenancy-in-common can be a very good thing in certain circumstances, but it can also open a huge can of worms! Frankly, it depends on whether you're the one who dies first or whether you're the survivor as to how you might want things to pan out. It depends on what your circumstances are and how much control you fancy exercising from the grave.

There are certain advantages. For example, you can leave your half-share of the home to your children in your will, while allowing your partner to live there for as long as necessary. This means that if your surviving partner ever has to go into a nursing home, the local authority would have the right to use only *his* half of the house to pay for it. It would also mean that, if your partner married again or entered a new relationship, he wouldn't be able to leave the whole house to Your Replacement! In both cases, your children would still get the half-share you've left them.

But what happens if your kids aren't as trustworthy as you thought they were? What if one of them is desperately in debt and tries to force the sale of the house to get his share? If you think it doesn't happen then disabuse yourself of that notion. Children can be greedy. Again, you could get around such potential problems by leaving your partner a lifetime's interest in your share, with it going to the children only when he dies.

Picture another scenario. You've left your half to the kids but have ensured that hubby has a lifetime's interest. What if, ten years after your ashes have been scattered all over the Lake District, one of your kids gets divorced and the exiting spouse is entitled to include the inheritance you've left your child as part of the matrimonial property? Your child can't get any money out of the family home because you've left your husband a lifetime's interest, so your child looks wealthy on paper but in fact has very little access to real cash. He or she would have to find the money from elsewhere – and that could leave him or her broke. Not what you had in mind, perhaps.

Obviously, in the case of friends or siblings who share ownership of a property, being tenants-in-common is probably a good thing. If you've inherited your parents' house with your sister, you'd probably prefer to leave your half-share to your husband or your children rather than her. She's already got her portion after all and you're entitled to do what you like with yours. It might prove inconvenient for her if you pop your clogs and she has to sell the inherited house in order to pass on your share to your family. But that's tough! At least, as a tenant-in-common you've got the choice about who gets what. On the other hand, if you're the surviving sister and you've got to sell the home you grew up in so you can give your money-grubbing brother-in-law, who's never done a day's work in his life, his half-share, you might wish you'd never heard of the phrase 'tenants-in -common'!

As you might imagine, where couples are concerned, joint ownership is probably the easiest and preferable option. Unless you've got such a huge house that planning for Inheritance Tax through the generations is a necessity, it simply doesn't seem fair to inadvertently shackle, or be shackled by, someone you've loved.

Who should manage the household finances?

In an ideal world, both partners in a relationship would have educated themselves about personal finances issues. They'll have discussed their short- and long-term financial goals and both would be sitting down at the kitchen table together on a regular basis to review the situation and check they're still on track.

Hah! It's more likely that one or both in a relationship are muddling along on the assumption that either the other partner is keeping an eye on things or that, as long as something's being put into an ISA or a pension fund, then their future is probably secure. In these days of burgeoning house prices, many people revel in the amount of equity they're accumulating in the family home and imagine that the roof over their heads will supply them with a retirement fund. This may be true if you eventually find yourself living in a large house with no mortgage and you're prepared to downshift to a smaller home, relocate to a cheaper part of the country or move abroad. It's what many retiring couples have done, but, in some cases, they've been forced to do so if they're not to live in penury for the rest of their days.

You'll not be surprised to learn that, generally, it's women who manage the general household budget – buying the shopping, keeping the children clothed and shod and choosing the colour of the paint, the fabric for the curtains and the style of sofa etc. Men tend to handle the 'big' things such as the mortgage, the family car, the pension fund etc.

Although things are beginning to change and women are becoming more involved in wider financial matters, there's a school of thought emerging in America that is actively trying to reverse the process. Laura Doyle is a writer who is being touted in the US as the new John Gray – the female version. Those of you who have read or heard about *Men are from Mars, Women are from Venus* will know that we're supposed to allow men to go 'into their caves' when we want to restore marital harmony. Doyle goes one step further. She proposes that we surrender all control and decision-making to our man if we really want to make our relationships work. (Stop laughing at the back!)

It's what she's done and, apparently, she now has a happier marriage because of it. You can find out all about it by reading her book, *The Surrendered Wife: A Practical Guide to Finding Intimacy, Passion, and Peace with Your Man*. According to Doyle, the basic principles of a surrendered wife are that she:

- Relinquishes inappropriate control of her husband
- Respects her husband's thinking
- Receives his gifts graciously and expresses gratitude for them
- Expresses what she wants without trying to control him
- Relies on him to handle household finances
- Focuses on her own self-care and fulfilment

Doyle goes on to add that a surrendered wife is:

- Vulnerable where she used to be a nag
- Trusting where she used to be controlling
- Respectful where she used to be demeaning
- Grateful where she used to be dissatisfied
- Has faith where she once had doubt

Her basic concept is, of course, nothing new. Treat your partner as you would have him treat you – as a decent intelligent human being. Women *and* men who constantly nag and criticise their partners probably deserve everything they get, which is likely to be not a lot. As Doyle points out, when you squash your husband's ideas, you kill his spirit just as he'd kill yours if it were the other way around.

The only thing we have a problem with is her recommendation to hand over all control of the finances to the man of the house. In her own case, she has followed it through to the extent that she says, while she knows where their bank accounts are held, she doesn't know how much is in them! Doyle thinks that control of the finances is the man's job and that by removing herself from involvement in all matters financial, she is showing respect for her husband. We're inclined to disagree.

Far too many women pop up on the Motley Fool message boards who have done exactly this, and have been left high and dry when their relationship has broken down. Money, or rather the lack of it, may well be one of the biggest single causes of arguments within a relationship, but it's usually because one or both partners are spending more than is coming in. So, handing over all responsibility for the bills to the man of the house, simply because he's a man, is frankly ridiculous.

The household finances need to be managed by the best person for the job – it's as simple as that. That doesn't mean the other partner in the relationship can then abdicate all responsibility. At the very least they should keep themselves informed and at no time should either partner ever relinquish the ability to make financial decisions. If you're the better person to manage the finances, then make sure you manage them *well*. If your partner is the better person to manage them, then make sure *he* manages them well. Ideally, work on them together.

As for all the other 'relationship' stuff Doyle espouses, to be fair, her main point is that women should express themselves to their men but not by telling them what to do. The idea is to tell them what you want, but not how to do it. She does claim that 'surrender' is not the same as 'submission', but, for us, we feel her approach is a regressive step for women – and for men too. It weakens the concept of compromise in a relationship.

To that end, it's vital to know what's happening with the finances as early as possible in a relationship to ensure that, whether you spend your retirement in sunny climes on the Costa Blanca or in the home of your dreams overlooking the seafront in Clacton, with or without a partner, you don't have to penny-pinch.

There are many approaches to money management between couples but, in our view, the key things are openness and communication. You have to lay your cards on the table, be honest about what your priorities are in life and where your weaknesses lie. If you are truly embarking on a lifelong future together, you need to do things like let your partner see your bank statements – and take a good look at his! This doesn't mean that you can't have any privacy at all: it just means that you should know roughly how much each of you earns, how much each of you has saved and how much debt each of you has incurred.

Money matters in a relationship – and not just where debts are concerned. It matters particularly if one partner stops working, for whatever reason, because that's when you really have to learn how to share what you have. It's very odd asking other couples how they manage their finances. Most don't want to talk about it or else one partner claims that 'everything's fine', even though we know from discussions with the other partner that it isn't. The couples who were open and direct about how they managed their finances were the only ones who agreed that they never had rows about money. They had successfully negotiated an arrangement with each other that suited them both – mainly because they'd actually talked about it.

For example, one woman told us that, when she gave up work to look after her first-born, she negotiated a 'monthly salary' from her husband – it went into her personal bank account and she knew it was hers to spend or save as she wished. She said it made her feel valued as a house-wife and mother because her husband accepted her need for some form of financial independence after giving up her career – and he recognised the fact that she earned it! Another stay-at-home mother was perfectly happy to access her husband's bank account whenever she wanted to because he had, after much insistence, managed to convince her that his money really was her money too.

What is difficult to understand are the men who say, 'Oh, I give her what I think she needs and I deal with everything else.' This is demean-ing. Who wants to be given a bit of pocket money along with a metaphorical pat on the head?

But what are the alternatives if you're both working, regardless of whether there are children or not? There are a number of options but it makes sense to agree from the start about what should be considered a joint household expense. The roof over your head, the electricity, gas and Council Tax, for example, are benefits or services that both of you enjoy. But what about things like clothes, CDs and books? Is he going to get angry if you regularly spend a fortune on fashion items when you know the boiler needs replacing? Are you going to get angry if he has a passion for collecting DVDs when he knows that you desperately want a new sofa so you can at least watch the damn things in comfort? What about savings? Do you both have ISAs and pensions that you regularly pay into? If so, should these be considered joint expenses that will enable you to enjoy financial independence when you retire?

There's also the thorny question of what to do if one of you is earning more than the other. Should you both contribute equal amounts to the joint expenses, leaving the lower earner to struggle on the remaining pittance while the higher earner enjoys the freedom to spend for England? Should you contribute jointly in direct proportion to what you earn? Or should you perhaps give yourselves an equal amount of 'pocket money' each month and just pool the rest?

As we pointed out earlier, there are no easy answers, although we would like to think that all but the most frivolous expenses would be considered a joint responsibility and that the higher earner would be generous in accepting a greater responsibility. After all, if you're freely sharing your bed with someone, in theory, you should surely freely share your money!

It's quite possible, however, to lead deliberately separate financial lives that meet at a common point. If your partner is financially lax but you aren't, then forcing your own ways of handling money onto him by insisting on completely joint finances can drive you apart eventually. It's a case of trying to find common ground.

If you can work out what your agreed joint monthly outgoings are and who's going to contribute what, then open a joint household account and make sure your agreed contributions are direct-debited into it. Ensure that all bills are direct-debited out of it (or use standing orders) so you know that you're not going to forget to pay something vital like the mortgage. Keep a personal account for your own money so that you can retain a modicum of privacy and independence; let him spend his non-household money how he likes.

The important thing is to communicate, communicate, communicate!

Should you make a Will?

The simple answer is yes, yes and yes! If you own anything at all of any value, even if it's just a few hundred quid in the building society, it is essential to make a Will. Death is something most people like to ignore but, unfortunately, it comes to us all. The mess of pottage you might leave behind for your loved ones to deal with if you don't make a Will is hardly something you'll want to be remembered for once they've come to terms with their grief. There are quite an extraordinary number of people who really don't think about this. Making a Will isn't something that costs a lot of money, yet the problems that dying intestate can cause are vast.

Apart from anything else, if you're that way inclined, it's the one time in your life when you can truly exact sweet revenge on the people you can't stand without any personal consequences! What, for example, was Shakespeare thinking when he gave unto his wife his 'second-best bed'? And what do you think her reaction was? What about the American who left his wife nothing 'but her lover and the knowledge I wasn't the fool she thought I was'? Others like to try to exert control from beyond the grave: witness one Bing Crosby, who tied up his estate in such a way that his surviving wife and children have virtually no control over their legacy and have to rely on hand-outs from the trustees of the estate.

So what does happen if you don't make a Will? Essentially, if you die without making a Will, the State makes one for you. It decides who will get what. If you don't have any dependants or relatives to leave your money to at all, it's the State who gets all the dosh! We're sure that you'd rather it went to the local cat's home at least.

If you die *unmarried* but with a partner and children, your children will get everything and your partner may get nothing at all. Obviously, if your home is in joint names, then your partner will at least automatically get the house via the survivorship rules. But if the house is in your name only, he could face problems.

Many people think, if they're *married*, that everything will automatically go to their spouse when they die: this simply isn't so. It's true that couples often hold their main asset – their home – in joint names, so when one dies the other automatically inherits their half-share. If this isn't the case, i.e. your holding it as tenants-in-common, it can lead to difficulties for your partner when you die. As usual the rules are different if you're married.

If you die intestate, your husband will be entitled to only a few personal things, the first £125,000 of your estate and a lifetime's interest in half of the remainder. Any children inherit the rest of your estate when they reach the age of 18. If most of the estate is tied up in the family home, your children could force your husband out of it in order to realise their own inheritance (though spouses do now have some rights of occupation). If you have no children, then your spouse gets the first £200,000 of the estate plus half the remainder. The rest goes to the surviving parents, siblings or other relatives.

One thing to get clear is the thorny issue of Inheritance Tax. At present, you are allowed to leave £250,000 (according to the 2002/03 tax rate) before your estate is subject to Inheritance Tax, which is at a flat rate of 40% on the remainder. The exemption may seem like a great deal, but with house prices as they are in this day and age, the exemption limit can easily be exceeded.

Leaving everything to your husband is an option, as there is no Inheritance Tax payable between spouses. Alternatively, you can get around the problem by giving away bits of your property before you die. As long as you live for at least seven years after making the gift, it doesn't form part of the estate at all and even if you die rather more quickly than you'd hoped, the liability diminishes on a sliding scale.

If you are single, you can always do what 90-year-old Brit Ian Patey did. In December 1999, he married the 41-year-old daughter of his former car mechanic just because he didn't want the State to get any of his £500,000 estate. His new wife merely had to nurse him through his remaining years and drive him around a bit, after which she got the lot!

Another important function of a Will is to appoint guardians in the event that both you and your partner die leaving young children. Guardians take over the parental role, usually looking after the children and deciding on issues such as education and religion, while the trustees of your estate will take care of any money you've left behind for the children. You can exert a certain amount of control from the grave: for example, you could grant powers to the trustees of your estate to make loans to the guardians to cover the cost of buying a bigger house. Either way, it's important that you think hard about whom you would want in either role and how you would want your money to be used for the benefit of your children.

Professional Wills cost about £50–£70 for a single person and £95–£150 for duplicate Wills between husband and wife, depending on where you go and how complicated your finances are. You could pop round to your local stationers and get a ready-made Will that you just fill in yourself, but we don't recommend it. We have heard of too many problems associated with Wills that were not drawn up by professionals. If you decide you need to take legal advice, make sure the lawyer you use is a member of the Society of Trust and Estate Practitioners (STEP). This is a self-regulatory worldwide society for those who specialise in this particular field; not all lawyers know all about Wills and Probate and those who aren't specialists could make mistakes. Members are entitled to use the initials 'TEP' after their name, which means that their expertise has been proven. A list of members can be obtained from STEP at 26 Dover Street, London W1S 4LY (phone on 020 7839 3886 or look at www.step.org).

To sum up, the moment you have anything worth giving or anyone who may need to be cared for, you should make a Will. Not only that but you should update it when your circumstances change – when you get married, get divorced or have children. If you don't, your last Will will be the one the lawyers use to distribute your goods, and if you weren't married that could mean your worldly possessions going to the ex you can barely think of without feeling violent.

Finally, once you've drawn up your Will, make sure someone knows where it is! There's no point in making all these arrangements if no one knows they exist. It's hardly fair to put one's partner, children or parents in the unfortunate position of having to ransack the house in search of paperwork when they're presumably a little overwhelmed by your loss. Jane's father rather sweetly reminds her every time she visits that all the 'necessaries' are in a cardboard box in a particular place should she ever need access to such information 'for any reason' – and she's glad to know it.

The bottom line is *never ever die without a Will*. Make sure you review it frequently, particularly if children arrive on the scene or your circumstances change!

Getting married – the 'Big Day'

Ah! The best day of your life, right? If you haven't been put off by our dreadful cynicism about the relationship failure rate, you've decided that you really can put up with your awful mother-in-law-to-be and you're prepared to stand up to your mother about how she wants to organise your wedding, then it probably will be one of your greatest memories!

First, the bad news. The average cost of a wedding in the UK is around £12,000. Yep! That's as much as most people would spend on a car. If you decide to trade in your model when the three-year warranty runs out, that gives you a monthly cost of around £330! Yes, there's no escaping the fact that weddings are big, expensive and legally binding. Given that rectifying an impulse purchase requires rather a lot more than an advert in *Exchange & Mart*, it clearly pays to try to get it right first time!

Before you write marriage off as a totally bad job, bear in mind there is a clear distinction here between the cost of marriage and the cost of weddings. In England and Wales, you can marry at a register office for just under £100. This leaves some £1,900 accounted for by the wedding industry.

If you've got this far through this book, you'll no doubt consider yourself a true Fool – with a capital 'F' – who now knows how and when to spot a con trick when you see one. Good for you! Up and down the country, thousands of shops, companies and publications beaver away tirelessly with a single aim in mind: to help you, or rather your parents, spend as much money as possible in their quest to make the perfect day, thus warding off the bad-luck pixies that cause marriages to fail.

Flicking through any bridal magazine, you'll be hard pushed to find any practical details on the ceremony, financial planning, legalities and so on. What you will find are pages and pages of glossy advertisements interspersed with advice on where to buy everything from silk thongs to vacuum cleaners. Prospective brides stepping into a wedding-dress shop are swept away by staff into a dreamy white fairyland of silk and satin, with photographs of the happy brides (who have passed through this till) pinned visibly to the cash desk. Against this kind of emotional onslaught, even the most miserly bride-to-be would struggle to keep a lid on the costs.

There's nothing romantic about starting your life together heavily in debt. Then again, as the wedding industry would say, it's the most important day of your life. Besides, spending money is fun and now you have the perfect excuse. So how do you get the fairytale wedding without the nightmare overdraft?

The most important rule is: be realistic. The wedding industry is based on fantasy, but if it rains, if you break out in acne the day before or if the bridesmaids are sick on the vicar, there's nothing you can do about it regardless of how much money you have spent. That's not to say that anything or everything will go wrong, but, no matter how hard you try, you can never make things truly 'perfect' in the abstract sense. Many wartime brides will tell you they had a 'perfect' wedding in spite of very 'imperfect' circumstances.

Apply this sense of gritty, down-to-earth realism to your budget:

- Make sure that everyone who is paying for the wedding is happy with the budget.
- Try deciding what you really want and then see how inexpensively you can get it.

- Shop around for everything: a bridal shop may not be the best place to buy shoes, for example.
- Try deciding whom you really want to be at the wedding and then working on the invites, rather than deciding on 100 guests and then inviting people at the office who make your life hell or relatives you last saw when you were six, just to make up the numbers. Remember: you are buying copious amounts of food and alcohol for these people.
- It's common practice in many areas of business to label up the most expensive packages as 'Premiere' or 'Regal'. Start with 'Budget' and work upwards. Watch out for hidden costs such as when you've hired the room but chairs are extra.
- There's such a thing as 'wedding insurance', with policies priced from around £48 to cover up to £3,000 worth of cancellation expenses. None of these policies will cover being left standing at the altar or having to cancel the wedding because his divorce didn't come through in time. When deciding whether to take out cover and how much cover you need, work on how much out of pocket you would be if you didn't turn up on the day. This will generally be any deposits or payments up front, plus any cancellation penalties. Bear in mind that items like dresses and cakes may survive to be used at a later date, but flowers and so on will probably have to be re-ordered.
- If you're changing your name, expect administrative chaos for at least the next six months. Your passport, your bank account, your ISAs, your driving licence etc. will all need to be changed.

A rough guide to wedding costs

Church ceremony. Church of England standard fees set by the Archbishops' Council are £142 for the marriage service, £15 for the publication of banns and £9 for the banns certificate. If you would like to marry in church, talk to your local vicar as soon as you plan to get married to check that he/she can and will marry you, to confirm availability and to get an idea of costs. Although the Church of England is now moving towards accepting the marriage of divorcees, vicars may still choose not to marry couples if they aren't regular members of the congregation, for example. Churches tend to lend themselves to larger, and therefore more expensive, weddings. Watch out for hidden extras like flowers, choirs and bells. Do you really want to spend £200–£300 extra just so the congregation can listen to Mrs Needham coaxing a tune out of an asthmatic organ while the choir – who clearly look the type to enjoy morris dancing in their spare time – struggle to be heard above the wheezing?

Register Office ceremony. It costs a mere £97.50 for a Register Office ceremony: £30 each to give notice of the wedding and £37.50 on the day, which includes a copy of the marriage certificate.

Licensed-venue civil wedding. This can cost anything from around £250 upwards. If you aren't concerned about having a church marriage, you can get a lot more flexibility with licensed premises. These vary dramatically in every aspect, including cost, not least because you'll get slapped with a registrar's attendance fee, which can be over £200. Most licensed venues will also provide the reception.

You can search for licensed premises nationwide on the Internet at www.confetti.co.uk. Otherwise, ring up the local Registrar of Births, Marriages and Deaths anywhere in the country and they'll send you the full list of licensed venues in your area free of charge.

The National Trust has a wide selection of great premises, but prices are steep compared with hotels or community centres. You're looking at around £500 and more to hire the room for the ceremony only. You can search for National Trust properties available for weddings on their website at www.nationaltrust.org.uk or contact their central office in London on 0870 609 5380.

Some local authorities own rather grand properties that can be hired quite cheaply, so it's always worth giving them a ring – you may be pleasantly surprised. These properties will often have kitchens and bars, which make them ideal for larger, buffet-style receptions. Room hire is usually charged by the hour.

Hotels with wedding licences will often offer a discount for your room hire if you have both the ceremony and reception there. They may also lend you a cake stand and knife, print place cards and so on, but if they charge for this then check against prices elsewhere. Hotels may also offer discounts for guests who stay overnight or offer a free room to the bride and groom (just make sure you put your new mother-in-law in the local Travelodge!).

Whether you want a small room at a hotel or your own personal castle for the day, shop around. Some venues have an inflated opinion of their scenic value. Don't book any venue that you haven't first checked out in person. You'll need to get an accurate idea of the room's size, quality of décor, light level, ambient temperature and even smell, as brochure descriptions can be a little optimistic. Also, bear in mind the location of your chosen venue against the present location of you and your guests. If you want to marry in Derbyshire and live in Surrey, there will be travel and accommodation costs to add into the final bill.

Reception. Assuming you're marrying in church, at a register office or at a licensed venue where there are no reception facilities, venue hire for the wedding reception can cost from around £50 to silly money, catering from around £15 a head for a fairly standard set menu or buffet to restaurant-level prices. In fact, a top tip is not to tell them it's a wedding reception! If you describe it just as a private party, you could cut your costs by up to half! Another top tip is to get married on a weekday rather than a Saturday. It's much more likely to be cheaper and if your friends and family won't take a day off work to attend, then you're probably better off without them there anyway.

Rings. Plain 9ct gold bands start from around £30. Men's are often a little more expensive than women's, so tell him to buy his own! You can get some real second-hand bargains, but only from reputable jewellers.

Dress. Standard wedding dresses start from around £20 from a charity shop (no reason why not, it's only been worn once!) up to... well, just add a nought or three. Throw in the tiara and/or veil, underwear, shoes, net underskirt, make-up, hair, stole or wrap (essential for cool-season ceremonies), handbag, gloves and you are looking at at least the same amount again. And then there are the bridesmaids to kit out...

Flowers. Basic bridal bouquets start from around £30, simple button-holes from around £2. Floral-arrangement prices will depend on size, the flowers used and so on. Depending on your ceremony style, you may need to allow up to a few hundred pounds for flowers.

Photographs. Allow around £500–£600 for this. It's vital to examine the previous work of prospective photographers with a critical eye. Try to look beyond the setting or the bride's poor dress sense and get a feel for the actual composition of the photograph, the exposure level and colours. You may not be able to make a silk purse out of a pig's ear but, if even relatively elegant brides look plain and dumpy, you have to question the skills of the photographer. Taking pictures involves a lot more than pointing the camera in the right direction and pressing a button.

Beware of inflexible photographers – 'I don't do indoor photos' – and grumpy photographers who don't like your guests taking their own photos. Worst of all, however, are photographers who charge per exposure. You're paying for the time and skill of an expert, not film! (Jane is still steaming about that one from her own experience!) Consider sitting for a studio portrait, particularly if your wedding party is very small. If you've got guests, however, don't keep them waiting too long – it may be fun for you posing prettily as your veil whips around your face in the wind, but it's boring for those waiting for you to finish so they can get on to the reception and the drinkies!

Wedding presents. Gifts are not mandatory, but if your friends and relatives do want to get you both something, wedding lists are the best way to avoid 20 toasters. Try to have a good variety of gifts on the list, as some people why not have as flexible a budget as others. In many cultures it's perfectly acceptable to give hard cash – some pin bank notes to the bride's gown whilst others give cash in decorative envelopes.

Apart from being ultimately flexible, cash can be given in such a way that it has a nice ring of anonymity – useful if not everyone can afford the Gucci luggage you want. If you'd prefer cash but don't know how to ask for it, suggest these new and mysterious euros. They're still cash and you can convert them back to sterling if you don't want to hang on to them for holidays in Europe. If children are present or imminently planned, anyone other than parents can put cash gifts into an investment fund for them instead, without tax penalties.

Anything involved with the 'W' ceremony, particularly if it's in white, tends to fetch a premium. If possible, try to avoid special wedding packages or services if they don't really seem to offer anything extra. Beware of 'tie-ins', such as the wedding car services that insist on supplying their own flowers. The less 'traditional' your wedding, the more freedom you have to use your own imagination and creativity, and it'll probably work out cheaper too. If the customary meringue isn't your style, take a look at the evening wear available as this may be particularly appropriate for an informal wedding. Teenage bridesmaids will probably love you forever if, instead of the ubiquitous violet-frilled lampshade, you dress them in a stylish ballgown or evening dress that will be wearable on other occasions. Bridesmaids' dresses have a habit of resurfacing years later at university balls.

Avoid like the plague any premises, florist, dress shop, caterer or anyone else who tries to make you ashamed or embarrassed about marrying frugally. Spend only what you think is appropriate, not what they would like you to spend. High levels of expenditure are not a status symbol, an indication of wealth or a magic charm to bless your nuptial union. For every celebrity *OK!* spread with cherubs in attendance, there is the chic couple who are happy to have sausage and mash at the local pub. Just as Kate Winslett did. (Mind you, she's divorced now, so perhaps not!)

So, a final quick guide to a frugal wedding:

- Decide on your budget and stick to it.
- Before buying any information or advice, check out whether a local authority or religious organisation will give it to you for free.
- Shop around.
- Be critical and bargain hard.
- Don't confuse 'white' with 'ivory' or wedding dress saleswomen will become very upset.
- Keep a poker face while listening to high-pressure sales tactics.
- Be creative.
- Remember whose day it is and who's the boss!

Congratulations! You can now enjoy lots of marital rows for the rest of your life knowing that it's far harder for him to fly the coop in the middle of an argument!

Finally...

On a more serious note, here is a top tip as a wedding present from the Fool: The number one cause of rows in any relationship is money, whether it's the lack of it or disagreements about how to spend it. If you can work to eliminate that particular bone of contention from your repertoire, it'll be one reason fewer for problems to arise.

If you're both bad with money, the outlook is debts, more debts, bailiffs, extreme anger and unhappiness. Go back and re-read Chapter Three immediately. If you are good with money and your partner isn't, the outlook still could be debts, more debts, extreme anger and unhappiness. With the promise of some nookie, dupe him into reading Chapters Two and Three just in case it makes him see the light! If you're both good with money then keep reading in the knowledge that you have a very good chance of enjoying a financially secure life together as well as a decent retirement. As they say, may all your troubles be little ones.

Establishing your independence in the first place and *maintaining* it once you've found your soul mate gives you something that many other women don't have – the ability to stand on your own two feet if you want to walk away or should your partner leave you in the lurch. So think ahead. Whether or not he turns out to be The One, you can at least be confident that you're going to be standing tall in your own right. Trust us, it's a win–win situation all round, really. However you look at it, you will be in a position of strength and that is a very good thing at any time in your life.

Kids

I wanted to go out and change the world but I couldn't find a babysitter.

Anon

Maggots, ankle-biters, blobblings, sprogs, kidiwinks, Little Miss Perfect and Little Lord Fauntleroy – whatever you like to call them, an awful lot of us want to have children. It's pretty much what we were made for, although, as neither Jane nor Jasmine has any children nor any immediate plans to reproduce, we clearly don't think it is the *only* thing we were made for.

Children are a joy (much of the time) and it makes perfect sense that you should want some. Our main interest, for the purposes of this book, is that you have enough money to keep them and yourself supported.

The cost of a child

We almost hesitate to talk about the actual cost of having a child and bringing it up because if you really sat down and thought hard about the financial implications, you may never give birth at all and that would not be helpful for the country as a whole. With the greying of the population and the increasing shortage of young working people paying their National Insurance contributions to subsidise their grandparents' pensions, we need those children to pay for *our* pensions. So do the decent thing, girl. Lie back and think of England.

Think through the implications first because the fact is that, for most people, having a child is the most expensive thing they will ever do – even more money-draining than buying a house. As well as the obvious costs of feeding, clothing, educating and entertaining a new little human being for several years to come, there are the hidden expenses of loss of earnings (most likely to be yours), lost work days because of child sickness, babysitting costs even if you don't have nannies and many other surprises that only children can dream up for you.

Raising a child in London will cost a middle-class family nearly £318,000 over the 21-year period according to a report in the glossy freebie *The London Magazine* in January 2002. The study found that the biggest drains on a family's income were on private education (£93,600) and child care (£92,928) covering nannies, nurseries and babysitters. The cost of higher education, including living expenses, was estimated at £25,125, while pocket money amounted to £4,056, uniforms £13,000 and extra-curricular activities, such as music lessons, were £13,260. Researchers compiled the figure for clothes and general expenses on the premise that they cost parents £3,000 a year per child. But the report stressed that this failed to take account of the 'ruthless consumerism' of young children and the spread of 'pester power', which has seen parents spend thousands of pounds on designer clothes and computer games.

This is not to put you off having children, although if you are put off the idea because of money considerations that's probably a good thing. It will mean that you are either not yet ready to have children or you don't honestly want them at all. If that's the case, you can now go off and book that cruise round the world, dinner at Claridge's and all the designer clothes you want because that is the kind of money you will save. However, if you are not in a rush to give birth but you *do* want one at some stage, do a few sums first. Having a basic idea of the costs and therefore how much you'll need to put aside, can cut out a lot of the worry and pressure once you are pregnant.

Saving up for a child

Frankly, it's unlikely you can save up enough money fully to pay for a child for the next 20 years or so. Certainly not before your biological clock strikes twelve, anyway. It is worth putting aside as much money as you can for a couple of years – or just a year, if you can't wait that long – before *really* trying for a baby. The more money you have in your savings, the less stress you will have and the easier life will be, even when you go back to work (if that's what you want to do).

Only you know how much money you might need and how much you can afford to put by right now. However, the things that you (and your partner) will need to consider are:

- Your loss of earnings for the length of time you stay off work once you have had the baby. Also, your loss of earnings if you decide to go part-time if and when you return to work.
- The various costs associated with babies and children (see later in this chapter).
- How your pension and savings contributions are going to be paid while you are not earning.
- The cost of moving house – possibly to a bigger place to accommodate the new baby – if that's something you're considering.

Of course, many babies are not planned and you may be reading this now emitting short bitter laughs as you rest your bulging stomach and aching ankles. Even if you do suddenly find yourself pregnant, you have nine months to save and set aside as much money as you can to make things easier for yourself later on. You can put quite a bit away in that time if you concentrate. Happily, there are also other ways of boosting your income once you have had a child, and we suggest you get every penny that it is your right to have from both your employer and the Government.

Rights and benefits

Maternity rights (and paternity rights) have gradually improved over the years, although we still generally lag behind the rest of Western Europe as we seem to do in most social provisions. There is money there, but, unfortunately, every year millions of pounds' worth of benefits go unclaimed – quite often because women don't know they exist and that they are entitled to them. Check wherever you can about any money or benefits that you are entitled to. Quite often the personnel department at work, if you have one, will be able to give you good advice, but quite often they won't. Not all personnel execs have quite as much brain as they should have, so double-check anything they tell you. Similarly, your local benefits office may give you all the information you need about what you are entitled to, or they may be staffed by people with the IQ of a mollusc with learning difficulties who wouldn't know what day it is, let alone what benefits you could have. So, as with everything else, we recommend that you do some homework yourself first: read the terms of your employment contract thoroughly, as well as the numerous leaflets available from your local Benefits Office, so that you know what questions to ask about what you can have and how you can get it.

Here are a few pointers to get you started on your road to riches – well, bits of money, anyway – once you start a family.

Maternity rights, leave and pay

The rules will be changing in April 2003, which will make a significant difference to the amount of time you can take off as maternity leave as well as how much money you can expect in maternity pay. It's a big improvement on what you're entitled to now – possibly even enough to persuade you to hold off having a baby for the time being until the changes are implemented – so we'll mention them as we go along. For the time being though, let's cover your maternity rights as they stand now.

When it comes to time off, *all* female employees are entitled to 18 weeks' maternity leave regardless of how long they have worked for their employer. This entitlement is increased to 29 weeks – counting from the time the baby is born – for those who have worked for their employer for at least a year before maternity leave starts. This latter point may sound a bit confusing because the statutory 18 weeks' maternity leave can start any time from 11 weeks *before* the birth of the baby, whereas the

29 extra weeks count *from the date* of the baby's birth. Essentially, all qualifying employees are allowed a maximum of 40 weeks' leave under the rules; if you want your full whack, you need to start your maternity leave 11 weeks before the scheduled birth.

The good news is that, from April 2003, the statutory period of maternity leave will be extended from 18 weeks to 26 weeks. Note this doesn't extend the 40-week period but it does mean that mothers can claim a further eight weeks of maternity pay. Put simply, from April 2003, you'll be entitled to 40 weeks of maternity leave, 26 weeks of which will be paid. You'll also be pleased to know that, from April 2003, fathers will also get a look-in: they'll have the right to two weeks of paid paternity leave, which will be at the same flat rate of pay as Statutory Maternity Pay.

When it comes to pay, the entire system is rather complicated but it works something like this: you have a statutory right to be paid during the first 18 weeks of your maternity leave but you will get the relevant amounts only if you got pregnant after you started your job (effectively, if you've worked for at least 41 weeks before the actual birth). The full entitlement is split into two parts:

Currently, during the first six weeks of maternity leave you are entitled to receive 90% of your salary. For the next 12 weeks of maternity leave, the Statutory Maternity Pay is at a flat rate of £75 a week. (From April 2003 this will zoom up to £100 a week, which is the rate fathers will be entitled to as well during their fortnight's paternity leave.) Some employers (though not many) will pay your full salary throughout the entire 18-week period, which is why it is worth checking the terms of your employment contract yourself, just in case you're one of the lucky ones! All maternity leave after the 18-week statutory period (or 26 weeks from April 2003) will be unpaid.

As you can see, the changes that will apply from April 2003 will have a significant effect on new mothers who, until recently, might have felt forced to go back to work just six weeks after the birth because they simply couldn't afford to extend their leave period. With six weeks at 90% of pay and a further 20 weeks with £100 a week coming in, however, it should make it easier for them to enjoy more time off with their babies.

It's worth remembering that the laws regarding maternity rights were brought in to stop working women from being penalised for having a baby. This has effectively been achieved by assuming that the period of leave is part and parcel of your employment contract. As such, during the statutory 18-week period (apart from the pay aspect) you're entitled to all the rights and benefits you would be enjoying if you were still going to work every day. So you can keep your company car and your company mobile phone and know that your employer's occupational pension contributions will continue to be paid while you're away. You should also benefit from any pay rises or bonuses that crop up in your absence and your holiday entitlement will continue to accrue.

Your employer also has rights, though, and it is important to stick to the rules as, in some instances, you could lose your entitlement to the full statutory allowance if you break them. For example, you must provide written notification to your employer of your intended leave of absence within a specific time period, and the same goes for when you decide you want to return to work.

The amount of money you are entitled to will vary if you have worked for your employer for less than six months or if you were already pregnant when you started work. It will also vary if you are a part-timer who isn't earning enough to pay National Insurance contributions or if you are self-employed or unemployed. In these circumstances, the Government will pay a Statutory Maternity Allowance, which is similar to the £75 (or £100 from April 2003) rate. Your partner's income is irrelevant.

If you've not been earning at all during the 15 months immediately prior to your expected week of childbirth, you will not be entitled to Statutory Maternity Allowance and will need to look at Incapacity Benefit, Income Support or Family Credit. The Benefits Agency should automatically check to see if you qualify for any of these, but it's worth giving them a nudge to make sure.

You can get some extra help from the Government if you're on certain benefits, though. It's a one-off payment of £500 – called a Sure Start

Maternity Grant – and you can claim it if you, or your partner, are getting one of the following:

- Income Support
- Income-based Jobseeker's Allowance
- Working Families' Tax Credit
- Disabled Person's Tax Credit

Whatever situation you are in, you'll find some very helpful information, including the recent changes, on the Department of Trade and Industry's website at www.dti.gov.uk or, of course, from your local Benefits Office.

Finally, as an aside, there are some new benefits now that allow *both* parents to take 13 weeks, unpaid leave each for each child. This new 'parental' leave can be taken at any time until the child reaches the age of five, so it doesn't strictly come under maternity rights. However, you could use them to extend your time off work without losing your right to return to your job. If you do some sums, and you qualify for the full Monty in the first place, you'll realise you could take more than a year off without losing your right to return to work (particularly if you include your paid holiday entitlement, too). It's just a question of whether you can afford it.

Child Benefit

Every child up to the age of 16 (and then up to 19 for those in full-time non-advanced further education) is entitled to weekly Child Benefit paid to his or her parent(s). For the 2002/03 tax year, Child Benefit amounts to £15.75 a week for the first child and £10.55 a week for every subsequent child. You can claim this benefit whatever your financial circumstances. Lone parents can claim £17.55 for their eldest child and, again, £10.55 for each subsequent child. For many parents this is invaluable extra income, which helps towards essentials such as food and clothing. For others, for whom money is not so tight, it's a rather useful source of free money which can either be used to pay for little luxuries like toys and outings or, even better, can be invested sensibly to produce a tidy sum for their offspring at a later date (if they go to university, for example). See later in this chapter for ways to best invest your Child Benefit for your kid's future.

Other benefits

There are several other benefits designed to help families with children and, needless to say, these will all change in April 2003. These are designed to help families on low to moderate incomes. The Working Families' Tax Credit, which has been in existence for only a couple of years, will become known as the Working Tax Credit as it will also apply to people who don't have children. The Children's Tax Credit, which was also introduced only a couple of years ago, will become known as the Child Tax Credit (for reasons apparently known only to the Government).

In spite of the myriad benefits, allowances and tax credits available, there are numerous people who struggle on low incomes and don't claim half of what they're entitled to – mainly because they simply don't know about them. For example, at the end of December 2001, about 5 million families were eligible for the Children's Tax Credit and yet only 3.7 million had actually claimed it. Frankly, it's not that surprising when the system chops and changes every couple of years – just as you get used to hearing about one thing, you suddenly find that it doesn't exist any more and something else has been introduced instead.

It's even more confusing when the Government changes the name of a benefit just to make it sound better. For example, what we used to call 'the dole' was known as Unemployment Benefit until it was changed to the supposedly prettier title of Jobseeker's Allowance. If you're under the age of 60 you might be getting Income Support, whereas if you're over 60 it suddenly and magically becomes known as the Minimum Income Guarantee. When it comes to help with getting back into employment, there's a New Deal for Lone Parents, a New Deal for Partners, a New Deal for Young People and a New Deal for Over-25s! In fact, on the Government's website about benefits (www.dss.gov.uk, although it's now known as the Department for Work and Pensions, of course), we counted more than 60 different types of grants, allowances and benefits in their A–Z list before losing track, ranging from Cold Weather Payments for pensioners to Child Benefit for kids.

So if you're confused, tell us about it!

Anyway, let's start with unravelling what you might be entitled to before April 2003 and then we'll cover how it's expected to work after that. Bear in mind that this comparatively new system of 'credits' comes mostly in the form of tax relief rather than in actual money. It's much easier for the Inland Revenue not to take so much off you in the first place than have the Benefits Agency actively pay money into your bank account (although this will change slightly after April 2003).

Working Families' Tax Credit

The current Working Families' Tax Credit (WFTC) is the Government's attempt to encourage people on low incomes to stay in work. It means you or your partner will get more in your pay packet. The amount of WFTC you get depends on the number and age of children in your family, the income coming into the household, the hours you work and the amount of childcare charges you pay. You can now apply for this while you are on maternity leave and your Statutory Maternity Pay of £75 a week will *not* count as income. At the moment, it's paid for six months, after which time you have to re-apply.

To qualify, you or your partner must be working for 16 hours or more a week – whether as an employee or as a self-employed person – and have one or more dependent children under 16 (or under 19 if in full-time education) living with you. You must have savings of £8,000 or less and be resident in the UK. In the 2002/03 tax year, if your current income is £94.50 a week or less you could get a combination of:

- £60 for one adult (even if there are two of you)
- £11.65 if one of you works 30 hours or more a week
- £26.45 for each child up to 16 years old (or £27.20 for those over 16)
- Childcare tax credit worth 70% of eligible childcare costs, up to a maximum of £135 for one child or £200 for two or more children

If you earn more than £94.50 a week, your maximum WFTC will be reduced by 55 pence for each £1 of income above £94.50. In theory, it's possible to earn more than £30,000 a year and still be entitled to receive WFTC. So, if money is tight, and the sums for WFTC work out for you, you could at least have the certainty of some extra cash for six months. There are other benefits too: for example, if your income amounts to less than £222 a week, you're entitled to various NHS benefits such as free dental care.

You can find out if you qualify for WFTC by contacting your local Benefits Office, any Inland Revenue enquiry offices or the WFTC Helpline (phone on 0845 609 5000).

Children's Tax Credit

The Children's Tax Credit (CTC) is a form of tax relief that could put an extra £529 a year into the pockets of low- to middle-income parents each year. As always, it depends on how much you earn as to whether you qualify, but essentially CTC can be claimed by married couples, unmarried couples or by single parents with at least one child living with them who is under the age of 16 at the start of the 2002/03 tax year. The full credit of £529 works on a sliding scale and is reduced at the rate of £1 for every £15 of income taxed at the Higher Rate. So, for rough guidance, if one of you is a Higher Rate taxpayer, then the chances of getting this extra tax relief taper out once your income reaches around £42,000.

To increase support for families with the youngest children, the Children's Tax Credit is worth up to £1,049 in the first year of the child's birth. This new 'baby rate' is also subject to the tapered reduction of £1 for every £15 of income taxed at the higher rate, but it allows tax relief for household incomes of up to £49,000.

Don't forget that, for the time being, you don't actually receive a payment for the Children's Tax Credit. If you qualify, the Inland Revenue will simply adjust your or your partner's tax code so that you pay slightly less income tax via your salary. Also, it's irrelevant how many children you have: there is only one credit per household.

If you aren't sure whether you can claim, ring the Inland Revenue's Children's Tax Credit Helpline (phone on 0845 300 1036).

The changes to the tax and child credits system don't come in until April 2003, but they are spelt out in a Government document thrillingly entitled 'The Child and Working Tax Credits: The Modernisation of Britain's Tax and Benefit System'. This can be found on the Treasury's website at http://www.hm-treasury.gov.uk/mediastore/otherfiles/new_tax_credits.pdf. Alternatively, you can get a copy by ringing the Treasury (phone on 020 7270 4558). It's only 45 pages, if you can bear to read it!

There is a section in this document which details how awards will be calculated and the criteria for eligibility. An interesting change is that families with gross household incomes of up to £66,000 will be entitled to something, however small, so don't think that you won't qualify if you have an income approaching anywhere near this figure. If you're entitled, then claim it!

In the meantime, we'll cover a few of the basic reforms so you'll know what to look out for when they're implemented.

The new Working Tax Credit (from April 2003)

The main difference with the new Working Tax Credit is that it is applicable to working people *without* children as well as families *with* children. It's irrelevant who is or isn't working, since the credit will be based simply on the level of income coming to each household.

It's designed to guarantee a minimum income of £237 a week for, say, a family with one earner and one child. Couples with no children and, say, a single earner are guaranteed a minimum weekly income of £183. A single person over 25 with no children is guaranteed an income of £154.

Unlike the Working Families' Tax Credit, you won't have to apply for it every six months. The credit award will remain in place for the entire tax year, regardless of when you apply and even if you or your partner gets a pay rise (as long as it's not more than £2,500). If you suffer a sudden fall in income levels through, for example, job loss or because you've started paying for childcare, you can apply to be re-assessed. If you've got savings – even if they're more than £8,000 - you will still be eligible. The Inland Revenue will simply include the income from those savings as part of their overall calculation.

The new Child Tax Credit (from April 2003)

The new Child Tax Credit is designed to streamline all the various 'child' elements currently available via different benefits. For example, there are child elements in Income Support, the Jobseeker's Allowance, the Working Families' Tax Credit, the Disabled Person's Tax Credit and, rather obviously, the Children's Tax Credit. Phew! All the child-related elements will be taken out of these benefits and brought together under the single Child Tax Credit.

Again, it will be based on overall household income, thus removing an anomaly under the old system where a single earner on a high income was not entitled even though a dual-earning family on the same income was.

Another key change is that any Child Tax Credit will be paid direct to the primary carer in the same way as Child Benefit. So, in the case of a mother who stays at home with the children while the father goes out to work, all the child elements of the tax credit relating to his salary will be effectively removed and paid into the mother's bank account. For women with controlling partners or who dislike having no money of their own, this will at least provide them with a personal income stream.

For families with an income of less than £13,000 a year, you can expect a minimum of £54.25 a week (including Child Benefit) if you have one child, with a further £38.50 for a second or any subsequent child. Families with a household income of up to £50,000 can expect a minimum of £26.50 a week for one child (including Child Benefit). Depending on how many children you've got, for those earning slightly more than £13,000 or £50,000, it will work on a taper system with a deduction of 37 pence for every £1 earned over and above those figures. Essentially, it means that families with incomes of up to £58,000 are likely to be eligible. And, since the higher 'baby rate' in the first year of birth will apply, even parents earning as much as £66,000 will be entitled to something.

Child running costs

We decided very early on as parents that it was better to have a dozen second-hand baby grows than three brand new ones for the same money! My first daughter was a sicky thing who puked on her clothes several times a day in the first few months. We couldn't have managed without my mountain of charity shop bargains! Also they often have good toys. Loads of bargain presents for Xmas this year!

From the Motley Fool discussion boards

To run a child you need to be able to pay for its fuel, regular maintenance and check-ups, the cost of keeping the body-work clean and shiny and, of course, making it burglar-proof. Oh no, hang on, that's cars. Children, now, are a different matter.

Let's just start with the first year of a child's life – a particularly expensive time as you probably won't even be earning to offset the expenses. If you have the money, and don't mind spending it, there are lots of delightful and expensive things to buy for a new baby. If money *is* an issue, however, there are many ways of cutting costs and even sacrificing some things without depriving either you or your baby. These are some average costs for clothes and equipment for the first year of a child's life, although you may find them more cheaper or dearer depending on where you live and what your standards are!

AVERAGE COSTS		
	Cot	£49.99
	Cot bedding	£29.99
	Mattress	£24.99
	Moses basket	£49.98
	Pushchair and raincover	£178.99
	Lightweight buggy	£29.99
	Car seat	£29.99
	Baby bath	£20.00
	Steriliser	£9.99
	Breast pump	£19.99

Six bottles	£11.37
Monitor	£49.99
Highchair	£39.99
Changing bag	£15.00
Changing mat	£7.00
Disposable nappies	£268.00
Wipes	£240.00
Skincare essentials	£120.00
Medicines	£12.36
Milk	£412.56
Food	£471.84

Clothes (0–3 months)

Six sleepsuits	£24.00
Six vests	£14.00
Cardigan	£7.00
Hat and mittens	£10.00
Seven bibs	£3.99

Clothes (3–6 months)

Six sleepsuits	£24.00
Six vests	£14.00
Cardigan or jumper	£10.00
Two dresses or dungarees	£28.00
Coat	£15.00
Six pairs of socks	£6.00

Clothes (6–12 months)

Six sleepsuits	£24.00
Six vests	£14.00
Cardigan or jumper	£10.00
Three dresses or trousers	£24.00
Coat	£18.00
Hat	£5.50
Six pairs of socks	£6.00

You can easily spend much more than this, as we haven't included the cost of painting and furnishing a nursery, buying velvet babygrows embroidered with the family crest or the price of that necessary silver spoon, without which any baby is, of course, a deprived child. If you *want* to spend more, you certainly can.

However, you can also spend a lot less. Many items on the list are not strictly necessary. For example, midwives say that just a plain washing-up bowl will do to bath baby in the first few months of its life and many parents do perfectly well without a Moses basket or a changing bag. A lot of clothes can be bought second-hand and if you have friends, relatives or neighbours who have recently had babies they will often hand over clothes that are now too small but still have a lot of wear left in them. If you breastfeed, not only will you ensure the best nutrition for your baby (and lose any weight gained during pregnancy yourself) but you will also save yourself over £400 in powdered milk, bottles and sterilisers.

So there are always ways of cutting down on costs. The discussion boards on the Motley Fool website, such as Living Below Your Means and Family Fools, have several ideas, so, if you are not already a devotee, check them out.

As your children grow, the costs will change and vary depending on where you live and how you like to live. If you're planning on sending them to private school, you'll need to consider how you will pay their huge fees (we have never come across a private school that doesn't charge huge fees). Apart from that expense, the other drain on your funds – if you are planning on going back to work – will be paying others to look after your little ones until they are old enough to go to school.

Childcare options

This is where the costs really start mounting up. If you think you can manage on one salary, or you just can't bear the idea of someone else looking after your child, then skip this section. If you'd like to go back to work after having your baby, you may find that the cost of paying someone to look after the little one is the same as (if not more than) your or your partner's salary. Once you've looked at the options and done the sums, don't be surprised if you decide that you or your partner (whoever is earning less and would be the better child carer) would do better to stay at home and bring up your child full time, rather than pay someone else to do it.

There are various childcare options around and all of them – apart from blackmailing the grandparents to do it – will really cost. You won't be surprised to hear that Britain lags behind most of Europe when it comes to free or state-subsidised care for pre-school children, with working parents having to cope with expensive nursery places, long working hours and inflexible parental leave. You cannot put childcare costs against tax, something for which several organisations are campaigning, so far in vain.

If you do want to hand your child over to a carer, the cheapest option is a childminder, who will cost an average of £90 a week (£4,680 a year). One disadvantage of childminders is that they look after children in his or her own home, so you have to get your children there and pick them up in the evening. Another is that childminders can look after more than one child at a time, including their own, so you cannot be sure that your child will get the attention he or she deserves. Childminders are regulated and (supposedly) checked by the local authority so they are, on the whole, safe. The level of checking varies from local authority to local authority, however, and some are far more lax than others.

Nursery places are more expensive at about £110–£140 a week (£5,700–£7,280 a year), depending on where you live (which is more than the average couple spends on housing or food). Again, you have the disadvantage of having to take the child to and from the nursery, which may not fit in with your working hours. It's also hard to monitor what goes on inside a nursery while you are not there. Nurseries are very good for socialising children though and can be particularly beneficial for an only child who might otherwise miss out on playmates. To afford a nursery place for one child you would need to be earning at least £5,970 to £8,200 a year.

The most expensive full-time childcare option is to have a live-in or live-out nanny. Again, prices vary depending on where you live, but on average you should expect to pay £200–£300 a week (net) for a live-in nanny (£20,436 gross a year) and £250–£350 a week (net) for a live-out (daily) nanny (£24,260 gross a year). You can cut these costs almost in half by doing a 'nanny share', whereby your child and your neighbour's child are both cared for by one nanny and you share the cost. The advantage of nannies is that they look after your child in your house and are devoted solely to the care of your child – they will not be spending time looking after others instead. Also, they'll often look after your house while you are not there and can deal with workmen, deliveries and all the other nuisances of owning a home. However, according to Nannytax, a company that runs nanny payrolls, to afford a full-time nanny you will need to be earning £27,548–£32,819 a year. In fact, if you are just earning that you'll effectively be going out to work purely to pay for the nanny, so, realistically, you would want your salary to be some way above that.

Au pairs are not proper child carers and should not be employed as such. Unlike nannies, au pairs are not trained or qualified to look after children, although you might be lucky enough to find one with a bit of experience. They should *never* be left in charge of children under three and should really only be looked on as an extra pair of hands to you, whatever the age of your children. Au pairs are not paid a salary: they are given about £45 a week 'pocket money' as well as room and board with you, the chance to speak English and soak up some British culture, all in return for some *light* housework and help with the kids.

How to make your child a millionaire

So we've gone on about how to claw in extra pennies when you're struggling to keep the family fed and watered, but if you're some way above the breadline and you've got a bit of cash to spare, you're probably wondering how to invest it well for your offspring. The emphasis on having children to add to the household income has largely disappeared in the last few decades. For centuries, a large part of the reason for having children was so that they could provide for you in your old age and, in fact, this is still true for huge swathes of the developing world. In developed countries, however, the old process of scraping a living to keep the family fed while the kids are growing up and then sending the older children off to work to help to support their ageing parents has largely disappeared. Now many of us are becoming more and more able to shift some of our own resources in the direction of our children's long-term security. Rather than expecting them to care for us in our old-age, we are putting money aside for our own retirement *and* considering our children's greater needs in times to come when State Pension provision may be phased out completely.

As well as thinking about helping your child in their older years, you may be considering sending them to a private school a few years hence and so are wondering about the best vehicle in which to save money for that and, probably, for their university fees. There are hundreds of specialist savings pots on offer for people just like you. You've probably seen their advertisements in newspapers. Some will have sent you glossy brochures already with charming photos of happy parents and their beaming, school-uniformed children. Would you be being a loving and sensible parent to save money in one of these schemes? Sadly, you probably wouldn't. In fact, there are many, many investment vehicles that seem specially tailored for parents that, when you actually come to use them, are quite clearly specially tailored for the profit of the companies providing them. Be wary here and follow our advice on what to invest in and what *not* to invest in for your child's long-term benefit.

What not *to bother with*

Premium Bonds. These have been a great favourite of most people's grandparents because, as a Government-backed vehicle, they are very, very safe. Not only that but there's always the chance – somewhat greater than the Lottery – of winning 'the big one'. Even if you don't win the top prize there are enough little prizes to give you a long-term average return of around 3% per year. As it is tax-free that means it's equivalent to a 5% gross return for a Higher Rate taxpayer, although if your children are Higher Rate taxpayers we would like to know why anyone is bothering to give them Premium Bonds. Given that children can earn a lot of interest before being taxed anyway, the whole tax-free thing is not particularly impressive here. So, in terms of a useful product for investing for kids, Premium Bonds leave *much* to be desired.

National Savings accounts. These were similarly a great favourite with people's grannies a while back. Again, they are safe and easy to manage: it's just a question of depositing money at the Post Office. But the returns have been generally poor – just 2% on average. There are National Savings Children's Bonus Bonds that are fixed-term, five-year investments, which offer a guaranteed return with a bonus, but you can only invest up to £1,000. All in all a safe bet, but not really worth it.

Friendly Societies. These are like credit unions in that they were originally set up when local groups of people got together to form mutual savings societies. Everyone is entitled to hold one Friendly Society savings plan, which is not taxable. Children's plans can be kept in place until they are 18 or 21, although adults' plans can be kept for only 10 years. The maximum you can invest in any of these plans is £25 a month, which is probably quite enough for the majority of parents, particularly new ones. However, Friendly Societies' charges tend to be rather high – usually about £2 a month. Also, the investments are usually based on insurance products (a type of endowment) and their returns are traditionally very poor. Not only that, but as children have their own tax exemption the tax-free status is of no advantage to them. Not worth the bother.

Endowments. The majority of savings and investment plans that come neatly packaged for parents, bearing names like 'Send Your Cat to University – Jewel-Encrusted Bond', are basically dressed-up endowments. There are many of them on the market because the moneymen worked out long ago that they were a quick and easy way of making good profits.

Essentially they work like endowment mortgages (mmm... everyone's favourite financial product). Here you invest your money in a 'with-profits' insurance vehicle in the hope that it will provide a big enough lump sum at some future date to cover a specific expense – maybe when the sproggling has cheated enough at his exams to get into university. According to a recent estimate, between half a million and 3 million people who have endowment-based mortgages are unlikely to get enough out of them to pay for their houses. Perhaps this is because the first two years' worth of your payments are often creamed off by the investment company in charges and commission before any of it is actually invested in anything likely to give you some sort of a return. Would that make a difference? Ooh, we think so. Knowing this probably doesn't make you want to trust your children's investment money to an insurance company, now, does it? No. Good.

Banks and building societies. We're not completely ruling these out, at least as short-term depositories for your cash (see page 107 for more information on this). Unless you are only ever going to put really, *really*, small amounts of money aside for your little one's future, none of the banks or building societies can offer anything like a good enough interest rate for the long term. If you can afford to put regular amounts into your child's savings then walk straight past their portals onto more lucrative investments.

Anything on the telly. You'd be amazed at the amount of really bad financial packages that are sold on the TV, often thanks to the services of B- and C-list celebrities who clearly haven't bothered to find out what kind of rip-offs these products are. If you can watch any of these adverts (including the 'Need a loan?' or 'Have you been hurt in an accident that wasn't your fault?' ones) without shouting and throwing things at the TV, then you need to read more of this book. These advertisements are the modern equivalent of the door-to-door endowment salesmen who used to plague our streets. The only advantage is that the TV ads don't force you to get up out of your chair to answer the door.

Anything that offers a free gift. Yes, that's a bit of a giveaway, isn't it? 'We're so desperate for you to buy this without asking too many questions, we'll give you an engraved ballpoint pen as a bribe' is actually what they're saying. If you see a free gift attached to any financial product you know it will be a bad call. Don't do it. It's not worth it. This pretty much applies to every product from prettied-up endowment plans to basic bank accounts.

So what can I invest in?

Good question. Having knocked down a whole tranche of traditionally favoured investments, you may be wondering if there's anything left. Well yes, dear reader, there certainly is.

First of all, certain bank and building society accounts are a good place to start an investment plan for your children. Not that they are exactly fabulous investment vehicles on their own in the long term, as we have just pointed out, but in the short term they're very useful for collecting up enough cash to plonk into a serious product later on. You might be able to put some or all of your Child Benefit into it each month plus any bits of cash that Auntie Bertha or Grandma Ermintrude gives for birthdays and Christmases. It's very sensible to use them for just such a purpose, particularly if you find the highest-paying accounts to save in for the short term.

Interest rates will change regularly, of course, so any new parent needs to have a look around to see what is currently being offered before making a choice. From our experience we would advise you not to waste your time on the banks. In almost every case they underperform the building societies, particularly the dwindling number of mutuals, when it comes to savings accounts. Shop around and remember that, for the purposes of collecting a decent amount of money for your child over a year or so, you don't need instant access. This is good, as you generally get the highest interest rates on the 60- or 90-day-notice accounts.

Probably the best way to set up an account is to do it in your own name (and that of your partner if you like) but to designate your child as the beneficiary. This is known as a bare trust. This means that while you have control of the account, the money is treated as his or hers and he or she will be able to take control of it upon reaching the age of 18. Make sure you fill in the R85 Inland Revenue form when you do it, though, because that'll mean any interest is paid gross. You could open the account simply in your child's name, which would mean that he or she would effectively have control over it (unless you manage to hide the pass book cleverly enough). In general, banks and building societies offer slightly better rates for special children's accounts, so you might feel it is worth opening one, even if you don't legally have control over it.

One thing you will have to be careful of is making a gift to your child that earns them income of more than £100 in any tax year, as the whole amount will count as your own income for tax purposes. With two parents there is a £200 limit (described by the Inland Revenue as £100 in respect of gifts from each parent, not £200 shared, if you see what they mean). This rule applies only to gifts from parents, directly or indirectly, not other relatives or friends or on money given from other sources. Children have the same income tax allowance as adults. Admittedly, given the very small amounts of interest you can earn each year in bank or building society accounts, you would have to be depositing truly serious amounts of cash in the first place to earn that kind of money. So, income tax is unlikely to be something you'll need to worry about when it comes to savings accounts, although it could become a problem after a few years of investing money in higher-paying investment vehicles.

Time is on their side – and therefore on yours

If you've read all of the book up to this chapter, it's likely you'll already be guessing what we're going to advise as a good, sensible, higher performing investment vehicle for your child's money. But before we get to the best bit, let's just step back for a moment and look at what your children have going for them (apart from your brains and beauty and their father's... well... their father's... oh, come on, there must be something good about him). As far as investing is concerned, the major advantage your children have is *time*. As you will have noticed in earlier chapters, thanks to the Miracle of Compound Returns, even relatively small investments can grow exponentially into impressively large ones when given enough time to do so. As you will have seen from the graph on page 112, the longer you invest in the stock market (for yes, dear reader, that is what we'll be suggesting) the more its ups and downs are smoothed out and the more you benefit from its overall upward climb.

Our advice for a long-term investment for your children's future wealth is (cue fanfare) buying an index-tracker or else shares in good-quality public companies on the developed world's stock markets.

Shares, that's what you want, probably through an index tracker. If you go for shares in hand-picked companies then it will be good-quality companies that you're looking for, ones that you think will still be around and doing well in 30, 40 or even 50 or 60 years. Just think what kind of riches you would now be earning if your parents had had the foresight to buy you shares in, say, IBM, Coca-Cola or American Express when you were just a wee one. Isn't that what you would like for your children? Of course, none of us can predict the future, but by spending some time and effort studying companies and learning how to invest cannily for the long term, you and your family will unquestionably reap benefits.

What? Spend time and effort on it, you gasp? Surely you can't be trusted to learn about the stock market to the degree that you could invest in it for your children's future? It's one thing to risk your own money, but your children's? Surely a nice, educated, braces-wearing stockbroker who does this sort of thing for a living would be much better at it? Well, let's see. Who in the world do you honestly think has your children's future health, wealth and happiness most at heart? The school? The Government? A stockbroker? Your neighbours? No, of course, it's you and, probably, your partner. You care about their future more than anyone else and you'll want to do the best for them more than anyone else. You have a brain, you can read and, frankly, so long as you have access to the Internet and can learn from the Motley Fool website (www.fool.co.uk) or you can buy the Motley Fool training books, *The Motley Fool UK Investment Guide* and *The Motley Fool UK Investment Workbook*, you'll be making very good decisions in no time at all.

In fact, as a woman you have an added advantage when investing for your children because women are generally more patient than men. Gross generalisation, we know, and, if we're honest, we'd have to admit that neither of us is especially good at waiting for anything, but *on the whole* women tend to be among the more patient members of the population. You see, the thing is, if you are investing money for your children, the best strategy to adopt is to tuck the money away for a minimum of five years – preferably much longer – and forget about it until your child comes of age. Of course, you're not going to forget about it completely. Once or twice a year, you might like to check that the company is heading in the right direction, but apart from that occasional look you won't need to bother about it at all for several years. There, that's not difficult, is it?

The question is, how do you invest in shares and which ones do you go for?

First of all, if you are buying shares or units of a tracker fund for your child, buy them in your name. Normally, you add the child's initials after yours to designate that the shares, or units, are held on your child's behalf. This is known as a 'bare trust'. It's easy to set up and needs no involvement from a solicitor. As parents you act as bare trustees, looking after the investment on behalf of the child until they can be registered in the child's name. This will be when he or she reaches the age of 18 (16 in Scotland) and you, as trustees, have to hand over the assets of the trust. The bare trust essentially separates all the investments in it from your own investments for taxation purposes, but still gives you complete control over them. They offer the child no protection from irresponsible parents (although if you are reading this then you could hardly be described as irresponsible, could you?), but it's the best way for you to handle the investments without incurring tax yourself. Another advantage is that children have their own CGT allowance and there's also no Inheritance Tax charged charged if you are unfortunate enough to shuffle off this mortal coil before your child reaches the age of 18.

If you want to, you can register your bare trust (it costs just 50 pence) by getting a 'Declaration of Trust' from your local tax office, filling in the form and sending it off together with your shiny 50 pence piece. There seems to be no advantage in doing so but still some people like to.

Free money

You may feel that you don't have any money to invest for your children, but what about Child Benefit? Currently parents get £15.75 per week for the first child and £10.55 a week for subsequent children. Let's say you have one child. If you invest his or her Child Benefit, which comes to £68.25 a month, into an index tracker every month for the 16 years that you receive it, then, assuming an average return of 6.4%, you will have £22,477 as a lump sum by the time he or she has reached maturity (at least physically, if not emotionally or socially). If you are a lone parent and in the incredibly lucky position of being able to do without your £17.55 a week Child Benefit for your eldest child, you could create £25,046. Who says you don't have any material riches to give to your child?

Children's Tax

Children do sometimes have to pay tax and, like the taxation of adults, the rules can change year on year. The advice we're about to give you here is correct as of April 2002, so if you're reading this more than a year later then things could have changed. That said, the rules are not likely to change drastically and, anyway, you should always check with your local tax office if you have any doubts or queries.

As we've said, children have the same Personal Allowance and Capital Gains Tax allowance as adults, so exploiting these efficiently will go a long way towards maximizing your children's long-term wealth. You wouldn't want money that you have saved for your children falling foul of your own personal taxation limits, would you?

When you open any interest-bearing account for your children, whether it's a savings account or a stockbroker's cash account, make sure you fill in Form R85, as we mentioned earlier. This will make sure that any interest is paid free of tax. You need to fill in the details of your child's savings account and permanent address, and then sign it on his or her behalf. Once past their sixteenth birthday they can sign such forms for themselves.

Take a look at the leaflet IR110, 'A Guide for People with Savings', as well. You should be able to get this from any Inland Revenue office but you can also find it on their website (find at www.inlandrevenue.gov.uk). The current single person's annual income tax allowance for the year 2002/03 is set at £4,615 whilst the annual Capital Gains Tax threshold (the amount you can earn before paying Capital Gains Tax) is set at £7,700. Each of your children can earn these amounts from income and capital gains respectively before becoming liable for any tax (although remember, if income of more than £100 arises from a gift you made to your child, all the income will be treated as yours and not that of the child, as we mentioned earlier). If a child is lucky enough to make any taxable income or capital gains, they must be declared to the Inland Revenue using the usual tax return. Obviously children don't normally receive tax returns (lucky little so-and-sos), therefore it's up to you to request one and make sure it's filled in correctly.

Whatever you do, it's important to establish that the child is the beneficiary of the money you invest. If you just keep the money in the bank or building society accounts and any stock market investments that you make in your own name, with the intention of handing it all over to your loved one on his or her eighteenth birthday, you may be hit with taxation problems. To make the beneficial ownership of the investment clear, all investments should be made in the name of the child.

Pensions for babies

Weird? Unnatural? Maybe, but for a really long-term investment, setting up a Stakeholder Pension for your little one is a pretty good plan (although, admittedly, you may not be around to see it bear fruit). As we've explained in Chapter Seven, Stakeholder Pensions were originally set up to give those on little or no wage – such as women taking a break from work to have children, people on low pay or the unemployed – the chance to contribute to a pension, thereby taking some of the burden off the Government. What the Government hadn't bargained for was that a number of families with cash to spare realised that as *anyone* could have a Stakeholder Pension, regardless of age or earnings status, even babies could have one. The scheme is tax-efficient for you and for your baby, which, of course, will mean a lot to him or her at this stage. Since the Government will chip in an extra 22% it also gives you a chance to invest in something that he or she won't be able to get their chubby hands on and fritter away until they need a pension, by which time there will probably be little or no State Pension.

Another plus is that you can stop and start contributions as you wish, so if you start a plan on behalf of a child and your financial circumstances change, you can stop without penalty. There is also the advantage of granny and grandpa, if they have some money to invest, being able to pass on money that might otherwise be liable for inheritance tax to their grandchildren through a Stakeholder Pension.

Under the Stakeholder Pension scheme everyone can contribute up to £2,808 a year with the Inland Revenue adding a further 22%, thereby boosting the maximum annual contribution to £3,600. Given that time is very much on your baby's side, if you pay the maximum amount into their pension for the first ten years, you'll have possibly sorted out all their pension needs for life. Sounds incredible? Well, not if you remember that it'll be at least 50 years before he or she decides to draw down their pension; in that time even a smallish lump sum will grow to something impressive because of (everybody join in the chorus) the Miracle of Compound Returns!

Even if you can't afford to invest the full allowable amount each year, putting Child Benefit into a Stakeholder Pension for a rather longer period can create a sizeable sum too. Research from HSBC bank shows that if you invest the allowance from birth up to the age of 18 in a Stakeholder Pension then, assuming premiums increase in line with the retail price index, by the time he or she is 65 the total fund value could be worth around half a million. You can also console yourself with the fact that pension contributions, however small, made at this point in your child's life will be worth more than the equivalent contributions made during the 42 years of their own working life between the ages of 18 and 60.

Teaching children the value of money and saving

The easiest way to teach your children about finance is to get them involved. Teach them the Miracle of Compound Returns. Teach them how money invested sensibly will grow, and how, when the growth is added in, that will also start to grow. Children are amazing in their capacity to absorb and learn.

One of the most important things that you can teach your children is not to waste their money on the National Lottery, scratch cards or other highly improbable get-rich-quick schemes. And that means leading by example, too! Teach them not to run up credit-card debt, especially during those vital first few years away from home when they're at university or starting their first job. Teach them to save money. Open a building society account for them and get them to pay the money in themselves. Instil in them the importance of saving. Introduce the idea of buying shares in companies, especially in ones that they'll have heard of:

if he or she has a stake in the business, your Manchester United-mad child is going to become as interested in the financial performance of the company as the football results. Investing for children should be fun, and they should be involved in making the decisions.

From what we've read, it seems there's no other way of learning how to manage money unless children have a regular income out of which they can save as well as buy. Obviously, what the allowance money should be used for depends on the age of the child. A five-year-old can certainly put her 20 pence into a piggy bank and understand that she has to use her own money to buy something you don't want to buy for her. On the other hand a thirteen-year-old with her own bank account should be perfectly capable of deciding whether she wants to use her money on the latest top from New Look or a haircut. And if your seventeen-year-old wants to drive a car, she needs to learn the financial cost of doing so.

So, if they want something, make them save up for it. With five- to seven-year-olds, toys are always a good start. Something small so that they can save up enough money over just two or three weeks or, if it's a slightly more expensive item (for them), offer to go halves. You'll probably win in the long run because you won't be reaching for your purse every time your child has a tantrum in the toy shop and he or she will learn to stop demanding that you buy them stuff.

Make sure that the amount of pocket money – or in later years, their allowance – is always paid on time. Keep to your side of the bargain. After all, your boss doesn't pay you whenever he or she happens to remember and so your children shouldn't be given the runaround either. Knowing they have a certain amount coming their way every week helps them to plan. As they get older, open a bank account for them so they can learn about paying in and drawing out cash.

One method that parents often use to teach their children about money is to pay them for doing the odd chore around the house. It's debatable whether this is a good thing or not because you are really linking two separate issues. On the one hand, you give them chores to do so they learn to be a responsible member of the household while the pocket money or allowance enables them to learn how to manage money. Do you really want to hand out 50 pence every time your 10-year-old empties the rubbish? The same goes for withdrawing pocket money as a punishment for not doing the chores.

Perhaps this method would be better used when your child needs to earn some extra money for a special item and is willing to do over and above the usual around the house in order to achieve a goal. Finally, if you really want to get your children interested in money, try setting them up with a virtual online portfolio at the Motley Fool website. One of our regular Fools did just this with his family as a competition. Each of them had a virtual portfolio with the aim of seeing who would choose the fastest-growing shares over a given period. Not surprisingly, he suffered a bit of a blow to his ego when his nine-year-old daughter beat him, his wife and his older son hands down during the first year!

You can get more in-depth advice and information on investing for your children and teaching them how to run their finances later on in the Motley Fool book called *Make Your Child a Millionaire*. A must for any parent (although we would say that, wouldn't we?)

Paying for your student offspring

If you do manage to teach your kids the value of money and the importance of saving, they'll be streets ahead of everyone else when they come to take their place at one of the hallowed Student Union bars somewhere in the country. Financially, life is not easy for students nowadays, and it can be just as tough, if not more so, for their increasingly impoverished parents.

A good place to find out how much the Government will pay for your child's further education, and how much you will have to pay, is the Department for Education and Skills' website (www.dfes.gov.uk). There's a lot of helpful information there for students and parents, together with forms and guides that you can download.

As you will find out from the website, you have to start with your Local Education Authority (LEA) to find out what your child is entitled to from the Government. Once your son's or daughter's eligibility for support has been assessed by them, you'll be asked to complete a Financial Assessment form. Using that information your LEA will work out:

● **Any contribution you're expected to make towards the cost of tuition fees, based on your income and your child's situation.** At present the Government subsidises the amount of tuition fees that most students are asked to pay so the maximum amount that students must contribute towards their fees in 2002/03 is £1,100 (this represents about a quarter of the average cost of tuition fees). For 2002/03, students who are financially dependent on their parents and whose parents' residual income (parental income before deductions, minus certain allowances) is less than £20,480 will not have to pay any fees at all. On the other hand, students who are financially dependent on their parents and whose parents' residual income is more than £30,502 will be asked to pay the full £1,100 fee.

● **The amount of loan your son or daughter can take out.** Loans are available to help students with their living costs. All eligible students can take out up to 75% of the maximum loan available. The remaining 25% of the loan is subject to income assessment. Your LEA will calculate how much of this remaining amount your son or daughter will be eligible to apply for. The maximum amount (100%) of loan available for 2002/03 is £3,905 for students living away from home, £4,815 for students in London and living away from home and £3,090 for students living at home. These loans have a very low rate of interest (roughly equivalent to the rate of inflation). You can get more information on these in the Government leaflet 'Guidance on Terms and Conditions', which you can get through their website (www.dfes.gov.uk). The day-to-day management of loan accounts is handled by the Student Loans Company (SLC). For information you can check out their website (www.studentloans.gov.uk).

● **Extra help that your son or daughter may be eligible for.** There's also a range of other help available through LEAs for students going into higher education. This includes help for:

  - students with dependants
  - lone parent students
  - students with disabilities
  - students in care
  - students incurring extra travel costs

Once your child is at college, he or she can get extra financial help with living expenses or course costs through the college. This help is discretionary and is based on an individual's circumstances. Tell your child to contact the admissions tutors or student welfare services section if he or she needs a Hardship loan or other help.

There's a strong argument for your child to borrow as much as possible through the Student Loans Company, as it's very cheap. The interest rate is currently well under 2% because inflation is so low, so it's probably the cheapest loan they will ever get. If inflation takes off they need not worry because the interest on a Student Loan is capped at 1% above base rates. If they're clever they could even invest some of it and make a bit of money by the time they graduate, although most are not clever with their money and are likely to spend it all and more.

That said, it's still better for students to graduate with just a Student Loan to pay off rather than credit-card debt and expensive bank overdrafts. It could be better for you, too, if they borrow as much as possible through the Student Loans Company, rather than take money from you, as the student rate is much lower than the average interest on deposit accounts.

The best gift you can give your student offspring, though, is freedom from as much debt as possible. Point them in the direction of the Motley Fool website, make sure they register with us, learn how to get out of debt (so they know to avoid it) and keep checking the 'Living Below Your

Means' discussion boards. The Motley Fool's book, *How to Invest When You Don't Have Any Money*, will also give them lots of ideas on how to live frugally and get the most from their cash.

What students need to live on, 2002– 2003

(from the *Observer* newspaper, 26 May 2002)

2002

Final-year rates	What students need to live on	Maximum loan available	Basic loan available to all students	Parental contributions
London	£7,560	£4,815	£3,610	£2,305
Elsewhere	£6,140	£3,905	£2,930	£2,075
Living at home in London	£3,600	£3,090	£2,320	£1,870
Living at home elsewhere	£3,100	£3,090	£2,320	£1,870

2003

Final-year rates	What students need to live on	Maximum loan available	Basic loan available to all students	Parental contributions
London	£7,560	£4,175	£3,130	£2,145
Elsewhere	£6,140	£3,390	£2,545	£1,945
Living at home in London	£3,600	£2,700	£2,020	£1,780
Living at home elsewhere	£3,100	£2,700	£2,020	£1,780

(Calculations based on NUS figures for the 2001/02 academic year, rent inflated by 5% and other costs by 2.5% and excluding tuition fees.)

WHAT STUDENTS NEED TO LIVE ON

If your children are still relatively young, now is a good time to start saving for their university support. Naturally, the Wise have got there before you and will be trying to sell you their 'Pay Your Son's University Bar Bill Investment Fund' or whatever, but ignore all those. Why not set up a separate tracker fund – through an ISA if you haven't used up your £7,000 limit yourself – specifically ear-marked for the dreaded university days coming up in a few years? If you've got five or more years to go before they leave school and move up to higher education, that will be a good way of making your money work for you and your child.

If your son or daughter is about to plunge into the world of university fees and expenses within a year or less, start looking into the grants and loans situation now. There's a lot of excellent advice on the www.support4learning.co.uk website, including an independent view of different bank accounts, student loans, grants and advice on managing your money. The NUS website (www.nus.org.uk) also has a lot of helpful information.

Where there's a Will...

We really couldn't leave a chapter on caring for, paying for and investing for children without mentioning two boring, somewhat depressing, but oh-so-important subjects: making a Will and taking out life assurance.

First, re-read the relevant section in Chapter Eight about why it's so important to make a Will – particularly when you have children. Second, for life assurance, you need to decide who is totally dependent on you for income. If you've got a fair bit of equity in your home, you can always take a gamble that property prices will remain high enough that your family could sell the property and move somewhere smaller - in which case you may feel you don't need life assurance.

But if people are dependent on you, decide how much of a lump sum would be needed to pay off the mortgage and how many years' worth of your annual income they'll need to keep them financially comfortable for as long as necessary. Perhaps you've got children who'll need to be seen through school and university or a partner who can't take your place as the breadwinner.

If we listened to insurance companies, we'd all be paying out for life assurance worth up to fifteen times our annual income. A person earning £20,000 would end up buying £300,000 worth of cover. Don't use their calculations. Work out how much your own family actually needs. Although there's a strong temptation to turn your untimely death into a lottery win for your spouse and kids, there are good reasons not to do this. It's expensive, unnecessary and you'll feel uncomfortable being worth hundreds of thousands of pounds as a corpse, but not much as a living person.

The best way is to multiply your income by the total number of years you think your family will need support and – bingo! You have a do-it-yourself formula for life assurance. The basic rule about buying life assurance is to go for the cheapest deal. All the companies are offering pretty much the same thing, so there's no reason to pay over the odds. If you feel you do need life assurance and would like to know more about the different types available (Term Life Insurance, Whole of Life Policies etc.) then check out the very clear and readable explanations on the Motley Fool website (www.fool.co.uk).

And finally, a word about you

One of the best things about having children is that it takes our minds off ourselves a little and makes us more unselfish. Or at least, it should do. Mothers, particularly, often make the mistake of putting their own financial future in jeopardy by stopping their investments and pension contributions to cope with family expenses. Obviously, if money is really tight, you have to prioritise and you may have to cut down on your own investments and pension contributions. If at all possible, however, keep at least some of them going. The Government introduced Stakeholder

Pensions in 2001 partly to allow mothers taking time out from work to continue to contribute to a pension. Your husband or partner can make contributions for you, so make sure you discuss this with him before you stop work. Becoming a mother does not mean losing your financial independence.

10

Splitting Up

Take care to get what you like or you will be forced to like what you get.

George Bernard Shaw

One of the best things about getting divorced must surely be losing the in-laws, or rather 'out-laws', as some people like to call them. Just think, you won't have to do Christmas with them any more, although if you've got kids one assumes they'll be wanting to keep in touch with Granny and Grandpa even if you don't necessarily harbour that desire.

At least getting divorced can mean a fresh start whether it's been forced on you or whether you've demanded it. Embrace the opportunity. There may well be moments when you look back and think about all the 'might have beens', but wishes aren't horses and there's little point in pondering on the 'what if' factor. Grab your chance to make a new life for yourself with both hands and look to the future, not the past. Although it can seem like it at the time, splitting up with your partner is not the end of the world.

There's no doubt that relationship break-ups can cause ructions though. Aside from all the practicalities that have to be dealt with, not to mention the emotional trauma, the complexities of the law don't exactly help to smooth the way either. There must be very few amicable separations where neither party is profoundly hurt or miserable about it, and even fewer where the children aren't affected in some way. Let's face it: the divorce rate in the UK is currently running at 40%. That means that for every 100,000 couples marrying this year, there are a further 40,000 couples who will be filing for divorce. So you won't be the only one going through it. You've probably got family or friends who've been there, done that and presumably they came through it okay. You can too – particularly if, where necessary, you can find yourself a sympathetic lawyer who is more inclined to take a constructive approach rather than launch into a vicious battle on your behalf. Bitterness can prove expensive and now is really not the right time for you to start practising to be a bitch.

If you're a 'mere' ex-girlfriend and there is no jointly owned home or children involved, then your disentanglement from the relationship can usually be sorted out privately. While this chapter may prove useful as background information in such circumstances, its aim is really to give women who are facing divorce, or unmarried women who have property or children with their exiting partner, a rough idea of how the system works. There are squillions of books about divorce that explain the nitty-gritty of the legal system and we couldn't possibly hope to cover all the ins and outs in a single chapter. Nonetheless, perhaps we can help with a few of the basics and your approach to them. Your aim is to get out of the relationship intact with as much as you are entitled to so that you can set up on your own again without leaving too much damage trailing behind you.

The key is to focus on the future. That can be hard if you're in so much pain that you feel like a walking zombie on the verge of completely losing the plot. Succumb to the madness of misery now and you may regret it by the time you've found your sanity once more. While it may be hard to imagine ever being happy again, your time will come and you don't want to find that you've handled things with such anger that you've lost out not only emotionally but also financially because of a failure to be rational.

You may well be extremely angry but don't make the separation process about punishing your partner, especially if there are children involved. Whatever happens, he'll always be their father and the more generosity of spirit you can show, the better off they'll be. If he is a jerk, they'll find it out for themselves eventually after all, so there's no need for you to rain on their parade. There are too many parents who use their children as pawns in such situations because it's often the only way they can think of to pay back their ex-partners for all the hurt they've caused. They forget that children grow up and that their memories are not necessarily as short as the parents might hope. So, be better, not bitter. And get used to it.

None of this means, of course, that you should allow your ex to trample over you in the rush for the exit. An experienced family lawyer told Jane that five years after a divorce, men usually find themselves in as good a financial position as they were before the divorce. Women usually don't. So bear that in mind when your solicitor appears to be trying to get a better settlement for you than you think is fair.

As a married woman you have legal rights and, regardless of marital status, so do your children. Unmarried women face rather more uncertainty during a relationship break-up because, much as the term 'common-law wife' is bandied about, it's a myth that the courts recognise it. Either way, there'll be questions to resolve. Where will you live? Where will the children live? Who's going to pay for what?

What happens depends on the circumstances surrounding the breakdown of the relationship, but it may be possible to discuss these things and come to an agreement between yourselves or, if necessary, with the help of a counselling or mediation service. If you really wanted to, you and your husband could handle the entire divorce on a do-it-yourself basis: the relevant forms are available from the Court Service website (www.courtservice.gov.uk/fandl/menu_div.html).

Unless there are no children and your financial situation is absolutely cut and dried, we would strongly advise you to get yourself an experienced divorce lawyer so you can be sure of your rights and obligations. Your financial future will be dependent on getting the right settlement in the first place – it's an investment in your future – so choose wisely. Contact the Solicitors Family Law Association (phone on 01689 850227 or find at www.sfla.co.uk) for a list of solicitors in your area who use a non-confrontational approach to divorce. The Law Society's website (www.solicitors-online.com) will also let you search for family lawyers who offer Legal Aid. The important thing is to try to stay rational. Know what your rights are, seek advice and you may find the process is not as terrifying as you first thought.

When it boils down to it, only a court can decide who gets what in the dispute after a marital breakdown; it's difficult to work out what the end result might be because there are so many different factors to take into consideration. There are certain guidelines that will give you a rough idea of how the law will deal with such issues if one or both of you decide it's time to call an end to it all. Of course, many cases don't actually go before a judge, except, perhaps, to rubber-stamp any formal agreement that you and your ex have made via a solicitor (a sensible move, as it means you can enforce the terms should there be problems later on). It's only when disputes are so fierce as to seem unresolvable that the matter will be put before a family court judge. Don't let it get that far. It's expensive and time-consuming, and the inevitable bitterness merely compounds itself. Jane knows someone who has insisted on using the court system to delay a resolution for the last *five* years – some people do it for no reason other than revenge or greed. Those people should get a life and move on. No one wins in the end.

Grounds for divorce

Under English law there is only one ground for divorce, which is that the marriage has 'irretrievably broken down'. The spouse filing for divorce (the petitioner) has to provide evidence of irretrievable breakdown by proving one or more of the following five 'facts':

- Adultery: that the other spouse (the respondent) has committed adultery and the petitioner finds it intolerable to live with the respondent.
- Unreasonable behaviour: that the respondent has behaved in such a way that the petitioner cannot *reasonably* be expected to live with the respondent.

- Desertion: that the respondent has deserted the petitioner for a continuous period of at least two years immediately preceding the presentation of the petition.
- Two years' separation: that the parties to the marriage have lived apart for a continuous period of at least two years immediately preceding the presentation of the petition and the respondent consents to a divorce.
- Five years' separation: that the parties to the marriage have lived apart for a continuous period of at least five years immediately preceding the presentation of the petition.

As you can see, it's under only one of the first two evidential facts that spouses can seek a so-called 'quickie' divorce. You should bear in mind that you can't use either as evidence of irretrievable breakdown if you continue living with your husband for six months or more after finding out about the adultery or after the incidence of unreasonable behaviour has occurred. Adultery is the easiest fact to use, as it either happened or it didn't. Unreasonable behaviour is fairly subjective, ie: if you think the behaviour is unreasonable, then it is. But it's also extremely inflammatory and many lawyers suggest avoiding it if possible. A 'quickie' divorce still takes between three and six months from start to finish as a minimum, and that's only if there are no complications. If, for example, the respondent denies adultery or unreasonable behaviour and decides to defend the petition, the case will have to go before a judge in open court. Hardly anyone defends a divorce these days, not least because it costs a fortune but also because it means airing your dirty linen in public. It's cheaper and more private to confine divorce matters to your respective solicitors.

A divorce is granted in two stages: the decree *nisi* comes first, which is when you can still change your mind. At this stage, you're still technically married and it then takes at least six weeks for the decree *absolute* to come through. It's at this point that you are irrevocably divorced. Matters relating to children and money should always be discussed early on in the divorce proceedings and it's extremely important to have the finances sorted out before applying for a decree absolute. You can wait however long you like before applying for a decree absolute and, remember, you have more rights while you are technically still married!

This is why it's important to raise issues of finance as soon as possible with your solicitor, particularly if your husband holds the purse strings or if there are debts to contend with. For example, if the family home is in his sole name, he could, in theory, sell the roof over your head without your knowledge and make off with the money (and Jasmine knows of one lovely man who did just that to his wife and children). As a wife you have rights of occupation and your solicitor should immediately contact the Land Registry to ensure your name is put on the Register as an interested party to prevent any such problems until things are sorted out. (In fact, you can contact the Land Registry yourself if you are really worried).

If you're the victim of spousal abuse but can't bring yourself to leave your husband just yet, you should try to build up some secret savings in the meantime – even if it's just a small amount of cash kept at a trusted friend's house. Copies of important documents, such as birth certificates and passports, should also be made and kept somewhere safe so that if and when you eventually decide to make the break, you at least have some proof of existence and a little cash to start again. As an aside, it goes without saying that you should not under any circumstances put up with abuse, whether physical or mental. You're absolutely entitled to protect yourself and your children and there are now new laws that enable you to get him out of the house with an Occupation Order and to protect yourself with a Non-molestation Order.

Organisations such as Refuge (phone on 0870 599 5443) and Women's Aid (phone on 08457 023 468 or find at www.womensaid.org.uk) can help you take the first step.

These suggestions also apply to any woman who thinks her husband will react badly to the idea of divorce. Sometimes there may be no alternative to leaving the house instantly with absolutely nothing to your name, but if you're in a position to think about a little forward planning, then it makes sense to make some preparations. If you don't have a personal bank account, for example, then open one now! The moment he finds out you're seeking a divorce he may empty the joint account leaving you with no access to any money at all. Make sure you protect yourself as far as possible before the recriminations start, just in case.

So, let's look first at what might happen when you're a married woman.

Your rights on divorce

I learnt the hard way that no one goes into a relationship believing or even giving it one single thought of failure. Things look all too rosy – perhaps they really are – at the beginning. I would advise caution and scepticism aplenty. I more or less supported my husband and paid most of the bills for the better part of five years but when he turned violent it was definitely time to go our separate ways. I was shocked to find that he could ask for maintenance payments – he had nothing to lose and everything to gain whether or not we stayed together.

From the Motley Fool discussion boards

Assuming you're married and need financial support, whether you'll get anything at all will depend on which one of you has more income and assets. If you're the higher earner, for example, then you could find you're supporting him.

Your respective ages matter since the court will want to ascertain if you have much of a working life ahead of you and can eventually support yourself. The length of the marriage is also important, as you're likely to get more for longevity! (A reward for putting up with him for so long?) Your needs will also be taken into consideration, but they'll have to be reasonable ones. You may be entitled to help with the mortgage, for example, if you can't manage it by yourself and you've got children to house. The court must do its best to keep your standard of living as near as it was before, but just because you've had holidays in the

Caribbean twice a year doesn't mean the court will think your ex should pay for them to continue.

In theory, all joint and individual assets are added up, the debts deducted and then the remainder is split 50:50, although it doesn't always work like that, of course. There are two main areas for consideration:

Maintenance and assets

You're entitled to apply for maintenance for yourself or for your children. If it's for yourself, you'll need to apply to the County Court or High Court. You can ask either for regular payments for a given period of time or for what's called a 'Clean Break' settlement. In the latter instance you ask for a one-off lump sum in full and final settlement of all obligations. This is often the route taken by outgoing wives because it means they no longer have to be dependent on someone they don't necessarily like very much any more and whose circumstances may change for the worse. It's also useful if you think you may co-habit and/or remarry later. Maintenance payments are lost once you remarry or even if you cohabit for more than six months, so a lump sum is often the most sensible route to take.

The main asset is generally the family home, but you'll usually be entitled to a portion of any assets that are connected with the marriage. If you've young children who need a roof over their heads, and you are looking after them, then the court will often give you the right to live in the family home until they reach the age of 18 or have finished full-time education. While this may seem a good solution, remember that it means your ex still owns a share of your home and he'll want his portion when the last child is no longer dependent. If you go for this option, you could find yourself having to sell up to pay him his share many years down the line when you've practically forgotten you were ever married to him in the first place. This is one of the reasons why women often opt for the 'Clean Break' settlement, not least because ex-husbands sometimes use their ability to demand the sale of the house as a threat.

New laws have recently come into effect, that also give you the right to transfer immediately some of his pension fund into one of your own. Previously, you could claim some of it only once he'd actually retired, so, not surprisingly, women coming out of long marriages often took the family home while he toddled off with his pension fund. If you don't have much of a pension scheme in operation for your own needs (and it's usually older married women who don't) because you've spent years at home bringing up children, it could have a profound effect on your retirement income, so it's worth considering this option in more detail.

Let's say that your husband has been contributing to a decent company pension scheme for the last 20 or 30 years. He's built up a pretty significant fund, which means that, when he finally decides to consign his briefcase to the attic on retirement, you and he can look forward to a jolly comfortable lifestyle. Let's also say that you've not earned very much during those last 20 or 30 years of the marriage – mainly because you've been at home bringing up the children – and have only been in a position to take the occasional job every now and then. So, you've no real pension scheme in place. But, hey, that's okay, your husband's got one.

Suddenly he wants a divorce – or you do! What happens?

Pension schemes have long been considered part and parcel of 'matrimonial property' on divorce, but in the past, whenever a court has had to consider how to divvy up between the divorcing parties, it's been very restricted in its powers. Until the new law came into effect there were only two options pension-wise when looking at all the available marital assets. These were:

- Allowing the pension holder to keep the pension fund, but transferring a greater share of other assets to the 'outgoing' partner (the matrimonial home etc.), to make up for the loss of access to a pension.
- Earmarking part of the pension fund for the other spouse's benefit, so that some of the eventual payout will flow her way the moment he starts claiming from it.

In this situation, of course, the first option means the ex-wife has nothing to live on when she reaches retirement age (apart from state benefits), whereas the second option means she has to wait until her ex-husband decides to retire before she can take her share of his pension income (and if he drops dead before he does so, she gets absolutely nothing at all!).

Now, under the new law, as the 'pension-less' spouse you've the option of physically taking a chunk of money from your ex-husband's pension fund to pay into a pension scheme of your own – *if* that's how you want to play it. However, your entitlement is only up to 50% of the value of the pension built up during the course of the marriage. If you have been married for 10 years and he has built up his pension over 20 years, only 10 years' worth is technically available to you. There's also the fact that, as the money is part of a pension fund, it will have to remain as part of a pension fund. As we explained in Chapter Seven, you can't get access to the money until you retire and then you'll have to buy an annuity with it.

The new law won't result in a larger settlement for either side on divorce, but it does mean couples now have a real choice about how to divide their marital property. The value of a husband's pension fund is no longer an intangible asset – women can actually walk away with some of it. Which route you take depends entirely on your own particular circumstances: if you're young, for example, you'll have more time to sort out your own pension provision. A woman in her late forties or fifties may be more concerned about her retirement. In spite of the benefits of being able to claim some of his pension, you may still be better off taking a cash set-off. At least that way, you can invest it however you prefer or blow it on something you really want!

Child support

Did you know that there are now an estimated 1.6 million lone parents in the UK? It's a lot, isn't it? And 94% of them are lone mothers, about half of whom are on benefits of some kind. It's no wonder the Government has been trying, and often failing, to get fathers to provide some form of support for their former family.

It's been more than ten years since the Child Support Act was introduced and it's been accepted for a very long time that the whole thing was a complete mess. The Bill was whizzed through Parliament with only a skeleton outline of the principles being debated – that absent parents should financially support their children. It was left to the civil servants to sort out the details and, they being lovers of red tape, the result was a bureaucratic nightmare. So much so that the Child Support Agency (CSA) has spent more time over the last decade dealing with re-assessments and appeals than chasing those who were in arrears or refusing to pay.

According to figures published by the CSA in February 2002, there are just over 1 million active cases affecting nearly 1.5 million children on its books. They make interesting reading:

- 51% of non-resident parents in these cases comply fully with the CSA's assessment of what they could and should pay
- 22% only *partially* comply (this usually means they're in arrears)
- 27% do not comply at all

The above statistics show that just over half of absent parents – mostly fathers – provide the legally required financial support for their children in accordance with their means as assessed by the CSA. These responsible fathers do their best by their children and comply fully with the law. However, they also illustrate that 49% of absent parents do *not*. Keep these numbers in mind when you're sitting in front of your solicitor trying to work out what sort of help you'll get from your ex for the children.

It's obviously right in *all* cases that an absent parent should contribute financially – to the best of his or her ability – towards a child's upbringing. So why does such a large proportion fail to do so?

Many fathers start off well but find it harder to keep up the payments when they start a new relationship and perhaps go on to have more children. In some cases, it may be that they feel they can't afford the CSA's assessment of their finances (the current system is so complicated that the absent parent often feels unfairly treated). Or, perhaps, because they don't care about their ex-partner any more, they don't care about the children they produced together. According to the organisation Families Need Fathers, it seems more likely to be the result of the emotional fallout of parents splitting up. It's not unusual for the mother to deny access to the children – a move which doesn't exactly encourage Dad to pay up – or else Dad refuses to pay – which, equally, does not encourage the mother to comply with the access rights that have been granted to the father. The phrase 'vicious circle' springs to mind, does it not?

Whatever the reason, Parliament's solution to these eternal problems was to give the CSA strong powers to deduct the required child support directly from a father's salary via his employer to ensure it gets to the mother. The courts also have the ultimate power to imprison the mother if she refuses to comply fully with the Contact Order. Unfortunately, while the CSA uses its powers fairly freely, there are very few instances of judges using theirs. After all, it means taking the mother away from the very children she's supposed to be caring for. However, judges are now leaning towards giving more contact to the absent parent and, as a way of dealing with recalcitrant mothers, judges are beginning to take the children away from the resident parent and giving them to the other. So be warned!

New laws governing the way child support is calculated have now finally been passed by Parliament. The system for calculating support has been greatly simplified and it's hoped that it will be seen as fairer and so less likely to cause problems between the parents. Whether it's for the better won't be known until the changes are actually implemented and individuals start feeling the effect of the new method of calculation and the penalties for not complying.

In case you're wondering, this was scheduled for introduction in April 2002, but guess what. The new computer system wasn't up and running in time and, at the time of writing, there's still been no announcement about when the changes will be put into practice. However, to give you a rough idea of what sort of support you can expect when implemented, the new formula will be based on a percentage of the absent parent's net income and the number of children involved. Briefly, absent fathers (and, let's face it, we mostly mean fathers when we talk about absent parents) will be required to pay 15% of their net income for a single child, 20% for two and 25% for three children or more. The maximum income that will be taken into account will be capped at £2,000 net a week. If the father has a new family then similar allowances will be made for each child in his second family, including stepchildren. Rates of 15%, 20% and 25% will be deducted from the non-resident parent's net income and only the balance will be subject to the standard rates for the first family.

Those who don't or won't pay risk losing their driving licence (yes, really!), and if they lie or refuse to provide information, they could be fined up to £1,000. Late payments will also lead to fines. Under the current system, fathers who live abroad cannot be chased, but the new law will ensure that non-resident parents who work abroad for a UK-based employer can be held accountable.

The new rules are certainly much easier to understand, but there are some caveats that have been introduced which are likely to cause just as many rows between parents as the Child Support Act of 1991 managed to do. For a start, the income of the resident mother will not be taken into consideration, nor will that of her new partner. You may think that's fair enough – just because the mother earns a fair whack, that doesn't negate the responsibility owed by the absent father. However, the lone mother could earn huge amounts each year and still demand, and be entitled to, up to 25% of the absent father's income. Equally, the father could be a millionaire with a vast income but will never be required to pay more than £26,000 a year via the CSA, even if he can afford much more. (In fact, mothers can apply to the court for a maintenance top-up in these circumstances, if it's for the children.)

Maintenance payments will also be reduced on a sliding scale depending on how often the absent father sees the child. For example, if the child stays with the non-resident parent for 175 nights or more throughout the year, the payments could be halved. Again, that's fair enough on the face of it – if the father is looking after the child for half the year, then he should only pay half. But what if the resident mother can't afford to lose the full maintenance payment? Her mortgage payments don't halve when she doesn't have the children, do they? This is why it's vital to have proper financial arrangements in place before a divorce is finalised.

These factors also mean that, if both parents share residence of the children *and* earn exactly the same amount, the parent regarded as 'absent' will *still* have to pay support to the parent with the legal Residence Order (custody of the children).

While there's no doubt that changes to the Child Support laws are long overdue and should improve things for the lone mother who needs financial help from the father, the new system is not exactly encouraging for fathers who already do their duty. In fact, most of the legal profession thinks the new system won't work as intended and that further changes will need to be made once it's implemented. Still, at least it will be more transparent and easier to implement. This in turn should free up CSA resources sufficiently so they can focus on those fathers who flatly refuse to face up to their responsibilities.

Until the changes are implemented, and that could be any moment now, the level of financial support is based on a very complicated formula that doesn't always work out very fairly. There is still the problem that if Darling Daddy decides to do a runner to another country, at the moment, the CSA have no powers to assess child maintenance payments in such situations. This is rare, but it happens. Generally speaking though, both the courts and the CSA still have wide-ranging powers to deal with recalcitrant ex-husbands who refuse to stump up. For example, they can ensure that maintenance payments are deducted directly from his pay packet. They can also freeze his bank accounts if you discover he's trying to hide money away. If he owns another property, a charge can be put on it so that when it's sold, the proceeds can be used for maintenance payments.

Bear in mind when considering what we've outlined above, that if you're the one with the money and he's the one with the children, you'll have to pay your whack under exactly the same system.

Rights of the common-law wife

As mentioned above, in English law there is no such thing as a common-law wife. It's a little different in Scotland because if you can persuade the court that you lived together as man and wife and the world effectively regarded you as a married couple, then you'll have the same rights as a married couple who are divorcing. It's known as a marriage by 'habit and repute'.

As we've said, if she's not in a position to support herself, a divorcing wife has a right to claim some form of maintenance from her ex and to have a share in the assets considered to be 'matrimonial property'. The unmarried woman has no such right even if she has been living with her partner for a very long time. Once the relationship is over, it's over and, unless you've got children or jointly owned property, you'll have no reason to see him ever again. Note the caveats though: unless you've got children or jointly owned property. And let's add another one: unless you believe you've acquired a 'beneficial interest'!

We'll look at the last one in a moment, as it's the most complicated, and you should always bear in mind that the rights that you may have can work the other way around if you're in a better financial position than he is.

Children

If you've got children together then you obviously won't be hearing the last of him. Even if you're not married, in cases of dispute the court can still make orders about where the children should live and what should happen to the family home and other assets. You can make an application for financial provision for children under Schedule 1 of the Children Act, which means you could get a share of his property for the children. Either parent can apply to the court on the children's behalf to establish a claim and it's very useful if you cannot afford anywhere else to live.

An unusual situation that arises in the case of an unmarried father is that he needs to get a court order establishing his parental rights over the child. These are automatically granted to fathers of children born within a marriage but in an out-of-wedlock case, he actively needs to obtain such rights. Either the mother can grant these or, if she refuses, he can apply to the court for a Parental Responsibility Order and will almost certainly get one. Unless he obtains one he has absolutely no rights at all over the child. He cannot have a say in how the child is brought up and is not even considered the next of kin in the legal sense. In theory, grandparents would have more legal rights than the father to take over the care of the child in the event of the mother's death!

Nevertheless, whether or not those rights have been granted, when it comes to providing for the children, the CSA rules apply in just the same way as they do for parents coming out of a marriage. See above for more details.

Property

The sort of dispute that may arise when unmarried couples separate is usually over splitting assets, such as the home. Whether you are entitled to anything depends entirely on whether these are in joint names or, if not, whether you can establish that you've acquired some entitlement to those assets.

If you've assets that are quite clearly jointly owned then these will be split accordingly. If both your names are on the deeds of the house as equal owners, for example, then you'll automatically be entitled to your half-share. Either you buy him out or he buys you out, or you sell up and split the proceeds. If you can't decide how to do it, you can ask the court to make the decision for you. This will be at great expense, of course, so, as ever, it's always better to try to reach an amicable agreement in this sort of situation.

But what if only one of you owns the property. Who has the rights then? Let's assume for the sake of argument that you moved into his house when the relationship began and that it's entirely in his name. Usually you'll have no right to remain in the home if you're asked to leave by a partner who is the sole legal owner of the property. But if you can show that you have contributed directly to buying it or to improving it in some substantial way, you may be able to show that you've acquired a 'beneficial interest' even though legal ownership belongs entirely to him. For example, if you paid the deposit or have contributed directly towards the mortgage instalments, this would constitute a beneficial interest. You've actually 'bought' a little bit of the house even though the title deeds don't say you have.

However, difficulties can arise if your partner has been paying the mortgage and you've been paying all the other household bills. It may just have been the method you were both happy with at the time but you would somehow have to prove that this arrangement was based on an understanding or agreement that you were effectively making contributions towards the purchase of the house itself by freeing up his income.

To illustrate what we mean there's a well-known case called *Burns v. Burns*, which set a legal precedent in 1984. A woman had lived with her partner for 17 years in a house he'd bought in his sole name. They had two children but never married, although she'd taken on the use of his surname. During the relationship she'd spent a fair bit of money on the house and on buying furniture, but she'd never contributed directly to the mortgage payments and couldn't establish the existence of an arrangement whereby she was to have a proprietary interest in it. He hadn't promised her anything, in other words. Two children and 17 years of her life and she got nothing.

Conversely it's amazing what you may be entitled to on the basis of a promise. In the more recent case of *Rowe v. Prance*, a woman gave up her rented flat and moved onto a boat that had been bought by her lover on the basis that he was going to leave his wife and move in with her. When the relationship fell apart, the court ruled that she was entitled to a half-share in the proceeds of the sale of the boat – even though it was in his sole name – simply because he had assured her that it was theirs to share. In legalese, it's known by the fun phrase of 'promissory estoppel' and it essentially applies where you act to your detriment in reliance on a promise by someone else.

It's an extremely complicated and costly process if you have to take this type of dispute through the courts, so it's worth repeating that it's always better to try to keep things amicable so you can negotiate effectively. While these things may or may not apply to you in your current situation, it's worth thinking about them should you embark on another relationship at a later date.

If you move into your partner's house, make sure that you have a joint account for the household bills – including the mortgage – and that you keep the bank statements as evidence of your contributions. If someone moves into *your* home then make sure you do exactly the opposite: on no account let him anywhere near the mortgage payments unless you are absolutely certain that you want him to acquire a financial interest in your home. An alternative is to enter into a 'Declaration of Trust', otherwise called a Trust Deed, so that you can set out your shares of the property before you start living together.

Conclusion

Finally, remember that society has traditionally cast women in the role of the martyr, dutifully slaving away in the hope that a handsome prince will reward her benevolence and purity. You've just discovered that your handsome prince is rather more of a frog and that the only person you can rely on is yourself.

Just as when you first learned to walk, your ability to manage on your own and to achieve independence again will improve over time. You may have to fall on your backside a bit but gradually you will be able to move towards taking control of your financial and emotional well-being once more – and this time, without having to put up with any frogs.

11

Getting Older

Age is something that doesn't matter, unless you're a cheese.

Billie Burke

So you're 50, perhaps 60 or even a sprightly 70; maybe you're in your late forties and just about to hit your real 'years of experience'. You may have a Foolish pile of cash to do something with or you may, like the majority of us, have nowhere near enough money. You may perhaps have debts because of a messy and expensive divorce, you could have grown-up, but not yet independent, children to feed, clothe, house and soothe. In short, you may be nowhere near the stage where you can sit back and let your investments keep you going for the rest of your natural life.

Whatever your situation, our message is: don't panic! And whatever you do, don't imagine that you're old. The average life expectancy for women in Britain is currently 87 years, and more and more of us are receiving a telegram from the Queen, so please don't kid yourself that you are old and your life is over. You've probably got three, four or even five decades more to go and quite honestly, it's a bit of a waste of time to spend all those years thinking that you're past it. It's simply not true, however much life, and those around you, might kid you into believing it.

The question of what you're going to do with the next few decades – whether you will continue to work at the same job, switch careers or stop working altogether and become a lady of leisure – depends on many factors, not least the amount of money you already have in savings and investments. In this chapter we will go through ways of maximising the income from your investments, getting the best annuity rate possible from your pension pot, making money out of your home, finding new and enjoyable ways of earning a crust and making plans and provisions for your future. Pick the bits that are relevant to you or indulge yourself in the heady rhythms of our beautiful prose without missing a serendipitous sentence – we don't mind, honest.

What's wrong with working?

By 2020, more than one-in-four of the UK working population will be over current pensionable age. Pension shortfalls and fewer younger people will mean many people will have to work into their mid-seventies, health permitting.

MORI for BUPA Health Debate, March 2002

It depends on what work you're doing and how you're feeling at this moment. If you're doing a job that you love, or even if you're just one of those people who thrive on work, deadlines and activity (Jasmine is like this), then there's no reason why you should give up early. In fact, there are many good reasons why you should keep on going as long as you want to, not least because you can build up a bigger nest egg and keep your brain stimulated.

On the other hand, if the mere thought of dragging yourself into the office for another ten solid years makes you want to top yourself, it's probably time for a change of direction. If you've a tidy sum stashed away – or a generous partner with a tidy sum coming in – then, by all means, give up the nine-to-five and do what you like. If you can't afford to give up all work, then it's time you thought about finding some other form of employment.

You may even be in one of those stupid professions, or companies, where they consider you over the hill at 45 and start flapping the cushions to make you leave. This happens to men as well as women, so don't feel victimised. If you love your job then fight for it with every means – including recent anti-discrimination legislation – you have available. In fact, this whole way of thinking is already being challenged from various directions, including the Government, which has realised we're all going to *have* to work for longer as we are living longer and our savings for retirement are woefully inadequate.

If you're not so fussed about the job you're doing at the moment, though, why not use this as an opportunity to start afresh in a new career, new business or new company? If a voice inside your head is saying 'you can't teach an old dog new tricks', or words to that effect, you can certainly listen to it and give up if you consider yourself an old dog. Personally, we don't see ourselves in that way, nor will we when we are in our fifties or older. As far as we're concerned, it doesn't apply.

Interestingly, as far as many women in or approaching their 'third age' right now are concerned, it doesn't apply to them either. Many women at this age are enjoying a higher public profile than ever before. In a practical sense they really are going through a 'middle youth', partly thanks to their strength in numbers. These women are part of the post-war 'baby-boomer' generation. According to Rutgers University academic Helen Fisher, the people from this generation are like a hefty meal passing through a snake, 'changing culture as they grow older'. They brought in sixties counterculture and bought into eighties' consumerism. They're now changing ideas about what it is to be a woman in her prime of life.

Around 80% of the nation's wealth now resides in the hands of those aged 45 and over. This age group also constitutes two-thirds of the working population, according to the Chartered Institute of Personnel and Development. It's quite possible that you have more power, influence and potential in your hands right now than you could imagine. Why not reap those benefits?

Retire and run your own business

I recently went to a Women's Conference held in Essex. We had a full day of local successful businesswomen telling us how they did it and how they sometimes had to fight their families to be allowed to do it (but do it they did). I currently teach HTML and Dreamweaver for Business

Link/Chamber of Commerce. I teach mainly men – in a fast track scenario and it is great to see their faces when this little middle-aged lady walks in to take the seminar.

From the Motley Fool discussion boards

If you haven't already set up and run your own business, now could be a good time to start. You could either set up in business as a freelancer – doing aromatherapy, music lessons, business consulting or that kind of thing – or set up a whole, proper company with offices, staff and the works. You certainly should not allow age to stop you – many other people of the same age haven't.

In fact, a survey from Barclays published in 2001 showed that more people over the age of 50 are starting their own business than ever before. In fact, 60,000 new businesses in 2000 were started by the over-fifties, accounting for 15% of all start-ups in the UK. Interestingly, over a third of the people in the survey started their business after they retired, were made redundant from or were dissatisfied with their previous job. Only about half of them are in the same type of business they worked in previously. Surprisingly, two-thirds had not run a business before. However these 'third-age' entrepreneurs tend to do a lot more background research and spadework than most others, in the form of writing business plans, drawing up budgets, doing cash-flow forecasts and the like. This means that businesses started up by third-agers tend to have firmer foundations and, therefore, more of a chance of surviving.

The Government is very keen to encourage entrepreneurs, although mostly in a cack-handed kind of a way. If you're serious about setting up your own business you can get help from local CENTEC centres – Government-sponsored help and advice agencies for small businesses – and you can also get information from Business Link. Look in the Yellow Pages under Business Enterprise Agencies or click on www.businesslink.co.uk. For Scotland call 0845 6078787 for Wales it's 01443 845500 or www.wda.co.uk.

You may already have skills that are saleable on their own. Perhaps you are a hairdresser, an accountant, a teacher or a therapist. If so it would be easy to set yourself up as a freelancer, offering your services at an hourly, daily or weekly rate. All you'll need is advertising, contacts and word-of-mouth recommendation to get you into the business swing of things.

You may feel you don't have skills, but don't rule out training and higher education. Take a look at what you've done in your life. You may be surprised at what skills you have without realising it. If you've been a mother, you'll have child-caring skills and could train to be a nanny, maternity nurse, doula (birth partner and post-birth partner) or even a midwife. If you've run a home and a family you might be surprised at your organisational skills and could set up a party-organising business or one of those companies that sorts out other people's lives and offices for them. The possibilities are endless, if you're willing to look.

You can get more help and advice on running a small business from the Federation of Small Businesses (phone on 01253 33600 or look at www.fsb.org.uk), the Small Business Bureau (phone on 01276 452010 or look at www.smallbusinessbureau.org.uk) or the Big Small Business Initiative (phone on 0870 8701165 or look at www.bsbi.co.uk).

You could also consider buying a franchise. Statistically, franchises are more likely to succeed than new businesses, although you have to pick the right company and you need to know exactly what you're letting yourself in for. You can get information on the pros and cons of franchising and how to go about getting one from the British Franchise Association (phone on 01491 578050 or look at wwww.british-franchise.org.uk).

You can also find out about your local Chambers of Commerce at www.britishchambers.co.uk or get ideas about new enterprises from www.enterprisezone.co.uk. The Consumers Association has brought out a very helpful book called *The Which Guide to Starting Your Own Business*, which would be another source of useful help and advice.

What to do once you have retired

So, you really are determined to retire! And why not? You've earned it. Believe it or not, this is a pretty important moment and decisions you make now will determine your wealth (or not) for the rest of your life, so make sure you make the right moves so that you can get the maximum income from the money you have.

There are a few basic things you should do about your retirement income from the start. Here are some of the main ones:

● Split the income between you and your spouse evenly so that you maximise the benefits of tax allowances and income bands. It's best for the spouse with the lower income to hold taxable investments.
● Ensure that you opt for as much tax-free cash as is available to you on retirement. It can be up to 25% of the pension fund.
● Think about delaying the purchase of an annuity by using phased retirement or income drawdown schemes (see pages 173–5 in Chapter Seven for an explanation of what these are and how to do them).
● All other things being equal, buy your annuity as late as possible. This will ensure you get the best rates and that should you die before you purchase the annuity your estate will inherit the pension fund.
● If you are a widow, do you qualify for compensation for your spouse being mis-sold SERPS? If the worse comes to the worst, and you have savings of less than £8,000 and no pension, you can apply for the Minimum Income Guarantee. The current rate starts at £78.45 for a single person aged 60 to 74. Phone 0800 028 1111 or check out www. dss.gov.uk/mig to find out all about it, if you think you are eligible.

If you have no savings other than a pension then you can skip this next section and go straight to our section on buying an annuity (see pages 286–8), but if you have any shares, cash, bonds or other valuables, have a look at this first.

Pension Credit

This is something the Government has recently brought in to increase some people's pensions a little. Essentially, a Pension Credit is a drop in tax for those pensioners who still pay tax. The changes don't come into effect until 2003, but it will reward all those who saved during their working lives and now have weekly incomes of up to £135 for a single pensioner or £200 for couples. The Government has calculated that 5.5 million pensioners – half of all pensioner households in this country – will be better off as a result of the new ruling.

The Pension Credit will guarantee a minimum income, which by April 2003 will be at least £100 for a single person or £154 for couples. Also, for every pound saved, pensioners will receive an additional cash credit. This means extra cash of between £1 and £23 a week on top of the Basic State Pension depending on the amount of your savings and other income.

Although most pensioners pay no tax at all because their income is so small, for those who do in April 2003 the Government will raise the pensioners' tax allowances by £240 over and above inflation. It'll have made it a little more worthwhile trying to save and not being a burden on the State. A taste of things to come, we think.

Make the most of your savings pot

At the Fool we don't think that getting old is any reason to change your investment *approach*. Articles in the Money sections of broadsheet news-papers may like to tell you that you'll be wanting to invest in bonds, gilts and cash and other safe-ish, low-performing vehicles, but that's not necessarily the right way to go. Investing is about maximising returns and controlling risk. You work out the level of risk that you are prepared to accept and then try to maximise your return within those parameters. As you get older, your appetite for risk is likely to reduce, and you'll probably want to concentrate on income from your investments rather than just watch them grow. However, this doesn't really change your fundamental approach, so don't let others make you more chicken than you need to be!

As you get older, your investment time horizon reduces. As your time horizon reduces, shares have less time to even out their ups and downs, which means that you don't want to take so many risks. If your investments are made up purely of shares, then you have to live with the possibility of a market crash. Young people can deal with this since they have a long time horizon and can afford to be patient. However, if there were a crash when you were seventy, it could put a severe downer on your remaining years. While you're still in your 50's and even in your 60's, though, this shouldn't be worrying you too much.

But this doesn't mean that you should abandon investing in shares altogether when you are getting on in years. If you invest cleverly enough you could get a pretty steady, high income from them. The thing you need to get clear is that *dividends* from shares – in other words, that nice cheque you get from them once a year or so - are a lot more stable than their price, so a crash in the market isn't actually as bad as it sounds if you're really interested in income. Even if the price of a share went through the floor, if the company is basically sound it's likely that the income or *dividends* from them won't fall, which means that you will still get a decent amount of money even if the figures you see in the FT next to your share look upsettingly small. Of course it would still not be much fun and you may not want the worry, but think carefully about how worrying it really would be for you because the rewards of keeping your money in equities should outweigh the risks when it comes to getting a good income overall.

The thing is that bonds and cash, the typical 'safe' income investments, are also not without risk, *and* the likely income from them is lower than that of shares. If there is a sudden burst of inflation, then the income that they provide can start to look very sick. Of course you could go for index-linked (i.e. inflation-proofed) bonds. However, the income from these is so much less that it doesn't really make them a very good use of your capital either. In fact, even the income from non-index-linked bonds is less than the income from a good many shares.

The long-term returns from equities have, in the past, been miles better than the returns from bonds and cash and it's quite possible that this will remain the case. We would say, therefore, that the question of holding bonds and cash (except for emergencies) does not arise until your time horizon has fallen to about 15 years or less. And remember, as a woman, that time horizon may not hit you until you are well into your seventies.

The 'Retirement Investing' discussion board on our website would be a good place to find out more about higher yielding companies by discussing them with other investors. Also, our expert, Stephen Bland, has written many a helpful article on the subject of investing for a high yield income on our website so look them up if you can (just put 'Stephen Bland' in the 'Search' box and see what comes up). Either that or pick up 'The Old Fool's Retirement Guide' by Fool Rob Davies for more advice on making the most of your investments.

Buying an annuity

Some of the most vigorous discussions on the Motley Fool websites are about annuities. An annuity, as you know, is a guaranteed sum of money that you'll be paid every month until you die. You buy it on retirement with 75% of the money in your personal pension plan (or more of it, if you want). There are two choices to be made: the type of annuity that best suits your needs and which provider to buy it from.

The first point, and the most crucial one, to understand about annuities is that, although there are many different types – joint life, single life, inflation-proofed and so on – on the day you buy the annuity, the size of your pension pot is fixed. You can't add any more later on, which is why it's important to make sure you buy the annuity at the right time. It may be worth waiting a few years and putting in lots more money or it could be worth taking the annuity now and continuing to work to supplement your income and create other investments.

The difference between the types of annuity is just how that pot of money is paid out to you. One of the biggest differences is that between annuities for men and for women. On average, as we've said many times in this book, women live longer than men, so their pot must be spread out over more years and, as a result, the income for each individual year will be lower for us than for our male counterparts. Those annuity companies aren't soft.

Another important aspect to keep in mind is the effect of inflation on your pension income. An inflation-proofed annuity will pay out progressively more money over time as inflation goes up. So in the early years it will pay less than a standard annuity, but will pay more than standard in the later years. If you have a standard annuity that doesn't move with inflation you could find yourself very much poorer the longer you live as inflation starts to eat into the real value of your monthly income.

Remember, to provide a reasonable income in retirement from an annuity you need about £400,000 in today's money on the day you retire. Depending on age, that will give you an annual income of something like £20,000. It's possible to buy an annuity at any point from the age of 50 to 75, when it becomes mandatory. Buying it early, when you have a long life expectancy, will obviously give a lower annual income than buying it later, when your life expectancy is lower. Remember that every year you don't benefit is a year of lost income. It's a kind of juggling act that would be made so much easier if we all had that magic crystal ball that told us how long we're going to live and, therefore, which investment would be best for us. Ho hum!

Annuity income is partly a return on the capital you have built up in the pension, and partly interest generated from the gilts (Government bonds) that the annuity is usually invested in. That worked well when life expectancy at retirement was only a few years. But, now that a 65-year-old woman can expect to live for another 20 years at least, the story is a little different. Inflation needs to be considered, even if it isn't a problem right now. For example, an inflation rate of only 2.3% a year reduces the value of £1,000 to £776 in ten years. Imagine what it could do in 20 years!

Moreover, choosing to depend on gilts for a significant part of your income – which annuities do – might not be a good idea if real returns significantly outpace nominal returns. All the historical evidence shows that equities are the best place for investments on a time horizon of ten years or more. These days some people are retiring at the age of 50, giving a retirement that could easily last 30 or 40 years.

So one option to be considered is an annuity that is invested in equities rather than bonds, called a *unit-linked* annuity. A similar product is a *with-profit* annuity, where the money is invested in the with-profit fund of an insurance company. In this case, the income will vary with the level of bonuses declared by the manager. Given the problems that some of these are facing, though, that may be a risky route. On the whole, we at the Motley Fool are not great fans of with-profits funds. A slightly safer alternative is a *guaranteed with-profit* annuity. The income may still vary, but there's a low guaranteed income to form a base. Higher in risk, but probably more rewarding, are *self-invested unit-linked* annuities where you choose what the fund invests in.

Once you have decided what type of annuity you need, you can shop around for the provider that offers the best deal – *and make sure that you do!* You'd be amazed at the difference it can make to shop around and if you don't you could be losing out on thousands of pounds. Every provider will have a slightly different estimate of how long you're going to live, and hence how much of the pot to pay out each year, so don't get stuck with a miserly one.

In annuities, probably more than anywhere else, the phrase 'You get what you pay for' is very true.

Remember that you don't have to purchase an annuity as soon as you retire. It's possible to use income drawdown as explained in Chapter Seven, in which you take income from the pension fund, but without actually buying an annuity until legally obliged to at the age of 75. The attraction is that the fund can continue growing for the maximum time possible and, should you die in that period, the remainder of the fund can be passed to your beneficiaries free of Inheritance Tax. Of course a standard annuity stops when the recipient dies, so it's not good at all for passing wealth from one generation to the next. Have a look at our explanation of income drawdown on pages 174–5.

Pensions help

Let's face it you're going to need it. There are a number of places you can go to for help (check out Chapter Seven on pensions as well for more information). Here are a few of the agencies that will give you free advice whenever you need it:

Occupational Pensions Regulatory Authority, Opra, Invicta House, Trafalgar Place, Brighton BN1 4DW (phone on 01273 627600 or look at www.opra.gov.uk).

Age Concern has fact sheets covering every issue concerning retirement and old age: Information and Policy Division, Age Concern England, Astral House, 1268 London Road, London SW16 4ER (phone on 0800 009966 or look at www.ageconcern.org.uk).

The Office for the Pensions Advisory Service (OPAS) can give you information about any aspect of occupational, personal and stakeholder pensions. You can complain to OPAS if you are having problems with your pension scheme. Contact them on 0845 601 2923.

If you have a major problem with your pension you can contact: The Pensions Ombudsman, 11 Belgrave Square, London SW1V 1RB (phone on 020 7834 9144).

The Pensions Compensation Board can compensate you if a bankrupt employer has removed your pension scheme's assets dishonestly. Contact them at: The Pensions Compensation Board, 11 Belgrave Square, London SW1V 1RB (phone on 020 7828 9794).

Your home – a treasure-trove

If you're a homeowner, it's highly likely that you have a good deal of equity wrapped up in it. Over the last 30 years, house prices in most parts of Britain have risen exponentially and, perhaps unwittingly, if you bought some time over the last few decades, you'll have made an excellent investment. In 2001 it was estimated that the over-sixties in the UK have around £550 billion of equity tied up in their homes. It's also reckoned that about three-quarters of those aged 65–69 own their own property and 85% of these own the property outright.

But how do you make money out of it? After all, you've got to live somewhere! Well, there are various ways of making money out of your home. One obvious way is to downsize. If you are in a large, expensive house you could sell it and buy something smaller and cheaper in the same area or move to a cheaper region altogether. The difference between the two sales can be your retirement pot. Of course, there are several costs involved – estate agents, solicitors, removals – but if the difference between the prices of the two properties is great enough then it should be worth it.

Another way is to take in one or more lodgers. See our advice on pages 98–9 of Chapter Four about how to go about this and how much you can earn tax-free. Another possibility, if you live in a popular area and you have an interest in it, is to set yourself up as a Bed & Breakfast. Naturally there are various health and safety, as well as legal, issues surrounding running your home as a commercial operation, so if you are serious about doing this, contact the English Tourism Council on 0870 606 7204 for their free leaflet on the subject.

Equity release schemes

A subject that has been filling the pages of the Money sections in the broadsheet newspapers in recent years is 'equity-release schemes'. These are specifically aimed at older people who are 'property-rich, but cash poor'. These schemes are like reverse mortgages and there are several different types of plans you can go with, but they all basically divide into two main types.

The first is reversion plans. Here, you agree to sell all or part of your home to another party. When you move home or pass on, they then take their share of the proceeds. The main disadvantage with these schemes is that you'll have to suffer a substantial discount from the actual market value. In fact, it's estimated that you'll only get between 35% and 60% of the actual market value in most cases, as well as missing out on the likely future growth in the value of your home. It's clear that this is not a very cost-effective option.

The second type is the rolled-up loan. You receive the value of the loan (which you can take as either capital or income) and the interest you would normally pay is rolled up year after year. The loan plus the interest is then repaid when you move house or pass on. Here, the disadvantage is that the loan plus interest may roll up to such an extent that it could even exceed the value of your home. Many plans now guarantee that you will never be forced out of your home and they also offer fixed or capped rates of interest. The rates are, of course, higher than you would get with an ordinary mortgage (sometimes twice the Bank of England's base rate) because the lender is more restricted in the security it has over the property and its money is tied up for an uncertain length of time.

You can see how useful it could be to some people to get some money out of their home without ever having to move, but there are several disadvantages to these schemes and they should be approached with great caution. For a start, although they are regulated rather more than they used to be (there were many mis-selling scandals in the 1980s), the confusing and complex nature of many of the products means that it's easy to make a mistake with them and incur high hidden charges. Many of these products still fall between the gaps of regulation for mortgages and consumer credit. The FSA says it's planning to release a report on this area, but at the time of writing, it hasn't yet appeared.

Different schemes tend to have all sorts of different criteria you have to fulfil before they'll consider you. One will insist that you are over the age of 65, your home is freehold or has a lease in excess of 80 years. Another will say you have to be over the age of 70, your home must be worth over £40,000 and, if not freehold, that the lease must be in excess of 75 years. And so on. You get the picture.

You do also have to take into account the fact that, once you have sold out to one of these schemes, you'll not have a home to pass on to your descendants when you die. If you are childless this may not be a problem, but it's a big issue for many and ideally they should be consulted before you sign on the dotted line.

Interestingly, the main reason why people take out equity-release schemes is for home improvement, but many also do so in order to pay for insurance to cover them in case they need long-term care. It's a gamble but if you seriously think that you are likely to need long-term care later on, it can be worth taking it out in your fifties or sixties to cover you for your older years. However, if you don't take out this insurance and you go into a home, generally you will sell your house, pay back the equity-release company the amount they loaned you plus whatever interest was agreed and then the money that is left over will go towards the payment for your care.

The theory with these products (like many financial products) is fine, but the problems start in practice when a lack of competition and clarity mean that charges are far higher than the value they actually deliver. They need to be treated with more caution than most, especially while the gaps in regulation are still there. At least they do seem to be improving and the need for further improvement is recognised – both of these are encouraging signs.

If you *do* decide this is something you'd like to do, make sure the scheme you have chosen is registered with the Safe Home Income Plan (SHIP), which has a code of practice safeguarding homeowners. You can get more information from them by phoning 0870 241 6060 or checking out their website at www.ship-ltd.org. You can also find information on these schemes from Age Concern (www.ageconcern.co.uk), the National

Consumer Council (www.ncc.org.uk), or even the Actuaries Profession (www.actuaries.org.uk).

The not-such-fun stuff

Facing one's mortality is not the most enjoyable part of living. It's not surprising that, even by the time we're in our fifties, very few of us have a Will, let alone thoughts of a retirement home or contingency plans in case we need long-term care. But, like everything to do with money, the more time you give yourself to research your options and plan things, the more in control you'll be, the healthier your bank account will be and, frankly, the happier you'll be.

The rest of this chapter is devoted to joyful subjects such as avoiding Inheritance Tax, executing a Power of Attorney, organising your funeral (yes, really) and keeping the council's hands off your property if you need long-term care. If these are subjects you know you need to address, make yourself a nice drink, think happy thoughts, sit down somewhere pleasant and promise yourself a really fun treat once you've finished reading this chapter. There, that's not so hard, is it?

Inheritance Tax – and how to avoid it

You might think that you have so little to leave to your friends and family, it's not worth bothering about Inheritance Tax (or IHT, as the legal people call it), but if you own your own home the chances are your descendants will get clobbered. Rising house prices are creating Inheritance Tax bills for thousands of families who never thought they would be liable for the fixed 40% (yes, 40%!) tax on any estate worth more than £250,000. Now that the *average* house price in the South East is £242,000 you can see how an awful lot of homeowners could be far closer to the Inheritance Tax threshold than they could imagine.

Gordon Brown, on the other hand, knows all about it. Inland Revenue receipts from this tax have jumped by 54% since 1997 to £2.4 billion a year. Many of the estates paying it consisted of little more than a modest family home – and some of those who paid it became Higher Rate taxpayers for the first time *after* they died. How's that for galling?

So if, incredibly, you're not thrilled by the idea of offering up large portions of your wealth to the nation's coffers on your demise, it's best to take avoiding action well in advance. How you avoid IHT will depend very much on your circumstances, how wealthy you are, whether or not you are married and whom you want to benefit from your money before and after your death. The important thing is that you do as much research as you can and get professional advice early on so that you know what the rules are, and what you can and can't do.

First, you need to know fairly accurately how much you are worth. It's a good idea to tot things up every couple of years or so, just so that you know if and when your net worth goes over the IHT threshold. It'll add some spice to your conversations with your neighbour at your Derby and Joan clubs: 'So, what's your current net worth, Deirdre?' 'Well, Janice, I'm nearly up to the IHT threshold. I really must start making some complex family trusts. And have you seen the price of butter?' Don't forget to add in your investments and other assets, including PEPs and ISAs. These cease to be tax-free on the death of the holder, which is an important point for your beneficiaries to note.

All assets, with very few exceptions, are added up at the time of death – and this would include gifts made within seven years of the donor's death. After any liabilities – such as debts – are deducted, Inheritance Tax is assessed at 40% on anything above £250,000. Happily, transfers between spouses are exempt from Inheritance Tax, so if you die leaving squillions to your husband there'll be no IHT to pay (and vice versa). But if you've children between you, it's worth passing on some money to them when the first spouse dies, if you're able to, as this will help avoid or cut down on IHT when the surviving spouse goes. Giving no more than the nil rate band to individual family members and friends in each will and giving the rest to charities or a political party is a good way of cutting out the taxman.

There are many other ways of avoiding IHT, particularly if you plan early. Avoidance strategies can be as simple as making sure you have written a Will or, if you're fairly wealthy, that you have put some complex family trusts together. You'll need to enlist the help of an experienced solicitor to do this – ideally one who is a member of STEP (see page 205 for contact details). Money that you give away earlier than seven years before your death is also exempt from Inheritance Tax, although if you're giving *things* like property or art, you have to prove that you yourself are not benefiting from them after you've given them away. In other words, if you are living in the house after you've transferred it into your children's names then they will still have to pay tax on it when you die, unless you have been paying a market rent each month for the privilege. It is known as a 'gift with reservation of benefit' because you haven't really given it away. Arranging life assurance with a death benefit equal to the anticipated Inheritance Tax bill is another means of ensuring your heirs benefit more than the taxman and this is probably the route to take.

If you own a property jointly you can organise a Notice of Severance which will turn you into tenants-in-common. Most joint property is held as beneficial joint tenants, which means that in the event of the death of one of the owners then the other takes by survivorship. However, a Notice of Severance will 'sever the joint tenancy' so that each party owns 50% of the property (the percentages can be uneven). This means that you can deal with your share of the property as you please and also means that the value of the house can be divided in each individual Will thus potentially cutting down on IHT.

There's also something called the Annual Gift Exemption, which is a little-used planning aid that can help to significantly reduce an estate for IHT purposes. There's an annual gift exemption of £3,000, which can be given free of any IHT to any one person. There's also an exemption that applies to annual amounts of £250 to any number of people. There are special exemptions for gifts to children in the year they marry, as well as other special exemptions too. It's all a bit fiddly and complicated (so what's new?), so it's a good idea to get professional advice if you want to take advantage of these breaks. It doesn't take a genius to work out that if you gift just £3,000 per year for 20 years to your family, that represents a tax saving of £24,000 if that money had been in your estate at the time of your death.

Whatever you do with your money before you die – especially if your assets are worth more than £250,000 – we can't stress enough that you must at least do *something*. If you do nothing, the Inland Revenue could be the biggest single beneficiary of your estate. For example, say you're a wealthy widow (hey, you can dream) worth £800,000 and you want your three lovely children to benefit equally after your death. If you don't do any tax planning to reduce or avoid inheritance tax, your estate will give rise to a whopping tax liability of £220,000. After this is paid, that will leave just £193,000 for each of your children, who will not be remembering you quite so fondly. So:

- Make a Will
- Update that Will whenever your circumstances change
- Keep an eye on your total net worth
- Put tax-avoidance plans into effect whenever you can afford it.

What about now?

It may sound like an odd one, but you might like to consider setting up some sort of Power of Attorney while you're in a good position to do so. We've covered Wills, but they come into effect only when you die. So what if you have a stroke or a bad accident that leaves you physically and/or mentally incapable of managing your affairs? That's when you need to execute a Power of Attorney. This is a document that appoints someone or several people to act on your behalf if you are unable to do so yourself. There are currently two types, General and Enduring.

A General Power of Attorney applies where someone is physically incapable of managing his or her affairs. It can give general authority to the Attorney or it can be very specific. For instance, someone could be appointed to act as an Attorney in the signing of a contract if the donor is out of the country. No power is taken away from the donor but, quite simply, power is given to a third party or parties for that specific time. More than one person can be appointed to act and they can act independently of each other (joint and several) or both together (joint).

An Enduring Power, however, is far more wide-ranging because this is intended to continue if the donor becomes mentally incapable. This confers tremendous responsibility on the Attorney, who has a duty to register the Power with the Court of Protection if the donor has become, or is becoming, mentally incapable. The registration process is onerous and costs money, but this pales into insignificance compared with the process of appointing a Receiver for a patient who is mentally incapable and who has *not* set up an Enduring Power of Attorney. It takes many months and costs a fortune not only to set up but also to run. The Enduring Power of Attorney is a bit like an insurance policy: absolutely useless unless it's required, but if you need one but haven't got one, it's probably too late.

Protect your property from the council

An estimated one in three women and one in five men will eventually need long-term care, and someone – probably you – will have to pay for it. If you think you might need to go into a residential nursing home for a short or long time, you'll certainly have to put measures in place to protect your property from the local council. Since Care in the Community was introduced, people going into residential or nursing care have basically lost their assets in order to pay for their care. Present rules allow you to keep £18,500, but if you have assets above that then they'll have to be used. The cost of care can be at least £20,000 a year and it doesn't take long to whittle away your assets at that level of charge. If you live alone you could be particularly vulnerable.

Only the very poorest get help with the basic costs of staying in a home. Under new rules, you don't have to sell your home immediately to pay for care, but in most circumstances you will be expected to do so eventually unless you have made other arrangements. If you are in a residential or nursing home and you stay until your assets fall below £18,500 – excluding the value of your home – the council will start paying for the cost of the care but a charge will be placed on your home. This means that your home will have to be sold once you die so that the council can recoup the cost of the care from the proceeds. The only exceptions are where the home is occupied by your partner, a relative aged 60 or more or a relative who is incapacitated.

Don't try and hand on your property to avoid paying these bills – you'll be treated as having made a 'deprivation' and your family (or the recipients of the assets) will be pursued for the money.

There are some circumstances when the value of your home *must* be ignored for the purposes of the means test, if you move permanently to live in a residential or nursing home. Both the local authority and the Benefits Agency must ignore the value of your former home where it's occupied by one or more of the following:

- your spouse or partner
- a relative who is aged 60 or over
- a relative who is under the age of 60 but is incapacitated
- a child under the age of 16 whom you are liable to maintain

If you own your home and no one else lives there with you, then its value will be included in the means test as capital. The first twelve weeks that you are in a home is paid for by the local authority, whatever your assets, after that you will have to start paying.

The local authority can't force you to sell your property without a court order but you will eventually have to sell it even if it occurs after your death.

Some people in this situation might choose to rent out their property and then use the net rental income together with their existing income to pay towards the fees of the home. If you decide to let your property, you should seek financial and legal advice. In some cases, renting out might generate enough income to pay the fees in full. If so, you would then count as a self-funding resident and may be able to claim Attendance Allowance. For others, this might not produce enough income to pay the fees in full.

Age Concern has pages and pages of invaluable information on all aspects of funding residential or nursing care and what the Government's rules are on its website (www.ageconcern.org.uk). It also has a free helpline on 0808 808 6060. Similarly, you can get comprehensive advice from the Help the Aged website (www.helptheaged.org.uk) or from its helpline on 0808 800 6565.

Funeral plans

Funeral plans are a great idea and a wonderful investment *if* you can face dealing with it and *if* you care that much. Let's face it, you're not going to be there to enjoy it, so do you really mind whether they play 'Sheep May Safely Graze' or 'I Will Survive' as people gather to pay their respects? It's up to you. We have friends who, before they entered their forties, had already decided what music and readings they wanted at their funerals. We think they really ought to get out more, but hey, if it makes them happy...

However, there's a genuine financial advantage to sorting it all out well in advance. For a start, if you pay for it all now you'll make sure that your descendants or executors are not burdened with the expense. Also, you pay today's prices and, if you shop around, you'll find that some companies will guarantee that no matter how long you live neither you nor your estate will pay another penny more towards the cost. If you sort all this out now then you are bound to save a lot of money for your children when the time comes.

There's also, of course, the advantage that you get to plan your own funeral, hymns, flowers and cars, nominate your own undertaker, choose your own coffin, in fact do the lot according to *your* specification. If you don't quite trust your kids not to dress up in Mr. Blobby outfits and sing 'The Birdie Song' at your funeral because 'It's what mum would have wanted', then getting it all sorted while you're around to make the decision yourself is not a bad idea.

Postscript

Jane and Jasmine are in towelling robes reclining on sun-loungers in a spa. They have glasses full of something colourful next to them.

Jane: Ah, you've got to the end of the book – well done. That wasn't too hard was it? You know, Albert Einstein once said; "If you want to live a happy life, tie it to a goal, not to people or things". We believe this is true, although nothing can replace the happiness you gain from loving and being loved by others.

Jasmine: The problem is that women have a habit of tying their lives to *people* – their partners, their children, their friends – without making enough practical provisions for themselves. Men, on the other hand, have a habit of tying their lives to *things* – their jobs, their income, their cars and their gadgets – and then wonder why they're feeling lonely and unhappy. Those are sweeping statements, I know, but although things are changing this is still very much the case today.

Jane: That's not to say men and women don't have the same goals – they do. Most of us, male and female, just want to love and be loved by someone, to live fulfilling lives and to be happy and content – and there's nothing wrong with that. It's just that men and women go about getting there differently. And sometimes, we both take the long way round unnecessarily – or inadvertently go off the route altogether.

Jasmine: The two most important things we need in life are people to share our lives with, and enough money to pay for a roof over our heads and food in our mouths. The easiest way to achieve the former is to find a partner. But – make no mistake – love does not conquer all. Neither does money, actually, but it sure as hell helps when the chips are down!

Jane: ...and at least money is something you can control. Unlike men.

Jasmine: Quite. In fact, if you make enough of it, you might even find yourself living the life of Reilly, with or without a partner in life. Being able to see the light at the end of the tunnel and knowing that it's not an oncoming train means real freedom.

Jane: So now, having read the book you'll know that, really, there's no hard slog involved once you've got the basics. If you're still wondering why you really ought to make the effort to become financially independent, then let's remind you of the following facts:

● Women usually earn less than men

● Women usually give up their careers to care for the children

● Women usually outlive their partners

Jasmine: Wow, Jane, I didn't know you could talk in bullet points!

Jane: It's a little trick I picked up at convent school...about the only useful thing I *did* pick up actually.

Jasmine: So how you do you do it?

Jane: Oh, just put your mouth like this and start talking.

Jasmine: Great. OK. Here goes...

So, dear reader, if you need further convincing, then remind yourself of these extra little nuggets of information:

● The divorce rate is running at 40%

● Fewer children are being born – the 'average' family now consists of 1.7 children instead of the more commonly quoted statistic of 2.2 children

● One in five women will not have children at all, whether through choice or inability

● It's anticipated that, in 20 years' time, more than half the adult population will be living alone

Hey, that's good, I'll try that out at my next party.

Jane: Yes, well done. Not so hard is it? But to get back to the subject, the chances of a woman having much in the way of a family support network, let alone a husband, by the time she hits retirement age, are getting slimmer all the time. And yet less than 40% of women in the UK have *any* sort of pension provision – and those who do don't have enough for their needs. Sometimes we wonder if women are taking their futures seriously enough.

Jasmine: Too right. We've tried to help you to plan your life so that, if the worst happens, whatever misfortune it may be, the last thing you'll have to worry about is money. And if the best happens – well, you and your loved ones will happily enjoy the comfortable, nay, luxurious things that life has to offer. More chocolates Jane? *(she passes a large box of Belgian truffles).*

Jane: Thanks, but that's the last one. Waistline!

So, look, please let us know if we've helped you, or indeed if we've missed the mark entirely, by emailing us at agirlsbest friend@fool.co.uk. We won't give personal advice, because we're not qualified financial advisers and that isn't our credo anyway, but we will try to reply to all messages we receive.

Jasmine: We like getting mail – it makes us feel loved. And do say what you think about the book on the 'Woman's Finance and Investing' discussion board. Finally, though, and seriously, be smart about it all. There are no fast bucks to be made here – it takes time. Remember Aesop's fable about the Tortoise and the Hare? To be a proper Fool in The Motley Fool sense is to be a Tortoise. If you're prone to impatience like the Hare, just remember who won the race.

Jane: So cheers! And good investing.

Jasmine: Cheers m'dears!

Index

The following Motley Fool books are also published by Boxtree:

The Motley Fool Tax Return Workbook

Motley Fool UK Investment Guide, 3rd Edition (published November 2002)

The Motley Fool UK Investment Workbook

The Fool's Guide to Investment Clubs

The Fool's Guide to Online Investing

The Old Fool's Retirement Guide

Make Your Child a Millionaire: The Fool's Guide

Rule Breakers, Rule Makers: The Foolish Guide to Picking Shares

How to Invest When You Don't Have Any Money: The Fool's Guide

These are available from all good bookshops, or can be ordered direct from:

Book Services by Post
PO Box 29
Douglas
Isle of Man
IM99 1BQ

Credit card hotline +44 (0) 1624 67513

Postage and packing free in the UK

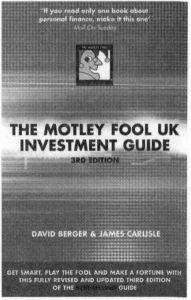

Published November 2002